Farmer, Soldier and Politician

The Life of Brigadier-General
Sir Owen Thomas, MP
Father of the 'Welsh Army Corps'

David A. Pretty

*Farmer, Soldier and Politician – The Life of Brigadier-General
Sir Owen Thomas, MP, Father of the 'Welsh Army Corps'*
first published in Wales in 2011
by
Bridge Books
61 Park Avenue
WREXHAM
LL12 7AW

© 2011 Text David A. Pretty
© 2011 Design, typesetting and layout, Bridge Books

All Rights Reserved.
No part of this publication may be reproduced,
stored in a retrieval system, or transmitted
in any form or by any means, electronic,
mechanical, photocopying, recording or
otherwise, without the prior permission
of the Copyright holder.

A CIP entry for this book is available
from the British Library

ISBN 978-1-84494-075-2

Printed and bound by
Gutenberg Press Ltd
Malta

I'r wyrion
Harry Teilo, Seren Lily ac Efa Medi

Contents

Acknowledgements	7
Preface	9
1. An Anglesey Background	11
2. Burgeoning Politician	31
3. Active Service	44
4. Colonial Travels	60
5. Brigadier-General	84
6. Removal from Command	112
7. Westminster	133
8. Final Years	158
9. Conclusion	169
Appendix 1: Nominal Roll of the Prince of Wales' Light Horse, 1899–1902	175
Appendix 2: 113th Infantry Brigade	190
Appendix 3: 38th (Welsh) Division	192
Bibliography	194
Index	202

Brigadier-General Sir Owen Thomas, Kt, MP, DL, JP.

Acknowledgements

MY INTEREST IN BRIGADIER-GENERAL SIR OWEN THOMAS began when researching the history of rural trade unions in Wales, with Anglesey as the starting point. I was also conscious of a family link. My grandfather, Hugh J. Pretty, and his brother, William J. Pretty (one of the founders of the Anglesey Labour Party), were fervent admirers, and both figure prominently alongside Owen Thomas's coffin in the photograph taken outside Neuadd, the Thomas family home, in 1923. More than two decades have passed since I first chronicled his career in a Welsh-language monograph entitled *Rhyfelwr Môn* (Warrior of Anglesey). Early retirement allowed me the freedom and time to plan for an enlarged English version. Initially, this meant retracing the footsteps of earlier research, but it was also an opportunity to incorporate much new material as well as to make minor revisions and corrections. Online searches provided considerable information from a variety of sources, not least the numerous websites relating to Africa and the Great War. As a result, I would like to think that I came to know Owen Thomas even better upon a second acquaintance.

Once again, I wish to register my thanks to individuals who supplied information: Clive Hughes, Christopher Wrigley and the late Richard Jones during the first period of research; and more recently, Owen Cock and Tom Arkell. At the outset, I succeeded in tracing the direct descendants of Owen Thomas's surviving daughter to Ireland. Unfortunately, there was to be no treasure trove of personal papers; all had been apparently lost during the Nazi military occupation of Jersey where Lady Thomas lived at the time. Nevertheless, Audrey Allen furnished me with family miscellanea, newspaper cuttings and photographs. I am very grateful to both Audrey and Bob Allen for their assistance.

My debt to the staff of libraries and archives where I conducted my research, or who responded to written queries, cannot be overstated: the National Library of Wales; Bangor University Library; House of Lords Record Office; National Archives; British Library; Imperial War Museum;

Bodleian Library; Derbyshire Record Office; Anglesey Record Office; Gwynedd Archives Service (Caernarfon); Denbighshire Record Office and the Royal Welsh Fusiliers Archives (Wrexham). Particular thanks go to Charles Parry who, following the publication of *Rhyfelwr Môn*, drew my attention to Owen Thomas's dealings with Frederick William Rolfe (Baron Corvo) and Charles Sydney Goldman. This information became the basis for two short articles subsequently published in the *Transactions of the Anglesey Antiquarian Society*. Debts to numerous historians are implicitly acknowledged in the works cited in the bibliography.

Perhaps more than anything, this second time round I appreciate the chance to put right a glaring failure on my part. Whilst I had a mind to write to the Kenya National Archives (they had nothing of value to my research), I neglected to follow the route to Neuadd, Llanbadrig, to question Robert Williams, grandson of Hannah Mary, Owen Thomas's youngest sister. Since his first letter to me, back in 1991, we have remained in touch, exchanging documents and information. Moreover, he and his wife Kathleen have been the kindest of hosts. Not only have I been honoured to spend a night in Owen Thomas's former bedroom, and photographed on the spot where my grandfather stood in 1923, but also, in July 2003, they arranged a get-together with Audrey and Bob Allen at Neuadd. In addition, Robert has acted as my guide to Carrog and historic Brynddu. With the kind permission of Professor Emeritus Robin Grove-White, he arranged for me to have copies of the letters written by Owen Thomas to the Hughes-Hunter family. For his support and friendship as we guard the memory of Owen Thomas, *diolch o galon*.

I also wish to express my appreciation of the interest shown by Alister Williams of Bridge Books in the subject and for his editing eye when preparing the work for publication. For any errors or shortcomings that remain, the responsibility, I need hardly add, is mine.

Given the tragic aspects to Owen Thomas's personal life, it has unquestionably strengthened one's own appreciation of family. *Rhyfelwr Môn* was dedicated to the memory of my parents. By now a new generation has made a joyous appearance, and it is with great pleasure that I dedicate this book to my grandchildren.

David A. Pretty, Tonteg, Rhondda Cynon Taf.
2011

Preface

Among the constants said to define and determine a person's character are family, environment and life experiences. All would feature in the making of Owen Thomas. His roots were deep in the farming community of rural Anglesey, where he spent his formative years. As a young man of rare quality, he immersed himself in public life to gain official recognition. While his interests were many and varied, he would achieve prominence in that Cromwellian blend of farmer, soldier and politician. Widely consulted by government and land settlement companies, his agricultural expertise was acknowledged both in Britain and on the African continent. Every inch the soldier, his military career, with its distinctly Welsh component, spanned both the Boer War and the First World War. Political ambitions took him from the county council to Westminster; elected MP for Anglesey in 1918, he was one of the very first Labour Party members to represent a rural constituency. During an extraordinarily eventful career, he became acquainted with an array of major figures at the centre of contemporary life. Bestowed with honour and office, he ended his days as Brigadier-General Sir Owen Thomas, MP. Naturally enough for a small county that venerated its favourite sons, he secured a rightful place in the pantheon of *'gwŷr mawr Môn'* (the great men of Anglesey). Indicative of an enhanced standing was also his inclusion among British Establishment notables in *Who's Who*, as well as the colonial celebrities of Edwardian Africa in *The Anglo-African Who's Who and Biographical Sketchbook, 1907*.

In many ways, history is but the biography of famous people. Events are best appreciated, and their significance better understood, when connected to the individuals who helped shape them. Owen Thomas's personal story offers a valuable insight into British colonial expansion in Africa; the response to military recruitment in Wales during the Great War; the first stirrings of a political labour movement in a rural county.

Disappointingly, it is an account lacking the sort of personal material that would allow a deeper understanding of the man, his thoughts and emotions. Though there is proof that he kept a diary whilst in East Africa, all personal papers have been lost, along with any evidence that he considered putting his personal recollections to paper. Scarcely a handful of his private letters have survived. To a considerable degree, therefore, this book is dependent on contemporary newspapers, supplemented by manuscript sources and official papers which provide the essential details for a portrait of a man and the world he lived in. His was a compelling life story that encompassed challenge, adventure, heroism, controversy, humiliation, personal triumph and profound loss.

1. An Anglesey Background

ANGLESEY'S RELATIVE ISOLATION AS AN ISLAND ended with the construction of two engineering masterpieces; Telford's suspension bridge (1826) and Stephenson's tubular bridge (1850) established a direct road and railway connection across the Menai Strait to stimulate contact with the mainland, and open all aspects of everyday life to outside influences.[1] Along the main routes, Menai Bridge, Llangefni, Amlwch and the port terminus of Holyhead, in particular, become the main centres of population and commercial activity. The rail link to Amlwch (1867) arrived long after the renowned Parys Mountain copper mine had gone into decline, ending the only instance of large-scale industrialisation on the island. Although ships and shipyards continued to maintain Anglesey's long maritime tradition and to provide valuable employment, opportunities were limited, resulting in a steady flow of emigrants that kept the population level at around 50,000 from the 1840s to the 1920s. Farming remained the chief occupation, and as various other industries declined, it grew in importance. In 1851, almost half the total number of males were employed on the land; even by 1911, over a third of the working population remained in agriculture.

Wealth and status defined the rural social structure and over the centuries the principal county families had accumulated extensive estates with profitable rentals. By 1880, two-thirds of the farmed land belonged to a handful of 'great landowners', the most prominent being Meyrick of Bodorgan and Williams-Bulkeley of Baron Hill, each owning over 16,000 acres, followed by Paget (later the Marquess of Anglesey) of Plas Newydd with over 9,000 acres. Notable among the proprietors of land over 5,000 acres was W. Bulkeley Hughes of Plas Coch, the red neo-gothic limestone mansion built at Llanedwen in 1569 that gave the estate its name. As so often the case, a shrewd marriage between Bulkeley Hughes's grandfather and the heiress of Brynddu, Llanfechell, secured the merger of the Plas

Coch and Brynddu estates. Until the latter part of the nineteenth century the landed gentry wielded unquestioned power over the tenantry and neighbouring communities. A paternalistic support of good causes, schools, churches and chapels perpetuated social deference and strengthened their political domination.

Tenant farmers, with holdings of fewer than 50 acres, occupied most of the cultivated land, farms being mostly let from year to year. A farm of over 200 acres would be considered a very substantial unit. Economic circumstances accounted for the general shift from corn growing to the more profitable business of livestock rearing. The revival of the Anglesey Agricultural Society in 1872 gave impetus to the annual county show where farmers could exhibit and compete. By now, the breeds of cattle and horses had greatly improved in quality and the coming of the railway facilitated the cheaper transportation of animals to new markets; agricultural districts bordering the branch line to Amlwch were said to have benefited greatly. For all the difficulties and insecurities surrounding rents, tenure and compensation for improvements, made worse by the agricultural depression of the 1880s and 1890s, it was observed that at the height of the Welsh Land Question more 'small fortunes' had been made by farmers in Anglesey than elsewhere in Wales. Fine houses and furnishings, the retinue of farm hands and domestic servants, the superior education they secured for their children, were testament to this prosperity. In no time, the line of demarcation between farmers and labourers widened to the point of open disaffection as simmering discontent over working conditions found a voice.

Another distinctive feature of Anglesey society was the overwhelming triumph of Nonconformity. Despite the patronage of the landed gentry, the Anglican Church had failed to stem the tide of religious dissent and by the time of the 1851 Religious Census, over 85 per cent of worshippers attended the 140 chapels that dotted the island. Of the three main denominations, the Calvinistic Methodists gained superiority with half the number of attendants. Claiming over 20,000 adherents by the 1880s, their numerical strength completely overshadowed the minority Independent and Baptist sects, who had 3,200 and 2,200 members respectively. Conflict between church and chapel gave the sectarian divide a potent edge, manifesting in resentment towards proselytising church schools, the payment of tithes and the growing demand for disestablishment. Denominational rivalry among Nonconformists, on the other hand, often bred resentment as Calvinistic Methodists increasingly monopolised public bodies and official appointments. For the majority, the chapel became the spiritual centre of the community, individual ministers exercising great influence; along with their allies among the farming and urban middle class they composed a formidable leadership élite ready to confront the traditional authority of the Anglican gentry.

Since the late eighteenth century the chief gentry families had carved out the county and borough parliamentary seats. In contrast to the Anglican landlords elsewhere in Wales, they were ostensibly Liberal in politics and at first acceptable to Nonconformist opinion. But, with the radicalisation of the Calvinistic Methodists, even Liberal grandees lost favour. Once Sir Richard Williams-Bulkeley announced his retirement, political activists immediately harnessed Nonconformist support for Richard Davies, the shipping tycoon and Methodist 'idol'. Nothing provided better proof of the political ascendancy of the Nonconformist middle class than his unopposed return as Liberal MP for the county seat in the momentous election of 1868. Though he failed to live up to radical expectations – he proved to be a 'silent member' in the House of Commons – Davies held the seat against Tory opposition in 1874. That same year, the Anglesey Liberal Association was set up as a formal party organisation, to be revamped in 1881 with the specific aim of consolidating the support of the farming class. Agricultural and religious grievances underpinning the Welsh Land Question were rapidly gaining political prominence.

Just as in politics, the Nonconformists also challenged the Anglican hegemony in education. They promoted the nonsectarian British schools in opposition to the National schools that many Nonconformist children were obliged to attend. The establishment of school boards under the 1870 Education Act paved the way for another demonstration of Nonconformist strength as they assumed control following contested elections. Nonsectarian education was secured, but the niggardly actions of rate-conscious middle class board members became another source of labour unrest. That said, formal schooling offered the best avenue for ordinary people seeking personal advancement. In an age that extolled the virtues of character and individualism, men who made their way in the world were celebrated, not only in the local weekly press, above all *Y Clorianydd* and *Y Wyntyll*, but more specifically the two separate volumes of *Enwogion Môn 1850–1912* [Famous People of Anglesey] published in 1913.[2] Among the disproportionate number of religious and literary figures came the rare farmer, soldier and politician.

Owen Thomas's life encompassed all three careers. Because the names of those still living were omitted from the collections, his imprint on history had yet to be recorded.

He was born on 18 December 1858 at Carrog, in the remote parish of Llanbadrig on the north-west coast of the island. Descended from an old Anglesey family, he could trace his distinguished ancestry back to the stock of Hwfa ap Cynddelw, the twelfth-century lord of the commote of Llifon and head of one of the Fifteen Noble Tribes of Gwynedd.[3] Among his forebears was Cwnws ap Hywel ap Iorwerth Ddu, who had fought and died (c.1406) in support of Owain Glyn Dŵr's revolt. Any threat to the family line was obviated by William ap Howel, 'the Patriarch of Tregaean', who died in 1581, aged 105, having fathered thirty-six legitimate children within three marriages, let alone another seven out of wedlock. Descended from Elin, the third wife, Owen Thomas's paternal ancestors remained settled around Llangefni. Thomas Pritchard (d.1733) of Tŷ Gwyn, Heneglwys, a yeoman farmer, was one of the first to espouse Nonconformity in Anglesey prior to the Methodist Revival.[4] All three sons also achieved prominence among the earliest Nonconformist pioneers. The line continued through Harry Thomas, the second son – forenames becoming surnames in the patronymic Welsh tradition. His daughter, Catherine, was the mother of Owen Thomas (1764–1833), born at Ty'n Llan, Heneglwys. By the early nineteenth century, the fortunes of the family would be based on agriculture and proven farming acumen. Three generations of well-to-do farmers became noted for their diligence and piety; all were held high in public affections.

Leaving Heneglwys after his marriage, Owen Thomas rented Carrog, a farm of 200 acres on the Plas Coch and Brynddu estates, in 1800.[5] As a leading member of the Independent denomination, he was instrumental

Carrog, Llanbadrig, the birthplace of Owen Thomas.

in founding, among others, the chapels at Ebenezer, Llanfechell, and Bethel, Cemaes, serving as minister following his ordination in 1814. Often he would leave the farm on horseback to undertake extensive preaching tours throughout Wales. His eldest son, Thomas Owen (1791–1859) followed in his father's footsteps as a farmer–preacher.[6] Ordained in 1828, he shared the ministry at Ebenezer and Bethel when his father's health deteriorated, and was an ardent promoter of the Sunday schools. For reasons not revealed, Thomas Owen later relinquished his calling as a minister. All the while, Carrog continued to flourish; in the 1840s he employed around eight farm labourers and three domestic servants.[7] Displaying the social ambitions of aspirational middle class farmers, his only son rounded his education at a private boarding school in Abergele.

Breaking with family tradition, Owen Thomas (1817–76) did not occupy the pulpit; instead, he would serve Bethel Chapel as a Sunday school teacher and loyal deacon for some thirty-two years.[8] Following his marriage to Ellen Roberts of Cemaes in 1843, there were to be eleven children: four sons and seven daughters. A few years after the birth of Owen, the third son, the family moved (*c.*1865–6) from Carrog to Neuadd, a farm of 185 acres, more conveniently situated on the outskirts of Cemaes.[9] This they did with a very heavy heart. Perhaps to add colour to an electioneering campaign years later, Owen Thomas junior would claim that his father had been forced to vacate Carrog, without a penny in compensation, to make way for the landlord's brother upon his return from military service in India.[10]

Whatever the truth of this, Owen Thomas served W. Bulkeley Hughes of Plas Coch as land agent for a good many years, efficiently running the northern portion of the estate without the hint of a rift. His personal qualities were an asset, his genial, compassionate nature endeared him to his fellow Welsh-speaking tenants, a man with whom they could discuss estate matters in their own language. At a time of sectarian tensions, the differences between an Anglican landlord and a zealous chapel-going agent raised no difficulties. Neither did politics, for W. Bulkeley Hughes was the Tory turned Liberal MP for the Caernarfonshire Boroughs. Ill-health precluded an active political role, nevertheless Thomas, Neuadd, figured among the leading farmers who gave Richard Davies, MP, a public show of support at Amlwch in 1873.[11] A year later, he was said to be 'dangerously ill' following a bout of increasingly debilitating rheumatic fever.

Owen Thomas, the son, was brought up in comfortable circumstances.[12] He first attended the local Church school at Llanfechell, one of the few to respect the religious sensibilities of Nonconformist parents. To broaden his horizons, he then received, as did all his siblings, a privileged education outside the island. As a boarder at the Clwyd Bank Academy, Ruthin, he was given a 'thorough commercial education' under the guidance of J. D. Jones, one of the foremost headmasters of the day.[13] Aged fourteen, he subsequently spent a year (1872) at Liverpool College, a prestigious Victorian public school offering 'sound religion and useful learning'.[14] However, his formal education was abruptly curtailed because of his father's failing health. Responsibility fell on youthful shoulders as he returned home to help out on the farm in the absence of his two elder brothers. Setting a family example for distant travel and enterprise, Thomas Owen Thomas and William Robert Thomas had been drawn by the economic possibilities in Argentina. Both were businessmen in Buenos

Neuadd, Cemaes, home of the Thomas family after the 1860s

Aires. Thomas Owen Thomas forged early connections with *Y Wladfa*, the Welsh colony in Patagonia, and was related, through marriage, to John Murray Thomas, one of the first pioneers. The two were together on an explorative journey in the Chubut valley in 1877.

Upon the untimely death of his father in 1876, Owen Thomas immediately took over the running of Neuadd as a yearly tenant alongside his widowed mother, employing three men and a boy.[15] Events moulded his character. Resourceful and self-assured, he rapidly matured into a confident young man with evident ambition, soon to make a name for himself. Owen Thomas excelled as a farmer, knowing what it was to work from dawn until dusk, turning his hand to every aspect of agricultural work, be it tilling the soil or erecting stone walls. Quick to adopt the latest implements and farming techniques, he established Neuadd as a model farm and his achievements were recognised and rewarded at premier agricultural events within the county and beyond. At the annual Anglesey Agricultural Show in 1881, he received the special prize offered for the best stocked farm.[16] Again, at the same show the following year, he was awarded a prize of £5 for being the tenant farmer with land in the best state of cultivation.[17] The permanent improvements were said to be too numerous to list. Further kudos came in 1883 when Jumbo, the aptly named $1\frac{1}{2}$-ton bullock, won second prize at the Smithfield Club Cattle

Show in Islington.[18] This was the very first time that an Anglesey farmer had ventured to compete in London against the top breeders, and hundreds assembled at Amlwch station to witness the departure. It proved a profitable journey for Owen Thomas; Jumbo was subsequently sold for 100 guineas. Everything considered, he possessed the right credentials to become vice-president of the Anglesey Agricultural Society in 1884[19] and president nine years later.[20]

His achievements had already caught the eye of the new landowner. On the death of W. Bulkeley Hughes in March 1882, his only child, Sarah Elizabeth Hughes-Hunter, inherited the Plas Coch and Brynddu estates which spanned 5,404 acres. Following in the footsteps of his father, Owen Thomas was appointed land agent in December with an annual salary of £160.[21] The desire for self-improvement was clear; to remedy the deficiencies in his formal education, he later sought permission to follow a course of land surveying.[22] He would hold the post of agent until December 1898, when he was succeeded by his younger brother, Hugh, then back at Carrog. As such, Owen Thomas wielded considerable authority over the tenantry. The steward was responsible for the collection of rents, the upkeep of the farms and outbuildings, as well as other duties associated with the day-to-day management of the estate. The hostility directed at 'landlordism' permeating the Welsh Land Question also tainted the estate agents, some of whom were depicted as unscrupulous English middlemen, guilty of petty tyranny over the Welsh-speaking Nonconformist tenantry. Owen Thomas stood as a direct opposite of the stereotype hate figure. Good-natured like his father, he fulfilled his duties without fear or favour to earn the lasting respect of the tenantry in difficult times. Estate tenants treated to a special dinner in 1893 could well toast their popular hero with cries of 'Jolly good fellow'.[23] It proved to be a broad-based appeal, spread among all classes within the rural community.

In physical appearance Owen Thomas was a dark-haired, well-built young man, some two inches short of six feet. To some he did not appear bookish or academically inclined.[24] He was by nature the quintessential countryman, with a passion for the traditional country pursuits of game shooting, fishing and hunting. Pheasant shoots enabled him to hone his skill as a marksman, thereby placing him in good stead to win trophies in military competitions. It was an interest he shared with his close shooting companion, the Revd John Williams of Brynsiencyn.[25] Together on the Plas Coch country estate their success with the gun forged a friendship, renewed in the Great War.

From the start, Owen Thomas immersed himself in every aspect of community life in the two adjoining parishes of Llanbadrig and Llanfechell. By 1881, their respective populations had reached 1,061 and 923, centred in the tight-knit villages of Cemaes and Llanfechell. Together they formed the *milltir sgwâr* [literally, square mile] that was to define and frame his early life. Paradoxically, it was in connection with the sea, not agriculture, that Owen Thomas first displayed his qualities as a natural leader. Over the centuries countless ships had been wrecked off the treacherous coast of north Anglesey with a great loss of life. Even after the inauguration of the first lifeboat service in 1828, the fate of the steam clipper *Royal Charter*, that claimed 450 lives, provided a grim reminder of the constant perils. In 1876, when only eighteen years old, Thomas took the initiative to organise a community volunteer rescue force composed of local farmers and traders.[26] Called into action, a rocket with an attached line would be fired to fasten a breeches buoy from shore to stricken ship. His sense of public duty was duly recognised by the Maritime Department of the Board of Trade with his appointment as Chief Officer of the Cemaes Life Saving Apparatus Station, a post he would hold until 1899.

Cultural and religious activities always received enthusiastic support. His name was among a number of local notables who gathered to arrange the eisteddfod held at Cemaes in July 1878.[27] Many years later, he patriotically provided each villager with a leek in celebration of St David's

Chief Officer Owen Thomas of the Cemaes Life Saving Apparatus Station.

Chief Officer Owen Thomas (centre front) with members of the Cemaes Life Saving Apparatus Station.

Day.[28] Steeped in religion, he maintained the family tradition of service to the Independent cause, as a Sunday school teacher and deacon at Bethel, and later Ebenezer chapel. His faith remained an important element throughout his life, and whilst living in Anglesey, he took a prominent part in denominational affairs. He donated the major prize awarded to pupils sitting the Independent Sunday schools examination.[29] In 1883, he attended the Independent quarterly meeting at Amlwch as official delegate, becoming president of the quarterly meeting held at Llanfechell in 1894.[30] A year earlier, the Union of Welsh Independents came to Holyhead for its annual assembly. On what was the Union's first visit to Anglesey, Owen Thomas had the singular honour of presiding at the public meeting.[31] He was again invited to preside at Llangefni in 1923 for the Union's second visit, but his death came a few months earlier.

This direct involvement in a range of interests gave him a high public profile at both community and county level. How he extended the scope of activities can only be explained by his close association with Colonel Charles Hunter (1844–1907), a link pivotal to his subsequent career. The colonel, who traced his family roots to Glencarse, Perthshire, Scotland, had married the heiress of Plas Coch in 1876, later adopting the style of Hughes-Hunter.[32] True to the tradition of social obligation displayed by the landed gentry, he soon became an active participant in local affairs. In the main, this involvement reflected his own personal interests and connections. From the time he became land agent, Owen Thomas found a father figure and key mentor. Hence the shared enthusiasm in freemasonry, sailing, the Oddfellows and, most especially, the military and politics. All dated from the formative period of the early 1880s.

With proprietary rights over the small harbour and foreshore, Sarah Hughes-Hunter, as Lady of the Manor of Cemaes, took an abiding interest in developing the village as a tourist resort. Middle-class holidaymakers, mostly from England, had only a short journey to travel from Amlwch railway station. Here at Cemaes, Owen Thomas first met his future wife, Frederica Wilhelmina Skelton Pershouse, the only child of Frederick Pershouse of Bowdon, Cheshire, described as a proprietor of houses and railway stock,[33] with family links to the Pershouses of Penn Hall, an ancient Staffordshire seat. However strong the anecdotal testimony that she ran away from home to marry Owen Thomas at Llanbadrig parish church on 31 August 1887, shortly after her father's death,[34] this belief can now be disproved. Her exquisite bridal dress, as seen in a wedding photograph, would suggest careful preparation. And, as it turns out, her father had in fact died in Angoulême, France, just a few months after her birth in March 1866.[35] Her mother, Wilhelmina Mary (née Darby) remarried a decade later, this time to Robert Newton Jackson, a mining engineer, who later inherited the Blackbrooke estate in Skenfrith, Monmouthshire.[36]

Within a year of the marriage, they had moved from Fron, Cemaes, to Brynddu, Llanfechell, on the Plas Coch estate, set in 94 acres, which was leased to Owen Thomas for 21 years at a rent of £100 per annum.[37] Synonymous with the name of the eminent diarist, William Bulkeley (1691–1760), Brynddu was a seventeenth-century mansion rich in history. Few were better suited to occupy the place of the former squire who, in his day, had proved to be something of a progressive farmer, generous and understanding towards the tenantry.[38] Brynddu became the early home of their five children. While Owen Thomas now attended Ebenezer chapel, the children were baptised in the parish church. According to the 1891 census, Frederick Leyton Pershouse, their first son, was listed and the household had four domestic servants: an English cook and housemaid,

Brynddu, Llanfechell, Owen Thomas's marital home from 1888.

and two bilingual nurses.[39] Robert Newton, Mina Margaret, Owen Vincent and Trevor were all born by the time their proud parents posed for an idyllic family group photograph in 1897.

The Plas Coch family were long renowned for their public spiritedness and social involvement. W. Bulkeley Hughes became patron of the church school at Llanfechell, also donating land for the building of Nonconformist chapels. Whether driven by altruism or self-interest, their largesse continued to benefit all sections of society. In time-honoured custom, they took care to alleviate the hardship of the most needy, with the land agent playing an integral role. When Sarah Hughes-Hunter donated coal to the poor of Cemaes and Llanfechell in 1886, Owen Thomas arranged its distribution.[40] As a member of the Anglesey Union Board of Guardians he would have been well aware of the scale of social deprivation; by 1892 the two parishes had as many as 150 paupers in receipt of poor relief.[41] Other charitable endeavours followed. Alongside Charles Hughes-Hunter, he became the chief promoter of the Oddfellows Friendly Society branch set up at Llanfechell in 1891.[42] As a mutual aid movement, it provided a degree of social security to working-class families before the advent of the welfare state. For a modest weekly subscription it handed out benefits to meet sickness and burial costs. Concerts, often presided over by Thomas, were regularly held to raise funds. Still going strong in 1920, the branch reported that £400 had been distributed over the previous decade.[43]

More select interests presented a social contrast. Both men shared a love of yachting, working together to organise the annual sailing regatta at Cemaes: Hughes-Hunter as commodore, Owen Thomas as secretary.[44] Well-known within Masonic circles, Hughes-Hunter held high rank as Grand Master of the Order of Mark Master Masons in the new Province of North Wales, first established at Llandudno in 1880. Soon after the St Eilian Lodge (N[o.] 360) of Mark Master Masons was founded at Amlwch in December 1885, Owen Thomas served as master and grand standard bearer.[45]

Less conventional, given his family background, was the way Owen Thomas came to embrace a soldier's life. He succeeded in reconciling fundamental Nonconformist values with a lifelong passion for the military. Once again, his induction came through the connections of his close

Owen and Frederica Thomas with their children, 1897. L–R: Robert Newton; Trevor (with nurse); Mina Margaret; Owen Vincent and Frederick Leyton

Lieutenant Owen Thomas, 2nd Volunteer Battalion, RWF, 1889.

mentor Charles Hughes-Hunter, a major in the 3rd (Militia) Battalion of the Manchester Regiment. Few records remain of the period immediately following its formation in 1881, but it is known that Owen Thomas was given his first commission as a militia lieutenant in the Manchester Regiment in 1886.[46] From the start of his military career, he reportedly displayed great energy and enthusiasm, fashionably sporting an army officer's moustache. By order of his superiors, he was soon authorised to raise a company of volunteers in Anglesey. Consequently, he transferred to the 2nd Volunteer Battalion, Royal Welsh Fusiliers, in 1887 to begin the task.

He faced a formidable challenge in a county distinctly lacking a strong military tradition. Despite the exploits of career-minded individuals from the gentry class, as personified by the first Marquess of Anglesey, the one-legged hero of Waterloo, soldiering held little appeal for the *gwerin* (the common people) at large. The Anglesey Militia suffered indiscipline among the rank and file and was amalgamated with that of Caernarfonshire in July 1860.[47] Anglesey became the last county in Wales to form a volunteer rifle corps in November 1860, but within three years the

Captain Owen Thomas, 2VB, RWF, at camp (possibly at Morfa Conwy), 1889.

companies at Aberffraw, Amlwch and Menai Bridge had been disbanded because of falling interest.[48] Units of artillery volunteers at Beaumaris and Holyhead encountered similar difficulties, leading to their disappearance by 1873. Only the specialist Royal Anglesey Engineers Militia remained. Another effort to revive the volunteer movement in the early 1880s came to nothing. For one thing, the Nonconformist ethos saturated the island, resulting in little love, if not outright disapproval, for the scarlet uniform.

With characteristic vigour, Owen Thomas set about organising a company of volunteers within his sphere of influence at Cemaes and Llanfechell.[49] It would be his first experience of raising troops. In only a few weeks he had single-handedly transformed local attitudes. To appease Nonconformist misgivings, he shrewdly persuaded a preacher and five deacons to enlist and as a result, 70 per cent of the new recruits were said to be Nonconformists, drawn from every denomination.[50] Most had agricultural connections, either as farmers or labourers. Amid the young men stood veterans of the Crimean and Ashanti wars. Designated K Company of the 2nd Volunteer Battalion, Royal Welsh Fusiliers, the Cemaes Rifle Volunteers succeeded beyond expectations. Within a year Thomas had 108 men under his command. As the only commissioned officer he kept his corps at full strength and in a 'most efficient state'. It could be seen as a model of inspirational leadership and an achievement probably unique in rural Wales. Attempts to replicate his success elsewhere in Anglesey had failed, whereas the Royal Welsh Fusiliers generally attracted recruits from urbanised north-east Wales and the English Midlands.[51]

When the 2nd Volunteer Battalion assembled at their camp on Morfa Conwy in the summer of 1886, Lieutenant Owen Thomas was accompanied by Charles Hughes-Hunter as honorary colonel.[52] By 1889, he had been promoted captain, and it was as Captain Owen Thomas, Brynddu, that he was generally known in Anglesey at this time. K Company regularly mustered for training, including rifle practice, at the designated shooting range over Neuadd fields. When the company's 'excellent band' received their new instruments, Thomas arranged a celebratory dinner for the men at the Crown Hotel, Llanfechell.[53] Tented camps at Valley, Conwy and Blackpool offered further training and annual inspection. Invariably, the unit was praised for its conduct and efficiency. In 1892, Captain Owen

Officers 2VB, RWF, at camp in Valley, Anglesey. Captain Owen Thomas is marked with an X.

Thomas and K Company were greeted at Plas Newydd by the then Marquess of Anglesey when the 2nd Battalion Royal Welsh Fusiliers made its way through north Wales en route from Ireland to Aldershot.[54] A 'sham fight' was held at Valley in 1893, with K Company winning the tug-of-war contest.[55] Similar success came in the rifle competitions. To cap the Cemaes men's achievement in winning both the Plas Newydd Challenge Cup and Counties Challenge Cup at Conwy in 1898, Major Thomas (as he now appeared in the list of officers attached to the newly-formed 3rd Volunteer Battalion) secured the Officers' Cup to confirm his prowess as a crack shot.[56] Here was a military leader in his element, and it said much about his personal command that K Company disbanded shortly after he had left the island.

NOTES

1. For a general survey, see E. A. Williams, *The Day Before Yesterday: Anglesey in the Nineteenth Century*, translated by G. Wynne Griffith (Beaumaris, 1988) and David A. Pretty, *Anglesey. The Concise History* (Cardiff, 2005).
2. R. Hughes, *Enwogion Môn 1850–1912* (Dolgellau, 1913) and R. Môn Williams, *Enwogion Môn 1850–1912* (Bangor, 1913).
3. J. E. Griffith, *Pedigrees of Anglesey and Carnarvonshire Families* (Horncastle, 1914), p.399.
4. W. Griffith, *Methodistiaeth Fore Môn 1740-1751* (Caernarfon, 1955), pp. 13–14.
5. T. Rees and J. Thomas, *Hanes Eglwysi Annibynnol Cymru*, Cyf.II (Liverpool, 1872), pp. 483–7.
6. Ibid, p.487; also *Y Dysgedydd*, 1860, pp. 445–6.
7. *Y Dysgedydd*, 1877, p.183.
8. Ibid, pp. 179–83.
9. Bangor University. Bangor General MSS 27, 002. Pedigree Notes on the family of Thomas of Carrog and later of Neuadd, by Captain O. T. Evans, Cemaes.
10. *Oswestry and Border Counties Advertiser*, 10 July 1895.
11. *Baner ac Amserau Cymru*, 8 Ionawr 1873.
12. A number of early details are gleaned from obituary notices, especially *Y Tyst* 14. Mawrth, 4 Ebrill 1923; *Who's Who in Wales*, 1920; *Who's Who*, 1923 and *Life in Pictures of Brig. Gen. Sir Owen Thomas* (London, nd., but 1922).

13. *Baner ac Amserau Cymru*, 19 Gorffennaf 1865, 21 Medi 1870.
14. Letter from the bursar of Liverpool College to the author, 25 June 1987.
15. 1881 Census return.
16. *North Wales Chronicle*, 3 September 1881.
17. *Holyhead Weekly Mail & Anglesey Herald*, 2 September 1882.
18. Ibid, 22 December 1883.
19. Ibid, 27 September 1884.
20. *North Wales Chronicle*, 18 August 1893.
21. Bangor University. Plas Coch MSS 3354. Rental of the Plas Coch and Brynddu Estates, 1882–1919; also Plas Coch Estate Account (kept at Brynddu).
22. Letter from Owen Thomas to Captain Hunter, 31 January 1885 (kept at Brynddu).
23. *Y Clorianydd*, 8 Mehefin 1893.
24. The words of the Revd Owen Parry. *Y Clorianydd*, 14 Mawrth 1923.
25. R. R. Hughes, *Y Parchedig John Williams, D.D., Brynsiencyn* (Caernarfon, 1929), p.143.
26. *Holyhead Mail & Anglesey Herald*, 2 February 1884.
27. Anglesey County Record Office. WDM/48. Reference provided by Glyndŵr Thomas.
28. *Y Clorianydd*, 9 Mawrth 1899.
29. Ibid, 13 Ebrill 1899.
30. *Y Tyst*, 18 Mai 1894.
31. Ibid, 23 Mehefin 1893.
32. *Burke's Landed Gentry*, 1894; *North Wales Observer & Express*, 8 February 1907.
33. Birth certificate of Mina Skelton Pershouse (bn. 11 March 1866). Additions and alterations to her name were made later.
34. Bangor University. Bangor General MSS 27,007. Autobiographical Notes by Captain O. T. Evans. Elsewhere, in a biographical note made by Lady Thomas in December 1949, she gives the year of her father's death as 1887, hence the initial confusion.
35. Information supplied by Wayne Roberts, Australia, 15 February 2008 (a Pershouse family researcher) citing Probate Records proved on 11 May 1868.
36. *Monmouthshire Beacon*, 26 December 1919, 3 December 1926.
37. Bangor University. Plas Coch MSS 3320–1, Lease 5 September 1888.
38. Emlyn Richards, *Bywyd Gŵr Bonheddig* (Caernarfon, 2002), pp.96–151.
39. 1891 Census return.

40. *Holyhead Mail & Anglesey Herald*, 19 March 1886.

41. *Royal Commission on Labour, The Agricultural Labourer, 1893*, vol.II (C.6894), Anglesey, p.137.

42. Ibid, p.135. See also *Y Clorianydd*, 18 Hydref 1894, 29 Hydref 1896.

43. *Y Clorianydd*, 4 Chwefror 1920.

44. *North Wales Observer & Express*, 19 August 1887.

45. Ibid, 21 May 1886; *Y Wyntyll*, 9 Tachwedd 1922.

46. The National Archives. WO 339/158715. Letter from Owen Thomas to the War Office, 15 August 1919, outlining his military service.

47. E. A. Williams, op.cit., p.88; Bryn Owen, *Welsh Militia and Volunteer Corps 1757–1908, 1: Anglesey and Caernarfonshire* (Caernarfon, 1989), p.28.

48. R. Westlake, *The Rifle Volunteers* (Chippenham, 1982), pp. viii-ix, 5.

49. *Royal Commission on Labour, The Agricultural Labourer*, op.cit., p.136; also *North Wales Chronicle*, 17 September 1892.

50. *The Times*, 1 October 1908, letter from Owen Thomas.

51. N. Evans, 'Loyalties: state, nation, community and military recruiting in Wales 1840-1918' in M. Cragoe and C. Williams (eds.), *Wales and War* (Cardiff, 2007), p.43.

52. *Holyhead Mail & Anglesey Herald*, 5 August 1887.

53. *Y Clorianydd*, 29 Ebrill 1897.

54. *North Wales Chronicle*, 3, 10 September 1892.

55. Ibid, 2 June 1893.

56. *Y Clorianydd*, 29 Medi 1898.

2: Burgeoning Politician

OWEN THOMAS'S INVOLVEMENT IN LOCAL POLITICS ran parallel to a host of other interests. He began his political career as a Gladstonian Liberal, highly regarded within the Anglesey Liberal Association, where his close relationship with Charles Hughes-Hunter again came into play. Like his father-in-law, W. Bulkeley Hughes, Hughes-Hunter was a leading light in Liberal circles and as political mentor, he appeared well placed to prepare the ground. Owen Thomas's first foray into politics came in February 1885, when he was elected vice-president of the Anglesey Liberal Association.[1] A few months later he chaired political meetings at Llanfechell and Pensarn addressed by Richard Davies MP.[2] As a newcomer to platform oratory, he expressed the pride he felt as a young man. At the annual meeting of the Association in September, both men shared centre stage. Hughes-Hunter, as president, seconded by Owen Thomas, proposed the motion of gratitude to Richard Davies as he prepared to defend his parliamentary seat (now merged with the boroughs).[3] The agricultural depression and Ireland were but two of the contentious issues Davies faced on his way to a fourth election victory.

Within a year, the Association faced a critical time, riven by deep division over the Irish Question. Richard Davies opposed Gladstone's Home Rule Bill. When the matter was discussed at a special meeting of the Anglesey Liberal Association in June 1886, Owen Thomas, in the absence of Hughes-Hunter, tried unsuccessfully, to defer a motion of confidence in Gladstone.[4] As it turned out, both men had strong objections to Irish self-government. Yielding to majority opinion, Davies, however, acted honourably and abstained from voting when the Bill was defeated in the Commons. After a heated discussion, the Association accepted his subsequent letter of resignation, a move that led Hughes-Hunter to relinquish both presidency and membership.[5] Thomas Lewis, a self-made merchant and Calvinistic Methodist, became the Liberal candidate. Whereas Hughes-Hunter publicly endorsed his Conservative opponent at the general election in July – when the Liberal majority fell disastrously – 'militia captains' reportedly stood silent among hundreds of Liberal 'deserters'.[6]

Taking his cue from Hughes-Hunter, Thomas also withdrew from the troubled Association to embrace emergent Liberal Unionism. Though he never divulged the nature of his opposition to Irish self-government, it is likely that he too shared the misgivings of an innately conservative landed interest. The launch of a Liberal Unionist Association in Anglesey in August 1887 came with Hughes-Hunter as its president.[7] Owen Thomas's noteworthy absence could perhaps be explained by the fact that it coincided with his wedding preparations. When Major Walter Yeldham, a Liberal Unionist agent, visited the island in September to gauge the strength of the cause,[8] it soon transpired that Hughes-Hunter was more intent on gaining a baronetcy. In his assessment of Owen Thomas, who pledged overt support, he foresaw the invaluable service he could render, being a 'good speaker' with 'great influence' among the farmers. Others doubted whether he would act independently of Hughes-Hunter.

Attempts to gain a footing in Anglesey were in vain. Following a joint meeting of Liberal Unionists and Conservatives at Llangefni in February 1888, Richard Davies declined their invitation to stand as a Unionist parliamentary candidate.[9] Neither Hughes-Hunter nor Owen Thomas were present. By the end of the year, Thomas, surprisingly, had returned alone to the Liberal fold. For an aspiring politician, this prompt decision (Hughes-Hunter rejoined the party in 1893) was rewarded with political dividends. The transfer of power to elected county councils offered him the ideal opportunity to play a public role in local government. And in the first county council election in January 1889, having drummed up support among Plas Coch tenants and employees,[10] he comfortably won the Llanbadrig seat by 156 votes to 93.[11] Albeit, as an Independent, it meant being in the denominational minority on a predominantly 'Calvin council'. After his short-lived deviation from mainstream Liberalism, Owen Thomas also reassumed influence within a reconstituted Anglesey Liberal Association. He was appointed delegate to the North Wales Liberal Federation,[12] where he would rub shoulders with Welsh national figures, and in February 1890, he once again became vice-president of the county Association.[13]

Soon after his return to active politics, Owen Thomas was caught up in an assertive farm labourers' movement that acquired political overtones. At the close of 1889, under the journalistic pen-name of 'Ap Ffarmwr', John Owen Jones had published a series of seminal articles in *Y Werin*, a halfpenny weekly newspaper targeting the working class, that made for a searing attack on the farmers.[14] He exposed the harsh plight of a docile workforce at the base of rural society: uneducated, exploited, alienated and often lorded over by their employers. Labourers worked up to fourteen hours a day for miserable wages. Family men lived in primitive hovels while the unmarried labourers were quartered in insanitary farm outhouses. As testified by the volume of letters and reports in *Y Werin*, the reaction, more especially in Anglesey, was phenomenal. To all appearances, they had raised the flag of revolt. Although Ap Ffarmwr propounded the idea of an independent trade union, majority opinion among labourers gave priority to a reduction in the working hours. Local meetings were held prior to staging a conference at Llangefni. The level of interest generated by the attendant publicity could not be ignored by either farmers or local politicians.

Owen Thomas, farmer and land agent.

Owen Thomas was involved from the outset. On 28 February 1890, he attended the first formal meeting of farm labourers, held in the neighbouring village of Llanfair-yng-Nghornwy, to support their plea for a reduction in the hours of work.[15] Accompanied by two sympathetic farmers, he gave similar backing to the labourers who met at Llanfechell the following month.[16] Speaking at Llannerch-y-medd he went further, to condemn sub-standard rural housing.[17] Most villages were blighted by

33

insanitary conditions and disease. His attendance at such meetings displayed a genuine concern; he cared about the injustices they suffered, and was fearless in expressing his views. Moreover, his presence instilled confidence in ordinary working men who wished to have their say. But as the farm labourers' campaign gathered momentum, prudence demanded that he tread carefully so as not to fuel the already charged debate. By now, the main body of farmers were up in arms, and he incurred their wrath by publicly siding with the labourers, some going so far as to accuse him of actually instigating the movement. For a time, his relations with fellow farmers came under severe strain and, responding to criticism in a letter to *Y Werin*, Thomas had good reason to moderate his position.[18] Appealing for conciliation and compromise, he coupled the men's demand for a reduction in working hours with advice to tenant farmers to unite in similar fashion when approaching their landlords for a reduction in rent. Seldom did a Welsh land agent openly advocate such action.

Events came to a head when some 5,000 farm workers gathered together at Llangefni on Easter Monday in a collective show of strength unprecedented in rural Wales.[19] At their conference, delegates voted unanimously to press the farmers into granting a twelve-hour day of 6 a.m. to 6 p.m. Though the radical idea of a trade union was mooted, it drew little support. Invited to preside at the subsequent public meeting, Captain Owen Thomas, county councillor, as he was billed, described their claim as 'fair and just'. Both classes within the rural community deserved justice, but he appealed to all speakers to steer clear of 'politics'. When the farmers met to consider the workers' demands a few days later, Thomas, regardless of the ill-feeling he had aroused among farmers, again pleaded their case.[20] In the event, it was agreed to reduce the working day to twelve hours, excepting harvest time. Heralded as a major triumph for the farm labourers' movement, the farmers had clearly made a prompt conciliatory gesture before the discontent became too difficult to contain.

By acceding to the men's request, they effectively forestalled calls for a trade union organisation that Ap Ffarmwr had continued to preach about. In further articles in *Y Werin*, he presented social and political reasons why combination would favour the workers. It provided the means to secure working-class representation on school boards and the county council. Reflecting an objective of the 'New Unionism', the prospect of them returning their own member of parliament was being aired; workers were in a position to outvote farmers.[21] Together with his die-hard supporters, Ap Ffarmwr drew up the framework of the Anglesey Agricultural Labourers' Union on 13 June 1890. In gratitude for past support, and to add status, Owen Thomas was invited to serve as its first president.[22] Among the local politicians in Anglesey his name stood out as the farm workers' champion. True, he had braved opposition to express a deep sense of social justice, but it was to be a measured response. His subsequent silence proved that for him, this might be a controversial step too far. More than once during his career, Owen Thomas would demonstrate the limits of his political radicalism. Even among the labourers themselves, there was little enthusiasm; most appeared well-satisfied with the immediate improvement in their working lives and before long the union foundered.

John Owen Jones – Ap Ffarmwr [Gwynedd Archives Service]

Despite the personal exhortation that politics be set aside, such was Owen Thomas's standing within the agricultural community that many saw him as a potential parliamentary candidate. Having won the admiration of the labourers, and restored his reputation among local farmers, he was in a position to bridge a widening class divide. So much so that at a meeting convened in Llanfechell on 6 June 1892, he received an invitation to contest the parliamentary seat in the name of both the workers and farmers of Anglesey.[23] Whilst several labourers spoke highly of Owen Thomas, none had a good word for Thomas Lewis who had boycotted their historic meeting at Llangefni in 1890. When he arrived to outline his political credo, Thomas favoured land reform and disestablishment, but remained emphatically opposed to Irish home rule. No decision was reached so he requested nine days to consider the matter. Projected in one newspaper as 'the proposed labour candidate for Anglesey', the radical press, in panic, misinterpreted his possible intervention as a barefaced Tory ploy to divert the working-class vote away from Thomas Lewis.[24] (Published correspondence would later prove that he had not been in league with former officials of the Anglesey Conservative Association.)[25] Rather than create divisions within Liberal ranks, Thomas declined the nomination. Praising 'the young squire of Brynddu' for his good sense, one editorial opined that his time was yet to come.[26]

Again and again, Owen Thomas sought to dispel any impression of partisanship. When the need arose, he gave equal support to labourers and farmers, a long-held principle that became an abiding theme throughout his political career. He convened a meeting of agricultural workers at Llanfechell on the day of the November hiring fair in 1892 to offer advice in the selection of spokesmen who gave evidence to the Royal Commission on Labour.[27] At a time of severe agricultural depression, when unity among farmers became paramount, he lent support to the Anglesey Agricultural Union formed in December 1892.[28] Farmers came to see the advantages of combination in their bid to secure rent reductions. When arrangements were being made to publicly recognise Ap Ffarmwr's unique contribution with an official presentation in May that year, Thomas initially agreed to present the testimonial.[29] Later, doubts arose whether he would be able to attend. Come the day, however, he shared the platform with other dignitaries.[30] As the first speaker to follow the passing of an unexpected motion to revive the Anglesey Agricultural Labourers' Union, it proved an awkward moment. Taken aback, he nevertheless paid a generous tribute to Ap Ffarmwr, understandably avoiding controversy by remaining silent on the subject. To all intents, the ceremony marked the close of a chapter and Ap Ffarmwr departed for south Wales the following year with bitter memories of his failed mission. Yet, like Joseph Arch in England, his name lived on to became synonymous with rural trade unionism. In Anglesey, it would provide inspiration for others to succeed, and ultimately allow Owen Thomas the opportunity to fulfil his political ambitions.

Meanwhile, the impending retirement of Thomas Lewis saw another attempt to persuade Owen Thomas to stand as parliamentary candidate in the interests of farmers and labourers.[31] To admirers from both classes, he was their ideal candidate;[32] his name appeared on a shortlist of possible successors presented to the Anglesey Liberal Association, but prior to the final selection meeting in January 1894 he withdrew his candidature.[33] Indisposed following a bout of influenza, this decision had been forwarded in a letter to the Association. In the event, Ellis Jones Griffith, the young barrister and Calvinistic Methodist, stood as the successful Liberal candidate in the general election of July 1895. The fact that Owen Thomas was an Independent in a preponderantly Methodist caucus aroused adverse comment,[34] but at least this did not deter his election as president of the Association once more in March 1894.[35] Not that his own denomination had any doubt that one day he would be rewarded with a seat at Westminster representing his native county.[36] Indicative of his social standing, it was noted with pride how he had been honoured with prestigious public positions, historically the preserve of the landed gentry or entrepreneurs. In 1893, he became the first Independent to be appointed High Sheriff of Anglesey.[37] A year later, his elevation to the Methodist-dominated Magistrates Bench as a Justice of the Peace was being warmly welcomed.[38] To add to this, in 1895, he topped the poll to elect county council aldermen.[39]

It was a signal achievement that he also received formal recognition much further afield. By dint of his experience in land management, let alone political connections, he was appointed to serve on the Royal Commission on Agricultural Depression in September 1893, initially as the sole representative from Wales.[40] Being a tenant farmer himself, Thomas was in a position to express the forthright views made public elsewhere.[41] To compete on equal terms with intense foreign competition he felt that legislative measures had to be taken to relieve farmers of the burdens of rents, rates and taxes. He remained committed to free trade, warning against a retreat into protectionism. As it turned out, the Commission's final report in 1897 failed to offer radical proposals. Disagreement among members marred its work, as evidenced by various memoranda on minor topics, such as the issue of tithe rent charges signed by Owen Thomas.[42] All the same, his stint on the Commission would serve him well and the experience and added knowledge enhanced his reputation as an authority on agriculture. Aside from raising his personal profile, he became acquainted with influential figures in the English 'Establishment', two of whom – Viscount Cobham and Sir Alfred Milner (who gave evidence on matters of taxation) – would feature later in his career.

Though often spoken of as a future MP, his political time had not yet come in Anglesey. So it was over the border, in the rural constituency of Oswestry, of all places, that Owen Thomas first contested a parliamentary election in July 1895. Invited by the local Liberal Association and some of the leading farmers, who viewed him as an exceptional candidate, he promised to 'fight like the soldier he [was]'.[43] Among the Welsh expatriates who signed his nomination papers was Owen Owen, headmaster of Oswestry High School, prominent in Liberal circles. For a decade since its formation, the seat had been held unopposed by Stanley Leighton of Sweeney Hall, the owner of 655 acres of land. Notorious for his anti-Welsh views and intervention in Welsh politics – he was chairman of the Clergy Defence Association at the time of the Welsh tithe disturbances – Leighton appeared the archetypal Anglican Tory landowner. As the 'Liberal and Agricultural' candidate, Thomas stood by his party's official programme (that included a just measure of Irish home rule) although he desired to be returned as the 'farmers' representative'.[44] Besides references to his membership of the Royal Commission on Agricultural Depression he spoke of his lifelong connection with the land and how well qualified he was to serve both tenant farmers and working men.

Far from Anglesey he could adopt a more forceful approach to landlordism by specifically aligning himself to the two classes.[45] As a tenant farmer he shared their concerns on such matters as high rents and security of tenure. And it was during the campaigning that he made an issue of his family's eviction from Carrog to make way for the landlord's brother after he took 'a fancy to the farm'.[46] To strike a chord with the farm workers he boasted a prominent role in the labour agitation in Anglesey that culminated in the improvement in their working hours. All his life he had taken the 'deepest interest' in the welfare of the labourers, and nothing would give him 'greater pleasure' than to advance their interests in parliament. Lest his hands-on experience of farming be questioned, he challenged any labourer to match him in a day's physical work.[47] Familiar faces were at hand to provide direct testimony of how he stood against the 'aristocracy' of his native county.[48] Following a meeting at Llanfechell, neighbouring farmers and labourers, together with delegates from the Anglesey Liberal Association, arrived, at their own expense, to sing his praises among their counterparts in north Shropshire.[49] The Tory press was less kind, portraying Owen Thomas as an unknown, untried, youthful 'carpetbagger', peddling the same speech, who sought to attain in the Oswestry constituency what he could not achieve in his own county.[50] Leighton, predictably, went on to win with 4,605 votes to 3,500.

Familiar issues brought him back to public attention in the context of Welsh politics. For years, the Land Question had been the nagging topic that soured relations between landlord and tenant farmer. Problems relating to rents, security of tenure and compensation for improvements mirrored the agitation in Ireland. Exploited, and exaggerated, by radical Nonconformist propaganda,[51] the situation was accentuated by the depression in agriculture. Though the Royal Commission on Land in Wales provided a vent for grievances, no legislative action could be expected from a Conservative government when it reported in 1896. Owen Thomas not only gave public lectures to advise farmers in these difficult times,[52] but in keeping with his reputation as a progressive land agent he launched an initiative that won the approval of the radical journal *Baner ac Amserau Cymru*.[53] On an estate where landlord–tenant relations had been of the best, and in consultation with Sarah Hughes-Hunter, he drew up a new and fairer tenancy contract by September 1899, that extended both the period of tenure and notice to quit. This gave added security along with defined rates of compensation for improvements undertaken by the tenant. Presented as a possible model for other landlords to consider, farmers were invited to study the reformist document, clause by clause, prior to a meeting of the Welsh National Liberal Federation in Swansea, when the Land Question, once more, came up for discussion as a policy issue.[54]

As for Owen Thomas himself, other matters preoccupied his mind at the close of 1899. A dramatic reversal of personal fortunes came with the crash of entrepreneurial ventures in which he was heavily involved. Since about 1890 he had been the principal owner of a small company at Llanfechell trading under the name of O. T. Evans & Co.[55] As ironmongers and dealers in agricultural implements, it flourished and began to diversify. In partnership with A. E. Barkworth and Captain H. R. Maxted, two wealthy Yorkshiremen who had settled locally, Thomas embarked on a course of rapid expansion in 1896, when the concern was ambitiously retitled the Anglesey Trading Company. Other local businesses were absorbed and their workforce integrated so that at its peak the company employed over 80 skilled craftsmen and labourers in various contracts, including the building of a school, hotel and private houses. But lacking business nous, the three directors presided over an unsustainable concern, compounded by mismanagement and profligacy. Gadlys Hotel had to be sold at a loss, and there was only a limited market for the thousands of coffin plates and shoe laces (still available in 1943!) which they ordered. Heavy losses forced the company into liquidation after only three years. The need for capital required Owen Thomas to press Sarah Hughes-Hunter into buying back the lease of Brynddu.[56] He then authorised the sale of costly furniture, carpets and wines at Brynddu in December 1900.[57] A public auction of the ironmongery stock, taken by the official receiver, followed in March 1901.

Owen Thomas had been continuously involved in local matters from a young age, and while his popularity remained undimmed, the collapse of the Anglesey Trading Company was, for a man of his social standing, a humiliating blow. Apart from the personal financial loss, it had potential implications for a wider community. To add to his woes, it appears that the brickworks at Cemaes, the 'little venture' initiated in March 1899,[58] also suffered a similar fate; the bricks were said to contain too much lime.[59] All in all, his public life had reached a nadir. 'Down on his luck, and on the look out', a description mistakenly ascribed to his personal circumstances in 1914,[60] would seem to have a greater resonance at this time. The outbreak of the Boer War in October came at an opportune moment for a man seeking to change the course of his life. The Cemaes Rifle Volunteers, by special proclamation, had already been instructed to stand by for active service in South Africa.[61]

Fortunate in his mentor, Owen Thomas had made the most of the opportunities that came his way. A range of activities and responsibilities moulded an individual characterised by energy, self-belief and ambition. To overcome his difficulties at this defining moment took an act of profound personal courage. Steeled by patriotic duty, he was prepared to leave behind a young family to become one of the first Welshmen to volunteer for service. Then again, perhaps there is another consideration. He may have had it in his mind to travel to southern Africa in any event, to report on the agricultural prospects at the request of Cecil Rhodes himself, before the war intervened to postpone his mission. Thomas claimed as much in a later press interview,[62] although no reference to contact between the two men appears in the Rhodes Papers.[63] Whatever the motivation, so began his deep involvement with Africa. A varied career had certainly equipped him with many of the skills and leadership qualities needed to meet the new challenges and opportunities that lay in an altogether different environment, half a world away from Anglesey.

Notes

1. *Holyhead Mail & Anglesey Herald*, 7 February 1885.
2. *Baner ac Amserau Cymru*, 15 Ebrill, 3 Mehefin 1885.
3. Ibid, 21 Hydref 1885.
4. *Yr Herald Cymraeg*, 8 Mehefin 1886.
5. *North Wales Chronicle*, 3 July 1886.
6. *Y Werin*, 17 Gorffennaf 1886.
7. *North Wales Chronicle*, 20 August 1887.
8. Bangor University, Bangor General MSS, 15,237, Walter Yeldham, diary and memoranda of interviews and conversations held in Anglesey, September 1887, pp. 9, 33, 37–8, 46.
9. *Holyhead Mail & Anglesey Herald*, 18 February 1888.
10. W. P. Griffith, *Power, Politics and County Government in Wales, Anglesey 1780–1914* (Llangefni, 2006), p.263.
11. *Holyhead Mail & Anglesey Herald*, 24 January 1889.
12. Ibid, 21 February 1889.

13. Ibid, 27 February 1890.
14. David A. Pretty, *The Rural Revolt That Failed. Farm Workers' Trade Unions in Wales 1889-1950*, (Cardiff, 1989), ch.II.
15. *Y Werin*, 8 Mawrth 1890.
16. Ibid, 29 Mawrth 1890.
17. Ibid, 5 Ebrill 1890.
18. Ibid, 29 Mawrth 1890, letter from Owen Thomas.
19. Ibid, 12 Ebrill 1890.
20. Ibid, 19 Ebrill 1890.
21. Ibid, 10 Mai 1890. The words of Richard Williams, an ordinary farm-hand.
22. Ibid, 21 Mehefin 1890.
23. *Y Clorianydd*, 2, 9 Mehefin 1892.
24. *Y Werin*, 11 Mehefin 1892.
25. *North Wales Observer & Express*, 13 October 1893.
26. Ibid, 17 June 1892; also *Y Clorianydd*, 27 Gorffennaf 1893.
27. *Y Werin*, 12 Tachwedd 1892.
28. *Holyhead Mail & Anglesey Herald*, 12 January 1893.
29. *Y Werin*, 18 Mawrth 1893.
30. *Y Genedl Gymreig*, 16 Mai 1893.
31. *Y Clorianydd*, 11 Ionawr 1894.
32. Cf. letters in *Y Clorianydd*, 8, 15, 22 Chwefror 1894.
33. *North Wales Observer & Express*, 22 December 1893.
34. *Y Clorianydd*, 8 Chwefror 1894.
35. *Y Werin*, 31 Mawrth 1894.
36. *Dysgedydd y Plant*, Gorffennaf 1894, p.189.
37. *Y Clorianydd*, 22 Mehefin, 27 Gorffennaf 1893.
38. *Y Celt*, 2 Mawrth 1894; *Y Tyst* 13 Ebrill 1894.
39. *Y Clorianydd*, 21 Mawrth 1895.
40. *The Times*, 11, 15 September 1893.
41. *North Wales Observer & Express*, 18 August, 1, 29 September 1893.
42. *Royal Commission on Agricultural Depression, Second Report, 1896* (Cd. 7981), pp. 20–1.
43. *Oswestry and Border Counties Advertiser*, 20 March 1895.
44. *Shrewsbury Chronicle*, 12 July 1895.
45. *Baner ac Amserau Cymru*, 10 Gorffennaf 1895.
46. *Oswestry and Border Counties Advertiser*, 10 July 1895.
47. *Shrewsbury Chronicle*, 12 July 1895.

48. *Oswestry and Border Counties Advertiser*, 17 July 1895.
49. *Y Clorianydd*, 11 Gorffennaf 1895; *Oswestry and Border Counties Advertiser*, 10, 17 July 1895.
50. Cf. editorials in *Shrewsbury Chronicle*, 19 July 1895 and *Montgomery County Times*, 13 July 1895.
51. David W. Howell, *Land and People in Nineteenth-Century Wales* (London, 1978), pp. 85–92, 152.
52. *Y Clorianydd*, 5 Mawrth 1896, 9 Chwefror 1899.
53. *Baner ac Amserau Cymru*, 20, 27 Medi 1899.
54. Ibid, 4 Hydref 1899.
55. Richard Jones, 'The Anglesey Trading Company, Llanfechell 1896-1899'. *Môn*, Cyf. IV, Rhif 2, Haf 1971, also his article in (eds.) Dewi Jones and Glyndŵr Thomas, *Nabod Môn* (Llanrwst, 2003), esp. pp. 272–7.
56. Letter from Owen Thomas to Sarah Hughes-Hunter, 13 November 1900 (kept at Brynddu).
57. M. Hughes, *Anglesey 1900* (Llanrwst, 2002), p.156.
58. In letters to Sarah Hughes-Hunter, 20, 31 March 1899 (kept at Brynddu) he gave details of the scheme in which she had invested £850.
59. Richard Jones, *Nabod Môn*. op.cit., p. 274.
60. R. R. Hughes, op.cit., p. 227.
61. *Y Clorianydd*, 19 Hydref 1899.
62. Ibid, 3 Mawrth 1915.
63. Confirmed by the archivist, Bodleian Library of Commonwealth & African Studies at Rhodes House, University of Oxford, in letters to the author, 6, 17 February 2009.

3. Active Service

WAR WAS DECLARED IN SOUTH AFRICA on 11 October 1899. Members of local militia who answered the call were obliged to temporarily enlist in a unit of the regular army and, consequently, Major Owen Thomas was attached to the 1st Battalion of the Essex Regiment stationed at Brentwood. Mobilized for immediate service, the battalion left for Southampton to board the transport ship S.S. *Greek* that sailed on 11 November. His personal patriotism was expressed in outright military commitment. It is doubtful whether he had given a thought for the Boers in the Transvaal and Orange Free State as they were manoeuvred by imperialist intrigue into waging war against Britain.[1]

Before Thomas left home, the conflicting political stand taken by Liberal politicians presaged divided opinion in Wales.[2] David Lloyd George courageously voiced sympathy and support for the Boer republics, but was in the minority. Even in the Nonconformist rural heartland, the popular spirit gloried in 'khaki and red' jingoism.[3] Regardless of the pro-Boer sentiment in the independent denominational press,[4] Owen Thomas, unquestionably, would have aligned himself with Ellis Jones Griffith, one of the first Liberal MPs to voice anti-Boer views. While the Anglesey Liberal Association was split on the matter, his continued support for Conservative government policy in South Africa allowed him to be returned unopposed in the 'khaki' election of 1900.

After taking on coal and supplies of fresh fruit at Tenerife, the next land sighted was Table Mountain and the S.S. *Greek* docked at Cape Town on 3 December where Owen Thomas made the most of his connections with friends in high places. He called to see Sir Alfred Milner, the British High Commissioner and Governor of Cape Colony, had lunch at Government House[5] and again met Cecil Rhodes.[6] Contact was thus immediately re-established with two of the principal power brokers in

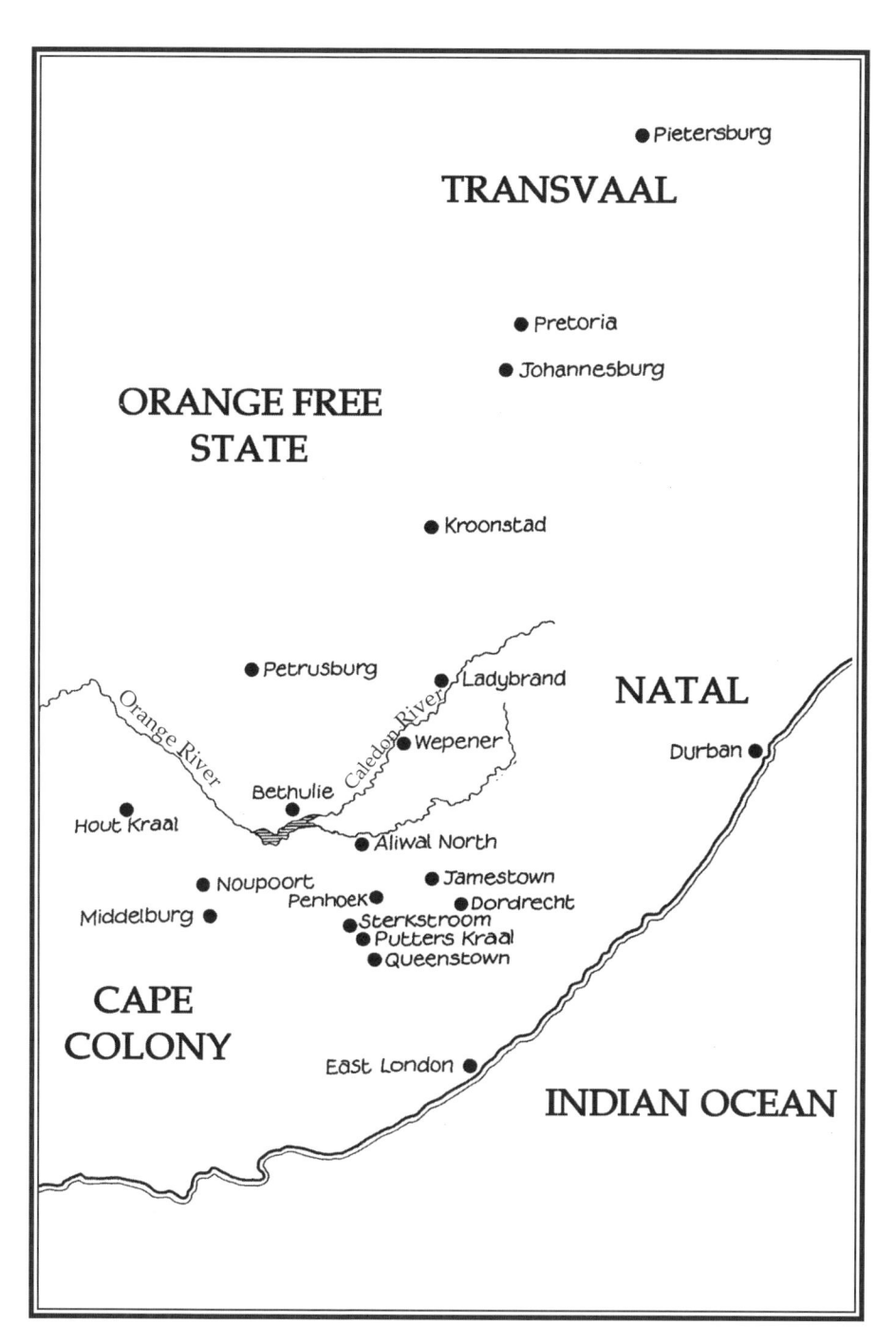

Area of operations, Anglo-Boer War.

South Africa. Empire building, capitalism and politics were intrinsically linked. Through the British South Africa Company, the Rand mining houses and colonial officials, Rhodes's grandiose imperialist vision of a land corridor painted red from the Cape to Cairo was perpetuated by an élite Anglophile clique.[7] Pre-eminent among them was Milner, Alfred Beit of Wernher, Beit & Co., the Transvaal gold magnate and financier, the 4th Earl Grey and Philip Lyttelton Gell. Having conspired to foment hostilities, they would subsequently be concerned with the task of postwar reconstruction, intent upon further economic and political gains. Once he had successfully fulfilled his military duties, Owen Thomas made his name in Africa serving these interested parties, thereby helping to prepare the groundwork for future empire building.

In letters from 'the front' published in the north Wales press, Thomas recounted his military progress in some detail, together with his impressions of the country and its people.[8] From Cape Town, he sailed on the troopship S.S. *Sicilian* to East London, a voyage of two days. After another two days by rail, he reached Lieutenant-General Sir William Gatacre's camp at Putters Kraal, twenty miles from Queenstown in Cape Colony. A Boer offensive was already underway, and Thomas arrived a few days before the disastrous 'black week' of 10–17 December when they inflicted three humiliating defeats on the British as they attempted to lift the sieges to towns in Cape Colony and Natal. Events pointed to a prolonged war and, as Owen Thomas averred, the strength of the enemy had been severely misjudged, underscored by their skill at guerrilla warfare and knowledge of the terrain. By now, his view of the Boers was unequivocal: they were 'the most cunning people on earth' and, brimful with xenophobic disdain, he confessed that he would never argue with 'the Dutch' unless he had a hand on his revolver.[9]

At his headquarters, Gatacre, commanding officer of the 3rd Infantry Division, had assembled a force of regular troops augmented by a colonial irregular contingent under Colonel E. Y. Brabant, a veteran of the Zulu War. Composed mainly of British farmers from the Eastern Province of Cape Colony, the two cavalry units of Brabant's Horse operated mainly as an independent force. Major Owen Thomas, who took command of a squadron in the 2nd Brabant's Horse, had no better companions to

Major Owen Thomas (centre) commanding a squadron of 2nd Brabant's Horse, 1900.

provide his first insight into agricultural conditions. Militarily, they were colonials of the 'best stuff'; excellent riders and marksmen, praised for their ability to adopt Boer tactics.[10] It was painfully apparent that infantry suffered a grave disadvantage in unfamiliar territory; Thomas considered one mounted soldier to be worth three or four men on foot in the open veld. Newcomers like himself had to acclimatise quickly to the harsh conditions, learning to endure baking heat as daytime temperatures soared to 104°F (40°C) in the shade. Flies infested their food; a mass of bluebottles not only covered their plates of bully beef and biscuits, but also followed the food into their mouths.

After his failure to relieve Stormberg in December, Gatacre was deployed in clearing the Boers from the north-east of Cape Colony early in 1900. Moving from Queenstown to Penhoek, the 1st and 2nd Brabant's Horse, now with a combined strength of 1,800 men, advanced on the right flank. Along with the Cape Mounted Rifles, the Frontier Mounted Rifles, the Kaffrarian Rifles, an artillery unit and 100 ox-drawn supply wagons, the column made for the small town of Dordrecht.[11] Running through Thomas's account is the sense of excitement and adventure. During their slow progress, his squadron formed an advanced guard, two miles ahead of the main body. The dangers of travelling through enemy country and camping in the open on cold nights meant they had to sleep in their uniform, boots and spurs on, weapons at the ready, lest the Boers attack. Morning roll call came at 4.00 a.m. The diet and strict military regime had made Thomas healthy and physically fit for action; training camps and rifle practice with the Cemaes Rifle Volunteers could only have been a

Major Owen Thomas (centre) and some of the officers of 2nd Brabant's Horse, 1900.

minor rehearsal for the reality now around him. At Dordrecht came his first experience of serious action when his squadron succeeded in driving back an enemy attack.[12] After three days of fighting, the Boers were eventually cleared from their laager on 5 March.

Following the later occupation of Jamestown on 9 March, they moved towards Aliwal North, a railway terminus on the Orange River captured by the Boers at the start of the war. Though the town was surrendered on 11 March, the column was pinned down by enemy shelling as they attempted to hold a road bridge across the river. In the melee Owen Thomas was thrown off his horse as it was killed under him. While he may have displayed courage under fire, he was to weave these events into a dramatic story in an effort to embellish his military image, when interviewed by the local press during the Great War.[13] Some 60 to 70 horses were said to have been ridden over him before he was given another horse by *The Times* correspondent. Whereas this incident cannot be verified – it went unrecorded in letters published in local newspapers in 1900 – another boast was plainly false. Coaxed by the journalist he further claimed to have personally captured and imprisoned at Aliwal North none other than Jan Christiaan Smuts, the Boer leader who later became prime minister of the Union of South Africa. In truth, Jan Smuts had remained in Pretoria until the British attack on the capital on 4 June.[14] The Smuts in question was his namesake, N. E. Smuts, the mayor of Aliwal

North, noted for his harsh treatment of the British during the period of Boer occupation.[15] It was on Brabant's instruction that Thomas personally arrested the Boer official.[16]

Brabant's Horse pressed north to Wepener, a town 85 miles away on the Caledon River, near the Basutoland (Lesotho) border. Progress was slow because the oxen had to be rested during the heat of the day. Owen Thomas, again part of the advanced guard, was among the first to enter Wepener, which was captured on 29 March.[17] Once the Union Jack had been hoisted, he kept the Boer flag in his possession as a battle trophy. Within a few days, however, the force of 1,895 men under Colonel E. H. Dalgety, that garrisoned at Jammersbergdrif, four miles west of Wepener, found itself surrounded by a numerically superior Boer force commanded by the redoubtable Christiaan De Wet. During the sixteen day siege (9–25 April), when Brabant's Horse held the northern position, Owen Thomas was once more in the thick of the fight. Day and night, they came under relentless heavy bombardment; men sheltered and slept in trenches, often flooded by rain. On the thirteenth day, no less than 450 shells were said to have been fired into the camp. In all, 33 men were killed and over 130 wounded. Only when a relief column approached did De Wet withdraw his force. Military reports later paid tribute to the gallant defenders of Wepener.

Over the next few months, Brabant's Horse was engaged in various operations as the war entered a vicious guerrilla phase. Acting on information, Major Thomas remained in the area around Wepener, tasked with searching several farms for hidden stores of arms and ammunition that were subsequently destroyed.[18]

A month's leave in October allowed him to return to Anglesey where a hero's welcome awaited. As he made his way from Rhosgoch station to Brynddu, in the uniform of Brabant's Horse, Charles Hughes-Hunter and estate tenants on horseback provided an escort.[19] After almost a year in South Africa, he appeared to be in great shape. At Llanfechell, windows were lit and banners waved in celebration. To the accompaniment of the band of the Cemaes Rifle Volunteers, he was enthusiastically fêted by the villagers. In turn, they were treated to an account of his experiences in the field of battle. Llannerch-y-medd, likewise, saluted his bravery with a public reception.[20] His leave also allowed him time to arrange the settlement of business debts and sever his tie with Brynddu. His wife and the four youngest children then accompanied him back to South Africa, to live in Middelburg, Cape Colony, and possibly link up with Pershouse relatives. Frederick Leyton remained with his grandparents at Blackbrooke, Skenfrith; one consideration may have been his perpetual ill-health. Such was their concern for his condition that he spent time at the renowned health spa in Bad Nauheim, north of Frankfurt, Germany, accompanied by his grandmother.[21] But further deterioration eventually resulted in his death from periostitis and septicaemia, aged 16, at Skenfrith on 28 January 1906.[22]

Owen Thomas remained with Brabant's Horse until 31 November 1900. Two days earlier, Lord Kitchener had taken over as the new commander-in-chief in South Africa. To counter the challenge posed by a few thousand guerrilla commandos, he developed a strategy of 'blockhouses and wire'. In a series of 'drives', designated areas would be methodically cleared of Boer combatants. For the surge to succeed, highly mobile units of troopers were of vital importance. As an experienced officer, Thomas was invited

Major Owen Thomas (right) during a recruitment drive for the Prince of Wales' Light Horse. Note the figure representing the cyclist element of the regiment.

Two views of the Prince of Wales' Light Horse on the march in South Africa.

by Kitchener to raise a regiment of Welsh cavalry. Sanctioned by the War Office, and with the Prince of Wales having telegraphed his permission on 19 December, the new contingent would be called the 'Prince of Wales' Light Horse'.[23] Assisted by Colonel J. Hanbury-Williams, a Monmouthshire man who served as military secretary to Sir Alfred Milner, and members of the flourishing Cambrian Society, recruiting began in Cape Town. Advertisements placed in South African newspapers were calculated to draw men into the ranks of a distinctively Welsh unit,[24] officially raised on 18 January 1901. They wore khaki uniform, a leather bandolier crossbelt and a slouch hat with a badge on the turned-up side bearing the three feathers and red dragon of Wales. A Welsh flag, inscribed with the motto *Y Ddraig Goch ddyry cychwyn* (the Red Dragon will lead the way), fluttered above Major Owen Thomas's tent.[25]

Within a few months, the regiment was 500 strong, almost half the total number being recruited in Wales, a high proportion of whom were

Nonconformists.[26] Their regimental chaplain, the patriotically named Revd Glendower Davies, was a Nonconformist minister. Use of the Welsh language and the singing of Welsh songs in social gatherings, generated a strong sense of identity and comradeship. Over time, the unit became a mix of nationalities, professional soldiers and volunteers. Other recruits were drawn from the far corners of the globe: Australia, New Zealand and Patagonia. Men from the latter region of Argentina, known in Wales as *Y Wladfa*, proved to be some of the most skilful horsemen and sharpshooters. One officer, Captain Lord Charles Kennedy, was a Scottish peer, while the higher tier of command, Majors H. Fielden and A. W. Jennings-Bramly, transferred from established regiments of hussars. A significant number of officers claimed Welsh roots, in Caerphilly, Wrexham, Pontypridd, Newport and Bangor-is-y-Coed, among whom were Captain Richard Lloyd Davies (the third son of Richard Davies, MP), and two Anglesey men, Captain John Henry Pritchard-Rayner, Llanddyfnan, and Captain W. Thomas, Llanfechell, the unit's medical officer.[27] In tribute to his long-standing mentor, the military protégé made Charles Hughes-Hunter an honorary colonel of the regiment.[28]

The men enlisted for six months. They received 5s per day in addition to their rations, clothing and equipment.[29] A gratuity of £5 would be awarded, together with a free passage back to their country of origin, at the end of their term of service. If they signed for an additional six months they could claim an extra month's holiday with their gratuity, or a month's pay with free passage. Recruits from Britain and the colonies usually came to South Africa at their own expense; rarely were they offered a paid crossing, though it would appear that Owen Thomas himself helped out. He later grumbled that expenditure on railway and sea passages from various places had left him £1,500 out of pocket.[30] Verbal assurances by Kitchener were of no value when the War Office subsequently refused to sanction payments that had not been agreed in writing beforehand. Evidently, one episode still rankled, a minor scandal involving certain ex-members of the Prince of Wales' Light Horse recruited in New Zealand and Australia.[31] It began when F. B. Hughes, late of Brabant's Horse, offered to enlist a squadron of men from both countries in April 1901. As the commanding officer, Owen Thomas gave his consent. The recruits, however, were led to believe that their passage fare of £13-13s would be refunded, and a daily allowance of 5s paid for their travelling time. Despite the 'excellent service' of the 'Australian squadron', Thomas was unable to offer reimbursement on termination of service, a refusal that they branded 'disgraceful treatment'. After a full investigation by the War Office in the spring of 1903, the men's claims were dismissed. Hughes, it concluded, had made unauthorised promises. As he did not hold a commission at the time of recruiting – his promotion to captain came in June 1901 – he could not be regarded as having been an official recruiting agent.

The Prince of Wales' Light Horse was but one of around 200 contingents of irregular colonial units raised in South Africa. The Welsh adventurer known as Owen Rhoscomyl, who had earlier attempted to raise a troop of Welsh Horse, served for a time in Rimington's Guides.[32] At full strength, Owen Thomas's unit totalled nearly 1,350, including 74 commissioned officers. The fact that he was able to recruit so many men in a matter of months was ascribed to his 'superhuman energy'.[33] Close family members are among the names on the nominal roll:[34] his nephew, Lieutenant O. T. Evans,[35] and two sons, troopers Robert (Robin) Newton Thomas (N[o.] 36236) and Owen Vincent Thomas (N[o.] 27147), all of 8 and 12 years. At the time of enlistment, however, both boys, who served as buglers, are stated

Lt-Col Owen Thomas with his twelve-year-old son, Robin, who served with him in the Prince of Wales' Light Horse.

to be 12-years-old.[36] (Intriguingly, Robert Newton's signature was witnessed by a Lieutenant William Bradney Pershouse.) Not listed was Trevor, said to have been 'under fire', as it were, at the age of five.[37] Their introduction to the military life at such an early age was certainly not unique. Child soldiers were a feature of the Boer War, the use of bugle boys being a long-standing army tradition. During the siege of Mafeking, Colonel Robert Baden-Powell, who later founded the Boy Scout movement, recruited and trained boys as young as nine to act as guides, messengers and lookouts.

As one of the leading Boer guerrilla commanders, Christiaan De Wet had continued to harass the British, much to the exasperation of Kitchener, desperate to bring the war to a quick end. Ready for action, the Prince of Wales' Light Horse was deployed in the major offensive against De Wet following his incursion into Cape Colony in February 1901. Having assembled at Nouwpoort for the operation, the regiment joined other columns in the 'great De Wet hunt' under the command of Colonel E. C. Bethune. During the pursuit, there were engagements at Colesburg and Philipstown. Replicating Boer tactics, the Prince of Wales' Light Horse operated as a small, mobile force, making inroads deep into enemy territory when De Wet retreated over the Orange river into the central district of the Orange Free State. Days of hard riding became a test of endurance for the men, with a very heavy toll on horses. According to the Revd Glendower Davies, it was during the skirmish at Petrusburg in early March that the 'Welsh fighting unit' drew its first blood. When a convoy on its way to Bloemfontein came under attack, a detachment of the Prince of Wales' Light Horse arrived as reinforcement. Displaying his leadership qualities in the firefight, Owen Thomas proved to be 'a general of the first order'.[38] For a fortnight, around the neighbourhood of Kroonstad, the unit fought daily skirmishes, and by the end, had sustained a number of casualties. On 31 March, Owen Thomas and his men had experienced five hours of hard fighting after the Boers laid an ambush. Thomas again proved his worth as a leader when he valiantly foiled their attempt to surround them; though in another encounter 25 of his men were captured and divested of their horses and equipment before being set free.[39] Following Kitchener's orders, the farms of those who gave shelter and support to the Boer fighters were then systematically burnt.

In April, both the Prince of Wales' Light Horse and Rimington's Guides were part of Major-General E. L. Elliott's mission to stamp out resistance in the Orange Free State. Thomas's mounted cavalry again saw combat during the north-eastern Orange Free State drive in May, when De Wet again evaded capture, and afterwards as part of the push led by Major-General Sir John French in Cape Colony in July. They were involved in mopping up small groups of determined Boer fighters who still continued to pierce British lines. Further skirmishing in November caused the unit to suffer casualties at Brande Kraal and Vogelfontein. During the overall course of the fighting, the Prince of Wales' Light Horse reported a casualty rate of 20 per cent; the total number of deaths reaching at least 30.[40] In December, Major A. W. Jennings-Bramly, the second-in-command, was killed in action in the Transvaal.[41] The South African War Memorial in Cardiff (unveiled by Major-General Sir John French on 20 November 1909) lists three from the unit among the 873 names of Welsh dead: trooper Joseph Thomas (N[o.] 27013) of Goodwick, Pembrokeshire; trooper William Thomas of St Bride's Major, Glamorgan, and Lieutenant Charles F. Berry.[42] Berry commanded the dozen members of the cycle section, used for reconnaissance and carrying messages.[43] Owen Thomas was to complain that not a single Welsh Nonconformist had been decorated despite the 'many acts of gallantry'.[44] Somewhat ironically, one officer mentioned in Kitchener's despatches – for 'dash and gallantry' – on 8 December 1901 was Captain F. B. Hughes.[45]

To strengthen their ranks, thinned by casualties and termination of service, Owen Thomas had issued an appeal in May 1901, published in Welsh newspapers, seeking further recruits for what he termed 'the strongest mounted corps in South Africa'.[46]

Two troopers of the Prince of Wales' Light Horse.
[The late Joseph Roberts via www.penmon.org]

Two posed photographs of Sergeant Joseph Goodman Roberts of Penmon, Anglesey, who served in the Prince of Wales' Light Horse. [The late Joseph Roberts via www.penmon.org]

Again in November, he was planning to raise 500 additional men, and with 300 volunteers already in south Wales, he considered the possibility of returning home for recruiting purposes.[47] As it happened, the Prince of Wales' Light Horse was disbanded at Middelburg on 31 December before the end of hostilities, prior to Owen Thomas receiving a new assignment.

Drawing on his experience as a farmer and stockbreeder, Kitchener appointed Thomas to the post of 'Military Director of Agriculture'.[48] Overseeing a staff of several hundred, he assumed responsibility for a network of military farms set up alongside remount depots. Such were the catastrophic losses of horses during the war – eventually totalling over 400,000[49] – that Kitchener was dubbed the 'largest horse killer in history'.[50] To cope with the ever-increasing demand, horses had to be procured from as far as Austria, India, Australia and Argentina. Shipments were costly and the quality often sub-standard. Thomas established and inspected 1,000-acre farms that provided forage for horses reared in the various colonies of South Africa, travelling over 1,500 miles each month to extend his knowledge of the land.

Kitchener's ruthlessly effective tactics eventually wore down Boer resistance and in May 1902 the peace treaty of Vereeniging was signed.

For Owen Thomas, it had been what might be termed a 'good war'. He overcame its challenges and emerged unscathed. Over a period of continuous service in South Africa, he had taken part in no fewer than 82 engagements.[51] With the exception of the encounters at Dordrecht, Aliwal North and Wepener, they had been, given the nature of the war, mostly minor skirmishes. For a second time, he had proved his ability to raise troops, and, once more, displayed his qualities of leadership. He was twice mentioned in despatches and subsequently awarded both campaign medals: the Queen's South Africa Medal and the King's South Africa Medal with six clasps.[52] In recognition of his services, he attained the honorary rank of lieutenant-colonel. As a seasoned soldier, his exploits provided a fund of tales. At Walton Heath, their Surrey retreat, David Lloyd George and Frances Stevenson were regaled with 'many interesting stories' of his experiences in the South African war.[53] The tales of derring-do not only improved with time, but grew distinctly taller.

NOTES

1. T. Pakenham, *The Boer War* (London, 1979), pp.xvi–xvii, 89, 119.
2. K. O. Morgan, 'Wales and the Boer War' in *Modern Wales: Politics, Places and People* (Cardiff, 1995).
3. E. Morgan Humphreys, *David Lloyd George* (Llandebie, 1943), p.31.
4. Specifically *Y Tyst* and *Y Celt*, cf. *Western Mail*, 14 March 1900.
5. *North Wales Chronicle*, 27 January 1900, letter from Owen Thomas.
6. Cf., *Y Clorianydd*, 3 Mawrth 1915.
7. See the thought-provoking views of Carroll Quigley, *The Anglo-American Establishment* (New York, 1981).
8. His letters are supplemented by T. Packenham, op.cit., L. S. Amery, *The Times History of the War in South Africa* (London, 5 volumes 1900–9), F. Maurice, *History of the War in South Africa 1899–1902* (London, 4 volumes, 1906–10), The Marquess of Anglesey, *A History of the British Cavalry 1816–1919*, vol. IV (London, 1986), W. Bennett, *Absent-minded Beggars. Volunteers in the Boer War* (Barnsley, 1999), and various websites.
9. *Y Clorianydd*, 25 Ionawr 1900, letter from Owen Thomas.

10. *North Wales Chronicle*, 27 January 1900, letter from Owen Thomas.
11. Ibid, 31 March 1900, letter from Owen Thomas.
12. *Y Clorianydd*, 5 Ebrill 1900, letter from Owen Thomas.
13. Ibid, 3 Mawrth 1915.
14. F. S. Crafford, *Jan Smuts: A Biography* (London, 1945), pp.41–2.
15. *The Times*, 14 March, 17 April 1900.
16. www.angloboerwar.wordpress.com/category/brabant-ey.
17. *North Wales Chronicle*, 2 June 1900; *Y Clorianydd* 7 Mehefin 1900, letters from Owen Thomas.
18. *The Times*, 7 May 1900.
19. *Y Clorianydd*, 25 Hydref, 1 Tachwedd 1900.
20. Ibid, 8 Tachwedd 1900.
21. Information provided by Robert Williams.
22. Death Certificate. See also M. N. J. (Jackson) *Bygone Days in the March Wall of Wales* (London, 1926), pp.33, 46. A lectern was placed in St Bridget's church, Skenfrith, and the bells rehung in 1911, in remembrance of Frederick Leyton.
23. *The Times*, 20 December 1900.
24. Ibid, 28 May 1901.
25. *Y Clorianydd*, 16 Mai 1901. Letter from Trooper J. T. G. Roberts; *North Wales Chronicle*, 1 June 1901.
26. *The Times*, 1 October 1908, letter from Owen Thomas.
27. *North Wales Chronicle*, 6 July 1901.
28. Cf., *Y Clorianydd*, 7 Chwefror 1907.
29. *The Times*, 20 June 1901.
30. National Library of Wales. Welsh Army Corps Papers, C12/34, letter from Owen Thomas to Lord Plymouth, 7 October 1914.
31. The National Archives. CO 417/395, 405, copies of correspondence, extracts from letters to the *Cape Times* and the War Office verdict, 26 October 1902–27 June 1904.
32. Bryn Owen, *Owen Roscomyl and the Welsh Horse* (Caernarfon, 1990), pp.13–14.
33. *North Wales Chronicle*, 6 July 1901, letter from C. H. Temple.
34. The National Archives, WO 127/16, nominal roll of the Prince of Wales' Light Horse.
35. Later, Captain Owen Thomas Evans, whose recollections are referred to above in Bangor MSS 27,002, and 27,007.

36. The National Archives, WO 126/104, Record of Service.
37. Cf., *North Wales Chronicle*, 21 January 1916.
38. Ibid, 1 June 1901. Also Louis Creswick, *South Africa and the Transvaal War* Vol. 7 (Manchester, 1902), p.8.
39. *Y Clorianydd*, 16 Mai 1901, letter from Trooper J. T. G. Roberts; also *The New York Times*, 29 April 1901.
40. *North Wales Chronicle*, 6 July 1901, letter from C. H. Temple; also www.justdone.co.za/ROH/abw_DeathByUnit.php.
41. *The Times*, 3 January 1902.
42. *Western Mail*, 20 November 1909.
43. Official records show Berry to have been a native of Taunton. Owen Thomas had hoped to have 50 cyclists, see *Caernarvon & Denbigh Herald*, 8 February 1901.
44. *The Times*, 1 October 1908, letter from Owen Thomas.
45. www.angloboerwar.com/units/pwslh.htm
46. *The Times*, 20 June 1901.
47. Letter from Owen Thomas to Charles Hughes-Hunter, 22 November 1901 (kept at Brynddu); also *The Times*, 20 December 1901.
48. *The Times*, 10 January 1902; *Y Clorianydd*, 30 Ionawr 1902.
49. T. Pakenham, op. cit., p.572.
50. The words of St John Brodrick, the Secretary of State for War.
51. Cf., *Y Clorianydd*, 3 Mawrth 1915.
52. *Who's Who*, 1923.
53. A. J. P. Taylor (ed.), *Lloyd George: A Diary by Frances Stevenson* (London, 1971), p.11, entry 16 November 1914.

4: Colonial Travels

APPARENTLY, SOMETIME PRIOR TO THE WAR, Owen Thomas had been asked to report on the agricultural prospects of the vast territories to the north of Transvaal – the future Rhodesia (Zimbabwe). Matabeleland and Mashonaland were being administered and developed by the British South Africa Company, founded by charter in 1889. As its managing director, Cecil Rhodes was intent that the company should encourage land settlement as the means to exploit its agricultural potential. Thomas claimed he had discussed the matter with Rhodes upon his arrival in South Africa, mindful that the war had put paid to their plans for a time.[1] During the course of extensive military operations, Thomas was presented with the ideal opportunity to directly observe much of the land in southern Africa at first-hand. Thus he traversed Cape Colony, the Orange Free State and the Transvaal on a dual mission: pursuing bands of Boer guerrillas, while examining the land, crops and stock, as well as collating relevant statistics in the process. It was more than a matter of casting an instinctive eye; officially or not, he served vested interests. Brief extracts from his findings were subsequently published by an unnamed correspondent in *The Times* in August 1901.[2]

In essence, it was advice from a 'well known authority on agricultural matters' to those seeking to partake in any postwar colonisation scheme. As the best farming land in Cape Colony had already been taken, future settlers were told to consider opportunities in the 'conquered territory' of the renamed Orange River Colony and Transvaal; newcomers having to be reminded of potential hazards, droughts and diseases. Significantly, this article was filed by Phillip Lyttelton Gell, a London-based director of the British South Africa Company, and a close associate of Rhodes and Milner.[3] Even before Rhodes's death in March 1902, and the end of hostilities, Milner and Beit were planning towards postwar reconstruction. As the two key players, they fostered Rhodes's imperialist vision. Milner,

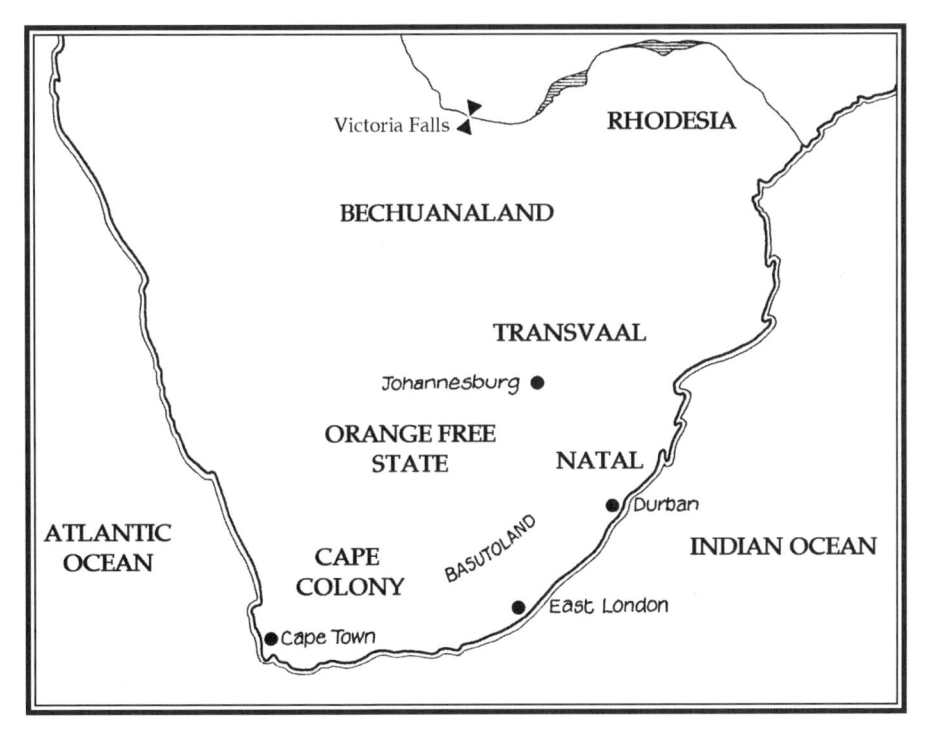

Southern Africa

the Governor of the Transvaal, based in Johannesburg, wielded considerable political power and began the process of setting up Land Boards to install English-speaking yeoman farmers 'on a large scale' in the former Boer Republics.[4] Transvaal was to be ethnically engineered into a 'thoroughly British' province where the Afrikaners would be outnumbered. Beit, a fellow trustee of the Rhodes Trust, and a director of the British South Africa Company, provided the essential financial backing.

Of Beit's many business interests in mining and land, the Transvaal Consolidated Land and Exploration Company held some two million acres in the Transvaal. Before he would accomplish the task initially mooted by Rhodes, Beit, as his successor, first commissioned Owen Thomas to report on the agricultural prospects of the company's landholdings, as well as the colony as a whole, as a result of which, like many other ex-soldiers who remained in South Africa, his career took a new turn. Accompanied by the 11th Marquess de Bucy, an experienced African traveller and military officer, Thomas embarked on his special mission at the close of the war.[5] Over a period of some nine months he covered an estimated 2,750 miles by road and 900 miles by rail, to complete an exhaustive tour of the Transvaal. It was not without its perils, none more than local diseases; in December 1902 he lay in a Pietersburg hospital suffering from malarial fever.[6] Thomas had ventured deep into isolated rural areas by cart to encounter poverty-stricken Boers on their remote farms, often completely unaware of the recent war. Uncivilized in both appearance and behaviour, he recalled that Boer children were more akin 'to apes than human beings'.[7]

In his confidential report (dated 30 January 1903), subsequently forwarded to Milner and Joseph Chamberlain at the Colonial Office, Thomas presented a sombre assessment.[8] All the drawbacks that faced prospective cereal growers were highlighted in a forthright manner: poor soil, climatic extremes, plant diseases, high transport costs and foreign competition. Farmers would have to sell their produce in Johannesburg, the leading market centre, at a loss. Transvaal was essentially a pastoral country, yet the stock farmers ran similar risks, made worse by contagious animal diseases. Tracts with the greatest agricultural possibilities remained with the Boers, whose fortitude he obviously admired. Due to the activities of mining speculators and government purchases, the land had greatly inflated in price. Moreover, farmers competed with rich mine owners for native workers. What he finally concluded cannot have pleased Beit and his fellow directors: land in the Transvaal, in general, had 'no great agricultural or pastoral value'. Many barriers were to be surmounted before colonization schemes could offer viable economic opportunities to prospective farmers. Otherwise, he warned, 'artificially to force agricultural development in order to satisfy a certain political expediency must result in the creation of a class of agricultural paupers …'[9]

If nothing else, this prognosis had been brutally objective. To justify his competence in making such judgements – 'a connoisseur who condemns a whole vintage' – Thomas invoked his qualifications. Never averse to self-advertisement, past triumphs were listed, twice in the case of the heaviest ox he had exhibited at the 'Royal Show' in Islington. Not only that, he was also 'an agricultural expert on land tenure and land values' – but even expert advice could fall on deaf ears. Such were the political imperatives that Milner pressed ahead regardless and Thomas would brand the *Handbook for Settlers* issued by the Land Board in the Transvaal as a 'pernicious' booklet full of 'erroneous promises'.[10] The eventual number of settlers proved disappointing, and only in the long term did the Land Board effect agricultural change. As Thomas rightly predicted from his knowledge of the 'cunning race', the Boer would never succumb to assimilation.

After revealing the realities of the Transvaal, Thomas was then employed by the British South Africa Company to undertake a similar survey of land mostly familiar to him during his military campaigning. The conclusions form part of his book, *Agricultural and Pastoral Prospects of South Africa*;[11] he found that incomers would have to take second place. Dutch farmers were already in possession of the best land in both Cape Colony and the Orange River Colony, whereas land in the rich fertile 'Garden Colony' of Natal had been allocated to the native African people. Prospective settlers were advised to concentrate on such alternatives as stock farming, fruit, cotton, tea and tobacco. Basutoland (Lesotho) remained in the hands of the native inhabitants; only a small portion of the vast territory of Bechuanaland (Botswana) offered long term potential. Derogatory remarks permeated his reports. Despite some redeeming features, most Boers were seen as indifferent, unprogressive farmers, who, in sub-dividing their farms, condemned themselves to poverty. Devoutly religious in character, yet they had a callous, untrustworthy streak. Though he acknowledged, on the one hand, that the indigenous 'Kaffir' was 'the best all-round cultivator' of the soil, he displayed, on the other, European prejudice of the worst kind. His reports were shot through with references to their limited intellect, immorality, unreliability, thievery and 'bestial idleness'. One 'English' farm labourer was worth four natives. He found no reason to condemn the white man's use of the *sjambok* (whip).

With the best land snapped up by either the Boer or the African, or else greatly inflated by the activities of mineral speculators and Land Boards, all three colonies presented problems to the potential stock farmer. Future prosperity lay in stock farming, but there were other considerations and financial credit had to be made available. If farmers were unable to secure absolute ownership, then, in an echo of the Welsh Land Question, he advocated fair rent, fixity of tenure and fair compensation for improvements. Animal diseases had to be eradicated, or at least controlled, and the land fenced off. Once these matters were dealt with, stock farming in certain parts of South Africa held great promise to settlers of 'English' origin attracted by the colonization schemes.

Only to the north of the Transvaal would colonists find a second Eden. Sometime around April 1903, Owen Thomas at last entered the extensive territories assigned to the British South Africa Company that Rhodes had requested him to visit. Under the auspices of the Rhodes Trustees, for a fee of £500, he spent a month in Rhodesia, previously a 'tract of barbarism inhabited by howling savages' in his blistering words. He also journeyed across areas owned by various other Rhodesian land companies, visiting the Victoria Falls, 'the eighth wonder of the word' on the Zambesi river. There could be no question that this was the best colony for the British settler. It had the most fertile soil, and a stimulating climate. There was political security; few Boers had ventured this far. With hardly any white people to speak of, new settlers had the pick of the land. Property here was infinitely cheaper than elsewhere in southern Africa, and it could well treble in value. Once animal diseases had been eradicated, the rich pastures of Matabeleland offered unrivalled prospects for the stock farmer. Alternatively, specialized crops such as tobacco, cotton and rubber could be cultivated on the fertile lands of Mashonaland. At the time, the mineral industry predominated, with gold and copper deposits awaiting further exploitation and development and the projected population increase would create a growing demand for agricultural produce. Landlocked Rhodesia had already established vital rail links for the transportation of goods to both the markets of South Africa and ocean seaports.

Owen Thomas subsequently discussed the development of Rhodesia with the Duke of Abercorn, president of the British South Africa Company, and leading company directors. At their request, he drew up a scheme for land settlement and colonization in Rhodesia, dated 15 March 1904.[12] Based on facts found in his report to the Rhodes Trustees, he re-endorsed its possibilities as a stock-raising country. The scheme

The Thomas children in 1906. L–R: Robert Newton; Frederick Leyton; Trevor; Owen Vincent and Mina Margaret.

concentrated on preparing the land for monied settler ranchers, and the means of attracting them to settle in Rhodesia. He dwelt in some detail on such matters as land tenure, the eradication of animal diseases, the establishment of an agricultural credit bank and a stockbreeding home farm. He recommended that the main body of settlers be recruited in 'England' [sic], from the 'more energetic class of farmers' found along the western periphery extending from Cornwall, Wales and Lancashire to Scotland. Practical information was to be disseminated by means of pamphlets, articles, lectures, and a 'Rhodesian Tent' prominently placed in the principal annual agricultural shows.

Upon analysis, P. Lyttelton Gell and Lord Gifford concluded that Thomas's scheme placed too narrow a focus on stockfarming.[13] Questions of cost and the presence of uncontrolled animal diseases undermined his main premise, which they variously described as 'theoretical', 'ideal' and 'utopian'. Cattle farmers faced too many hazards, while other options had not been sufficiently pursued. Many of his proposals could be useful to the British South Africa Company in the long term, but at the time neither director found merit in the scheme as a practical investment. It was therefore not in the interests of the company to accept his recommendations. They favoured a more realistic land settlement policy that attracted a greater number of self-supporting agriculturalists, the 'small cultivating proprietors' who would supply food, and ultimately grow tobacco and other exportable products. In this connection, Owen Thomas was invited to utilize his 'great influence' to renew contact with the Welsh colonists in Patagonia. They were the very type of 'hardy and experienced cultivators' that the company desired to see settle in Rhodesia. If successful, Thomas's services would be of great value.

As it happened, Thomas's investigations in the Transvaal in 1902 had coincided with a crisis in the Chubut valley, Patagonia.[14] Severe floods, together with the antagonistic actions of the Argentinian government, triggered discontent among the 2,500 Welsh colonists in this part of *Y Wladfa*. An Emigration Movement Committee was set up, leading to discussions of relocation to Canada or Zoutpansberg in north-eastern Transvaal, with British government assistance.[15] The prospect of attracting a large number of farmers of British extraction to settle in Boer areas naturally appealed to Milner. Pro-South African lobbyists among the Welsh colonists approached the British South Africa Company and Chamberlain, the Colonial Secretary. At Colonial Office expense, a three man delegation including R. J. Roberts and Llwyd ap Iwan (son of Michael D. Jones, who had provided the original inspiration for *Y Wladfa*) travelled to the Transvaal where they met Owen Thomas early in 1903. His recent bleak prognosis provided a salutary caution to any would-be settlers, not least fellow Welshmen. His own brother, Thomas Owen Thomas, it will be recalled, was closely connected with *Y Wladfa*. Though sympathetic to their aspirations he warned against such a move at a meeting of Welsh expatriates in Durban: it would be merely 'jumping from the frying pan into the fire'.[16] Little wonder, therefore, that the Transvaal offer was rejected out of hand.

Following his subsequent visit to Rhodesia, Thomas had waxed eloquently over the exceptional opportunities there. He foresaw a nursery for an 'independent and dynamic race of white men' who would contribute to the 'glory of the Empire'.[17] By the same token, he urged leaders of the

Welsh community in Patagonia to consider the possibilities of establishing an alternative *Gwladfa* within its borders. In a letter (in Welsh) to R. J. Roberts in August 1904, he summarised the superior economic conditions that could sustain a distinct Welsh colony.[18] It would be possible to offer them a 100–200 square-mile block of excellent agricultural land. Again, possibly at the behest of the British South Africa Company, he held out the prospect of farmers being granted 2,000 acres free of charge. They were invited to view Rhodesia for themselves, or else he was quite willing to visit Patagonia to elaborate further. For nothing would please him more than to see a colony of '*Cymry glân gloew*' (loosely, fluent Welsh speakers) in Rhodesia, drawn from both Patagonia and Wales itself. Despite his optimism,[19] this particular 'dream' was never realised.[20] Some colonists did move to Canada, but most were content to stay in Chubut when conditions improved.

Back in Britain, Owen Thomas and his family had settled in Fawley, near Henley-on-Thames, by 1904. In connection with the British South Africa Company, he worked from an office address in London and also made a telling appearance in print. At the request of the 4th Earl Grey, a director of the company, he prepared the mass of notes, compiled over three-and-a-half years in southern Africa, for publication in book form. Altogether, Thomas calculated that he had travelled 7,000 miles by road and 700 miles [sic] by rail, to penetrate the vast interior where only a handful of white men lived. With the Rhodes Trust contributing £240 towards its cost, the *Agricultural and Pastoral Prospects of South Africa* was published by Constable in October 1904. In his dedication, and elsewhere, Owen Thomas commended Earl Grey for encouraging the small farmer and husbandry rather than viewing the land through the 'Rand constructed spectacles' of gold speculators.[21] The book was well received and press reviews considered it a standard work: 'a searching examination'[22] and a 'really remarkable book full of epigrams and parables'.[23] It confirmed his growing status as 'one of the leading authorities on South African land and colonization.'[24]

Few knew that it came not from his pen, but that of Frederick William Rolfe, the self-styled Baron Corvo. In response to a newspaper advertisement, Rolfe had agreed to act as literary assistant in October 1903. His memorable description of Thomas as 'an obese magenta colonel of militia with a black-stubbed moustache and a Welsh-tongued proposition'[25] gives a hint of his florid style. Rolfe, as it turned out, was a paranoid, scrounging, vindictive individual – the supposed 'tormented genius' so beloved of the literati. He claimed to have spent over seven months expanding 'a 20 page pamphlet into a 500 page volume'. A characteristic exaggeration; for one thing the book had precisely 321 pages. It came embellished with classical references to Virgil and Columella, two Roman writers on agriculture, the Greek poet Meleagros, and quotes from Darwin, Kipling and Pasteur. Up to June 1904, Rolfe also composed articles, letters and much more besides. They included material relating to Rhodesia, chiefly the scheme for land settlement and colonization (March, 1904) and the article entitled 'The Commercial Future of Rhodesia' for the *Magazine of Commerce* (April, 1904). Subtitled 'the resources of a great territory attractively described by a writer who has personal knowledge of the country', the piece was in fact the scholarly handiwork of a ghost-writer, and it mirrored almost exactly the section on Rhodesia that would appear in the book.

What proportion Rolfe actually wrote is not known. Thomas, though, had little reason to doubt his own authorial talent; pre-Corvo, if original, his concise report on the Transvaal (30 January 1903) was stylishly sound, enlivened by some Latinisms, and mention of Autolycus of Greek mythology. In fact, a few of his memorable sentences reappear in the book.

Rolfe proved to be an unfortunate choice. No precise terms had been reached when the original verbal agreement was made. Payments amounting to £52 seemed a fair return for the work done, but to a man in desperate financial straits, it was an opportunity to exact a small fortune from Thomas or the Rhodes Trust. On 6 August 1904, he issued a writ claiming £999-9s-6d for 1,050 hours at 10s-10d an hour. Entwined with other matters, he sued for the excessively grand total of £2,000.[26] When the case eventually came before the High Court of Justice, King's Bench Division, on 16 January 1907, Baron Corvo's day in court proved unproductive. An attempt to dig up material at the War Office to discredit Thomas yielded nothing[27] (he possibly had wind of the minor scandal involving ex-members of the Prince of Wales' Light Horse). His bizarre behaviour hardly made him a creditable witness against a man of Colonel Owen Thomas's standing, and judgement was entered for the defendant with costs. Well could he 'feel exactly as though I had been beaten with beetroots and mangold-wurzels all over'.[28] An aggrieved man, he spent the remainder of his days in the slums of Venice, wallowing in debauchery. Meantime, only 406 copies of the book had been sold by November 1910, out of the 2,000 printed.[29] Little credence can therefore be given to Thomas's claim five years later that its reception had been so favourable that there was call for a second edition.[30]

Vast sections of territories administered by the British South Africa Company in Rhodesia were allocated to various land companies, and such business concerns as the Matabele Gold Reefs and Estates Co. Ltd and the Gwanda Railway Syndicate Ltd. Like the Rhodesia Consolidated Ltd, with its 700,000 acres, they offered lots of between 200–1,000 acres for sale or lease. The appropriation of prime land, of course, dispossessed the indigenous African people and created a pool of cheap native labour. Still, it probably never concerned Owen Thomas. Throughout 1905, he acted as the 'expert' agricultural adviser to the above companies.[31] Under his guidance, pamphlets and illustrated booklets were produced, detailing land and stock available to the prospective white settler at very favourable terms. In advertisements that appeared in *Y Clorianydd* he marketed these opportunities to Welsh farmers, this time combining the attractions of both stockbreeding and cultivation.[32] Export crops, primarily maize, cotton and tobacco, offered great possibilities. In due course, following his recommendations,[33] the 'high priced Turkish tobacco' (for which he had personally acquired a taste) became Rhodesia's main cash crop.

* * *

While there is no evidence to link Owen Thomas with two other colourful imperialists out in South Africa, their paths must surely have crossed: Charles Sydney Goldman served in the Boer War and had extensive goldmining interests in the Transvaal,[34] and the controversial and flamboyant Ewart Scott Grogan, a member of Milner's inner circle at the time of reconstruction, also mixed with Goldman, Beit and the business big shots

East Africa

of Johannesburg at the very time Thomas was in the Transvaal.[35] What is more certain is that Thomas rubbed shoulders with Goldman later in London. As a member of the Compatriots Club, a dining circle founded in 1904, Goldman joined a select group of ardent imperialists who supported Joseph Chamberlain's campaign for tariff reform and imperial preference. When Milner returned from South Africa, he became president of the club. Various aspects of the imperialist creed were aired in a weighty volume entitled *The Empire and the Century. A series of Essays on Imperial*

Problems and Possibilities published in 1905 with Goldman as editor. In his introduction, he extolled the 'dream of a United British Empire'.[36] Among the 50 contributors were Ewart S. Grogan and Colonel Owen Thomas. Though true believers in imperialism, not all supported Chamberlain's policy of imposing protectionist tariffs to favour trade with the colonies. Thomas sided with the minority of free traders – consistent with the position he held in 1893, and defended in 1918.

In his chapter on 'Land Settlement and Colonization in South Africa', Thomas trod on familiar ground, but without trace of Rolfe or academic references. According to his imperialist thinking, colonization could not be regarded as emigration because the Britons who settled in Canada, Australia, South Africa and other parts of the empire were 'merely moving within the family'. Predictably, much was made of Rhodesia and the 'magnificent opportunity' it offered to the British settler. Only this time he took heed of discussions with the directors of the British South Africa Company to announce that the outlook was equally bright for both the stockbreeder and cultivator of specialized crops.

Contact with Goldman, moreover, led to a geographical change of direction for Owen Thomas. Together with his business partner, Ewart S. Grogan, Goldman had spotted the commercial opportunities in the East Africa Protectorate (under British rule since 1895; and from 1920, the colony of Kenya). The completion of the railway linking Mombasa on the coast to Nairobi, and subsequently, the shores of Lake Victoria by 1901, opened up a vast area for settlement and economic development.[37] Once again, the expropriation of African tribal homelands meant cheap land and a plentiful supply of cheap labour. A large block of land in the Rift Valley was granted to the East Africa Syndicate in 1903. A year later, Joseph Chamberlain unsuccessfully offered land to Theodor Herzl, founder of the Zionist movement, as a possible choice for the persecuted Jews of eastern Europe. By 1906, the white population still only numbered around 1,600 among up to three million native inhabitants. The Colonial Office was plainly anxious to attract European settlers; more especially, companies with money to invest and expertise in African farming. The door was open to freebooting capitalists with an eye to the main chance. As with Rhodesia, the Protectorate came to be seen as a future 'white man's country' in the South Africa image.

As one of the leading pioneers in British East Africa, Grogan began to build up his considerable business interests in 1905, with Goldman crucially providing capital. One aim was to develop the port of Kilindini near Mombasa. To avail themselves of opportunities further inland, the Uplands of East Africa Syndicate Ltd was registered on 24 February 1906 with a nominal capital of £10,000.[38] The first directors included Goldman, Grogan and Sir Herbert A. Lawrence, a Boer War veteran and City of London banker, though Grogan, who came under investigation for the fraudulent transfer of land, soon resigned.[39] Set up to examine and explore territories in both British East Africa and Uganda, and develop business opportunities, the company had secured the services of Owen Thomas as their agricultural adviser. He would receive 25 per cent of the annual net profits after the payment of share dividends, plus a seat on the board.

Unlike South Africa, Thomas did not publish a public account of his travels in East Africa, but an outline can be pieced together from brief reports in the *East African Standard*. His arrival in January 1906 on the S.S. *Africa* meant that he was away when his eldest son, Frederick Leyton, died at Skenfrith.[40] After visiting Zanzibar, he journeyed by rickshaw along the coast of Kenya in March, accompanied by Sir James Hayes Sadler, the British Commissioner, to visit the northern ports.[41] Moving inland to Naivasha, he travelled with Goldman as far as Entebbe in Uganda, in June.[42] Talk here was of a railway concession to connect Entebbe with Gondokoro in the Sudan (and ultimately Cairo).[43] After a stay at the Government House in the capital Nairobi in July, Goldman and Thomas returned to the coast at Mombasa, en route to Shimoni to view the coastlands.[44] All the while Thomas was gathering information and evaluating the agricultural prospects of the region with a view to business investment.

Owen Thomas traversed vast swathes of East Africa a year or so earlier than Winston Churchill, who recorded his experiences in *My African Journey* (1908). Churchill praised both the beauty and fertility of the land and whilst on safari came across some warlike tribes.[45] Photographs capture Owen Thomas and his party in similar surroundings at a later date.[46] Accompanied by his son, Robert Newton Thomas, and others, they are seen in tented and hut camps, sporting pith helmets and safari suits,

Owen Thomas in camp during his travels in East Africa.

their retinue of African porters and carriers in the background. Across open plains and deep into jungle terrain, the arduous trekking was fraught with difficulty and danger. From lions to mosquitoes, to the fearsome natives encountered in the remote wild. On reaching one village, a hundred armed warriors charged towards him with their spears aimed at his heart.[47] Once the danger had passed, both he and the tribal chief took part in a ritual ceremony when their blood was mingled to denote a binding friendship as 'blood brothers'.

It soon became clear that the Syndicate had ambitious plans to expand its presence in the Protectorate. In June 1906, it applied for a lease of 358,000 acres (547 square miles), a colossal tract of land on the coastal strip between Mombasa and the border with German East Africa (Tanzania).[48] The commercial prospects for tropical products – cotton, sisal, rubber, fibre, coconuts – made for a sound investment. In addition to gaining railway and steamship concessions, Thomas was keen to develop parts of the Highlands, where the temperate climate proved more conducive to Europeans. Some 2,000 acres were acquired at Limuru, a fertile area to the north of Nairobi, a move that dispossessed the Kikuyu tribe of their rights. Though suitable for all cereals, Thomas concentrated his attention on the rearing of stock, and in a direct appeal to farmers in Anglesey he spoke of

Robert Newton Thomas and his father in camp in East Africa.

a future for the Welsh Black cattle.[49] Knowledge of the breed's qualities made him confident that settlers could command good prices. It also dawned upon him that conditions were also ideal for breeding pigs.[50] Not all the schemes contained in his *Report on the British East Africa and Uganda Protectorates for the Uplands of East Africa Syndicate* (privately printed, 1907) would be realised, though the proposal for a bacon factory in the Highlands found favour with Sir James Hayes Sadler, who had become Governor of the East Africa Protectorate.[51]

The need for capital was paramount. Already the Syndicate had attracted prestigious support from a major investor such as the Duke of Westminster, and both he and Viscount Cobham smoothed the way with the Colonial Office.[52] In July 1907, Thomas and Goldman attended a meeting of the British East Africa Association in London to discuss 'progress and prosperity' in the region.[53] After a lantern demonstration of slides and photographs, Thomas read a paper entitled 'A Few Notes and Observations on East Africa'. With its potential asset of 547 square miles on the coast – the largest concession that would be granted by the Colonial Office – the Syndicate secured the backing of influential money men. By August 1908, four eminent grandees, the Duke of Westminster, Viscount Cobham, the Earl of Plymouth and Lord Belper, were formally added to the board of directors.[54] In December, Owen Thomas was appointed the general manager. Reflecting wider ambitions, the company reconstituted itself in November 1909 as the East African Estates Ltd, with a registered office at Carlton House in Regent Street, London.

Financial depression and trade stagnation made 1907–09 difficult years for the company but, nevertheless, one venture proved eminently successful. It was not Welsh Black cattle that would thrive on the rich grazing found in the Highlands, but pigs. Thomas, with characteristic flourish, later claimed that £10,000 had been spent on importing pigs into the country, where they proceeded to 'multiply like rabbits' at little expense.[55] In 1909, the company invested £3,000 in the construction of the Uplands Bacon Factory at Limuru, installed with modern equipment. Praised for its high quality products, it soon established a profitable export trade.[56] During the war years, large quantities of bacon and ham were supplied to the military. According to one authority, this was probably Owen Thomas's most significant contribution to Kenya's economic development.[57] (The Kenya Farmers' Association would eventually take over the factory as a co-operative venture.)

Differences in attitudes to land ownership, and European ignorance of African life, culture and customs, were highlighted when white settlers adopted coercive measures to recruit indigenous workers at a time of severe labour shortage. Though a Native Labour Commission was appointed in 1912, the pressure from planter interest intensified. A delegation of leading landowners and company representatives met Lewis Harcourt, the Colonial Secretary, at the House of Commons in December with proposals to induce labour recruitment. Lord Cranworth and Colonel Owen Thomas were vociferous detractors of the African male. In his submission, Thomas adhered to the belief that the native African was fundamentally lazy and unwilling to work.[58] The Native Labour Commission later reported that settler treatment of Africans had been unduly harsh, 'warping ideals of justice and humanity'.[59] Collateral evidence proved the East African Estates Ltd to be among the worst offenders. In 1913, H. C. Belfield, the new governor of the East Africa Protectorate, uncovered the 'scandalous conditions' on its coastal estate at Shimoni.[60] Little medical provision was made for the native workers, and the company had failed to report 28 deaths. As a result, he forbade them to engage more labourers until conditions were improved. Otherwise, next to nothing is known of the workforce overseen by Owen Thomas. Native wages were incorporated under general plantation expenditure in company records. Replying to criticism of sweated labour on company plantations in 1922, Thomas asserted that the 2–3,000 native employees were being paid at rates fixed by the colonial government.[61]

Throughout the period of his involvement, the East African Estates Ltd remained a modest enterprise, with a market capitalisation of £120,000 in 1913, rising to £260,000 by 1923.[62] Now managing director, Thomas continued to sail to East Africa on periodic tours to view their business interests. His annual remuneration increased from £1,500 in 1913 to £3,080 (including expenses) by 1921, together with a substantial shareholding. Apart from the bacon-curing factory, the company also had land and property at Entebbe. He supervised the development of the 358,000 acres (later much reduced) along the coastal belt, where sisal-hemp, tiwi and 125,000 coconut trees were planted. In 1917, the company acquired the Gazi (British East Africa) Rubber and Fibre Estates Ltd that had sub-leased a portion of its land. Rubber, however, was not well suited to conditions in East Africa, and it failed to compete with Malaya and Indonesia, where future production would be concentrated.

In a colonial sideshow to the Great War, German forces had offered stubborn resistance in East Africa to the very end and the resulting economic turmoil brought work on the plantations to a halt. The conscription of native Africans into the military as porters had led to a severe shortage of labour, made worse by postwar famine and influenza. A rise in the value of the Indian rupee, the standard currency, against sterling also left the business heavily exposed. Financial losses of £4,435 for 1919 had almost doubled by 1923, when it reported a loss of £8,018. Owen Thomas's final responsibility in the early 1920s involved experiments with various tropical products, in particular cotton growing in the Voi-Taveta region,[63] and attempts were made to raise the necessary capital. But the economic future of Kenya lay in the Highlands, not in coastal plantations. Tropical diseases were prevalent on the coast, and there was heavy mortality among the native workers. As the problems mounted, the company decided in 1923 to surrender almost half of the unproductive, unhealthy coastal land in exchange for some 20,000 acres in the Highlands where maize, coffee and sugar were grown. In common with other pioneering companies, the East African Estates Ltd had encountered many difficulties during Owen Thomas's time. Thereafter, it operated on a smaller scale to become essentially a property investment company, which gradually liquidated its assets before it was voluntarily dissolved in September 1975.

At least in Anglesey and Africa, Owen Thomas received due recognition in his day. The progress of the *'teithydd Affricanaidd'* (African traveller) was noted in *Y Clorianydd*.[64] It opined that no other Welshman had seen as much of Africa.[65] Local admirers, who proclaimed his fearlessness and sense of adventure, ranked him with Stanley.[66] Indeed, it is possible to draw a few noteworthy parallels with 'Africa's greatest explorer'.[67] Both were Welsh-speaking Welshmen from rural Wales. John Rowlands, or Henry Morton Stanley (1841–1904) as he became known, made epic trans-Africa journeys of exploration during the 1870s and 80s to 'find' Dr Livingstone, trace the source of the Congo river, and under the auspices of the Belgian king he helped found the Congo Free State. Owen Thomas travelled to investigate the agricultural potential of both southern and east Africa. In the process, the two men undertook arduous expeditions that covered hundreds of miles deep into the wilds of Africa, though Thomas never experienced the 'unimaginable dangers' that faced Stanley. Both encountered native tribes and partook in ceremonies to enter blood brotherhood with a tribal warlord. They even shared the same penchant for exaggeration, falsehoods and self-mythologising, more so in Stanley's case, if only to mention his initial efforts to conceal his Welsh origins. Later, both had a final career in politics as members of the House of Commons; both received a knighthood. Amid the wealth of surviving material relating to Stanley are the detailed personal diaries he kept on his travels in 'Darkest Africa'. Alas, Thomas's East African diary, extending 'over many years'[68] has been lost to posterity.

Africa was in their blood in every sense. Tropical diseases dogged both men. Whilst malaria caused the death of most of his white companions, a nasty fever gave Stanley a near-death experience. For the rest of his life,

Owen Thomas became prey to bouts of malarial fever.[69] But there were also significant differences in their character. In contrast to his contemporaries, and certainly Owen Thomas, Stanley's attitude to the Africans was 'unusually enlightened'.[70] Perceived to be the embodiment of European imperialism he displayed no racial prejudice, whereas Thomas sneered at the 'idle native'; the 'kaffir' he regarded as 'nothing more than grown up children'.[71] Though steeped in Nonconformist values, and principled in the case of the downtrodden farm labourers of Anglesey, his ideal of social justice did not extend to the native people. He appears every bit the white intolerant racist of his age, paying little heed to African rights. His opinions, moreover, contrasted sharply with the views of Ellis Jones Griffith, who had visited South Africa a few years earlier than Thomas, and who would advocate citizenship for the black majority when the constitution of the Union of South Africa was debated in the Commons in August 1909.[72] It cannot be said that he tarred all races with the same brush. Thomas associated with leading figures among the notable element of Arab stock residing on the coast of East Africa. He regarded the governor of Mombasa, Sheikh Ali Bin Salim, of the royal clan of the Sultan of Zanzibar, as a 'valued and trusting friend'.[73] Indeed, it was Thomas who introduced Sir Frederick Treves, the celebrated surgeon (who had treated Joseph Merrick, the 'Elephant man'), to the sheikh when he arrived at Mombasa to begin his journey to Uganda.[74] In his booklet, *Stray Leaves from my East African Diary* (1920), Thomas presented a convincing case for employing 'educated Arabs', imbued with British ideals and loyalties, in the future government and administration of Kenya.[75] Having helped to stem the German military advance towards the East Africa Protectorate during the Great War, their services could further promote national interests. With the coastal zone only recently placed under the jurisdiction of the Sultan of Zanzibar, he may have also been minded by business calculations.

Whereas Stanley strongly opposed the appropriation of native lands by Europeans, Thomas, indisputably, played a vital part in the process of land grabbing that facilitated British colonial advance in Africa. Even before his contribution to the making of Rhodesia and Kenya could be appreciated, his role in the Boer War and as a land surveyor who reported on the agricultural prospects of the Transvaal had cemented his reputation. His name appeared among the 2,000 or so 'colonial African celebrities' listed in *The Anglo-African Who's Who and Biographical Sketchbook* (1907). Alongside Beit, Gell, Goldman, Grey, Grogan, Milner and Rhodes, he stood in illustrious company, increasingly well-connected to an imperialist coterie. Those involved in the early development of Kenya also burnished his credentials, one observer specifically mentioned Colonel Owen Thomas among the 'intelligent and highly qualified men' at work in the colony.[76] In preparing his classic Kenya memoir, *A Colony in the Making* (London, 1912), Lord Cranworth, one of the founding fathers, credited him with a special acknowledgement. To be sure, his knowledge and expertise had gained the highest respect of politicians and businessmen who sought his services. And the reports he produced for the major land and colonization companies did much to shape the agricultural development of key African territories of the British Empire. In Rhodesia and Kenya respectively, he is credited with introducing two successful export commodities: tobacco and bacon products. Together, they provide a key measure of his achievements on the continent.

By this stage, circumstances allowed him an affluent lifestyle in rural Buckinghamshire and later in the fashionable Montagu Mansions in Marylebone, London.[77]

A motor car, and a steam launch anchored in Cemaes harbour, added to the trappings of wealth. Throughout this time, he maintained close ties with Anglesey. In 1907, he was able to purchase Cestyll, a grand house near Cemlyn, as a second home on the island where he could relax with his family.[78] Also visiting his elderly mother at Neuadd (he was in Anglesey at the time of her death, aged 90, in June 1911)[79] and brother Hugh at Carrog, he reconnected with community life. Cemaes remained close to his heart, while villagers always expressed a kind word for '*y Cyrnol da o'r Brynddu gynt*' (the good Colonel formerly of Brynddu).[80] He would deliver the occasional lecture on Africa;[81] perhaps he brought along the elephant skull, a memento of big-game shooting, still kept at Neuadd. He also presided at an Oddfellows concert, and with characteristic altruism, in 1909 he gave hand-outs of 'many pounds' to destitute women of the locality who faced winter hardship.[82] As he entered middle age,

Owen Thomas could reflect on a successful career that had taken him far afield since his days as land agent to the Plas Coch estate. And with three sons about to make their way in the world, he had much to look forward to. Until another war utterly changed his life.

NOTES

1. *Y Clorianydd*, 3 Mawrth 1915.
2. *The Times*, 5 August 1901.
3. Derbyshire Record Office, papers of the Gell family of Hopton, D3287, BSA/5/23.
4. Shula Marks, 'Southern and Central Africa, 1886–1910. The Construction of the Modern South African State' in *The Cambridge History of Africa*, vol.6 (Cambridge, 1985), pp. 481-5. Also, *The Times*, 29 July 1902.
5. Walter H. Wills (ed.) *The Anglo-African Who's Who and Biographical Sketchbook, 1907.* (reprinted, Jeepstown Press, London, 2006), pp.96–7.
6. *Y Clorianydd*, 18 Rhagfyr 1902.
7. Ibid, 3 Mawrth 1915.
8. The National Archives, CO 291/55, 12658, Milner to Chamberlain, enclosing Owen Thomas's *Report to the Chairman and Directors of the Transvaal Consolidated Land and Exploration Co. Ltd*, dated 30 January 1903.
9. *Report*, p.19.
10. Owen Thomas, *Agricultural and Pastoral Prospects of South Africa* (London, 1904), pp.103–4.
11. Points made in this and subsequent paragraphs are drawn from the book; also *Cape Times*, 8 April 1903. 'An Expert Interviewed'.
12. Derbyshire Record Office, papers of the Gell family of Hopton, D3287, BSA/5/145. Scheme for Land Settlement in Rhodesia, Owen Thomas, 15 March 1904.
13. Ibid, BSA/5/153, Report on Owen Thomas's Memorandum by Lord Gifford and P. Lyttelton Gell, 27 April 1904.
14. G. Dyfnallt Owen, *Crisis in Chubut. A Chapter in the history of the Welsh Colony in Patagonia* (Swansea, 1977).
15. *The Times*, 19 February 1902.

16. *Y Clorianydd*, 8 Ionawr 1903.
17. Owen Thomas, 'The Commercial Future of Rhodesia' in the *Magazine of Commerce*, April 1904, p.299.
18. Derbyshire Record Office, papers of the Gell family of Hopton, D3287, BSA/5/161/2, letter from Owen Thomas to R. J. Roberts, 30 August 1904.
19. Ibid, BSA/5/161/1, letter from Owen Thomas to P. Lyttelton Gell, 6 September 1904.
20. Cf. Glyn Williams, *The Desert and the Dream: A Study of Welsh Colonization in Chubut, 1865–1915* (Cardiff, 1975).
21. *The Times*, 12 October 1904, letter from Owen Thomas.
22. *Times Literary Supplement*, 21 October 1904.
23. *East African Standard*, 20 January 1906.
24. *The Times*, 17 August 1904.
25. A. J. A. Symons, *The Quest for Corvo* (London, 1934), p.148, also D. Weeks, *Corvo* (London, 1971), pp.241–2, 257–8.
26. The National Archives, J54/1331, Statement of Claim, 29 November 1904.
27. M. J. Benkovitz, *Frederick Rolfe: Baron Corvo – A Biography* (London, 1977), p.194.
28. A. J. A. Symons, op. cit., p.161. At long last Rolfe has been given his due. When Nabu Press (Charleston, USA) reprinted *Agricultural and Pastoral Prospects of South Africa* in 2010, he is credited alongside Owen Thomas as co-author.
29. C. Woolf, *A Bibliography of Frederick Rolfe, Baron Corvo* (London, 1972), pp. 99–100. Constable (publishers) hold no contract or record of the book – letter to the author, 3 February 1987.
30. *Y Clorianydd*, 3 Mawrth 1915.
31. Ibid, 9 Tachwedd 1905.
32. Ibid, 9 Tachwedd, 14 Rhagfyr 1905.
33. *The Times*, 7 November 1906, Annual meeting of the Rhodesia Consolidated Ltd.
34. Ibid, 9 April 1958; also letter from John Monck (son) to the author, 31 October 1990.
35. Edward Paice, *Lost Lion of Empire. The Life of 'Cape-to-Cairo' Grogan* (London, 2001), p. 139.
36. C. S. Goldman (ed.), *The Empire and the Century. A Series of Essays on Imperial Problems and Possibilities* (London, 1905), p.xx and M. P. K. Sorrenson, *Origins of European Settlement in Kenya* (Oxford, 1968).

37. See C. C. Wrigley, 'Kenya: The Patterns of Economic Life, 1902–45' in V. Harlow and E. M. Chilver (eds.) *History of East Africa*, Vol. 2 (Oxford 1965).
38. Companies House, Cardiff. Company File 87,739. Uplands of East Africa Syndicate Ltd/East African Estates Ltd.
39. Edward Paice, op.cit., p.191.
40. *East African Standard*, 20 January 1906; *Y Clorianydd*, 8 Chwefror 1906.
41. *East African Standard*, 10, 24, 31 March 1906.
42. Ibid, 19 May, 16 June 1906.
43. Ibid, 23 June, 14 July 1906.
44. Ibid, 21, 28 July 1906.
45. Winston Churchill, *My African Journey*, (London, 1908), passim.
46. *Life in Pictures of Brig. Gen. Sir Owen Thomas*, op. cit.
47. Cf. *Abergele Visitor*, 17 June 1916.
48. *Colonial Reports, East Africa Protectorate 1906–7* (Cd. 3729), pp.39–40.
49. *Y Clorianydd*, 31 Ionawr 1917.
50. Cf., Ibid, 7 Tachwedd 1917.
51. M. P. K. Sorrenson, op.cit., p.109.
52. Ibid, pp.109–112.
53. *The Times*, 24 July 1907.
54. Companies House, Cardiff, Company File 87,739.
55. Cf. *North Wales Chronicle*, 2 November 1917.
56. *Colonial Reports, East Africa Protectorate 1909* (Cd. 5467), p.14; 1910–11 (Cd. 6007), p.16.
57. Letter from C. C. Wrigley to the author, 22 July 1987.
58. The National Archives, CO 533/113. Minutes of Proceedings at a Deputation to the Rt Hon The Secretary of State for the Colonies on the East Africa Labour Question at the House of Commons, 16 December 1912.
59. Anthony Clayton and Donald C. Savage, *Government and Labour in Kenya 1895–1963* (London, 1974), xviii.
60. Ibid, pp.55, 76–7 (fn 105).
61. *Liverpool Daily Post*, 11 November 1922.
62. Information on the company is based on documents in Company File 87,739; also reports of Ordinary General Meetings, see *The Times*, 17 January 1920, 11 August 1921, 26 July, 11 December 1923, 21 July 1925.
63. *The Times*, 17 January 1920.
64. *Y Clorianydd*, 8 Chwefror 1906.
65. Ibid, 20 Rhagfyr 1906, 25 Mehefin 1908.

66. Ibid, 9 Medi 1909.
67. Facts relating to Stanley are drawn from Tim Jeal's authoritative study, *Stanley. The Impossible Life of Africa's Greatest Explorer* (London, 2007).
68. Owen Thomas, *Stray Leaves from my East African Diary* (London, 1920), p.5.
69. He was reported ill in March 1916, February 1917 and September 1919.
70. Tim Jeal, op. cit., p.144.
71. Owen Thomas, *Agricultural and Pastoral Prospects*, op.cit., especially the section on 'Natives'.
72. T. I. Ellis, *Ellis Jones Griffith* (Llandybie, 1969), pp.84–5.
73. Owen Thomas, *Stray Leaves*, op.cit., p.13.
74. Ibid, p. 25. Treves made no mention of Thomas in his travelogue, *Uganda for a Holiday* (London, 1910).
75. Bereft of personal details, *Stray Leaves* is not so much a diary as a short treatise dedicated to this single message.
76. *The New Age*, Vol. 5, No. 20, 9 September 1909, article by 'Mombasa'.
77. 1911 Census return.
78. *Y Clorianydd*, 26 Medi 1907, 9 Ebrill 1908.
79. Ibid, 8 Mehefin 1911.
80. Ibid, 20 Rhagfyr 1906.
81. Ibid, 14 Ionawr 1904.
82. Ibid, 17 Medi 1908, 7 Ionawr 1909; *Y Wyntyll*, 13 Awst, 10 Medi 1908.

5. Brigadier-General

As Britain concentrated upon empire building, notably in Africa, continental alliances had divided Europe into two armed camps. A deepening Anglo-German rivalry engendered an alignment with France and Russia, and a subsequent series of crises raised the threat of war. The sequence of events in the Balkans in the summer of 1914 coincided with a short visit Owen Thomas made to Anglesey. On 22 July, a day before Austria's ultimatum to Serbia, he attended a public meeting at Cemaes called by Lady Hughes-Hunter to discuss a proposed promenade along the foreshore.[1] Maintaining his close interest in the development of Cemaes as a tourist resort, he reminded the audience that this was the place where he had first met his future wife. And he hoped to return within a year on the occasion of the promenade's official opening. Military agreements, however, produced a deadly momentum; in only a matter of days a mobilization of Russian, French and German forces led to declarations of war. When German troops invaded neutral Belgium on 4 August, Britain intervened.

To supplement the regular army, Kitchener, as Secretary for War, issued an appeal for 100,000 men between the ages of 19 and 30 to enlist at this time of national emergency.[2] Volunteers rushed to join the New Army to fight for 'King and Country', in a war widely expected to last a matter of weeks. As in 1899, Owen Thomas, consistent with his principles, was among the first to respond to the call to arms. Again the epitome of patriotic duty, he directed a personal appeal to fellow Welshmen to join a corps of cavalry.[3] Former members of the Prince of Wales' Light Horse were invited to contact him at his office in Carlton House, London. Still firmly tuned into the style of fighting in the Boer War, he foresaw a future role for a detachment of mounted troops. At first, organised recruiting was placed on a local footing, so at the end of August, he returned to Anglesey, residing at Cestyll, to assist the newly-formed county committee.[4] A series of thirty public meetings were being planned as part of the voluntary recruiting drive. Together with the great and the good of the island – Ellis Jones Griffith, Lord Boston, Dr Thomas Jones (chairman of the county council), the Revds John Williams, Thomas Charles Williams and others – Colonel Owen Thomas beseeched the young men of Anglesey to join the fight.

In his platform appeals, he employed incisive language to stir his audience into a positive response. At Llangefni he declared, in a chilling, and, in time, cruelly self-fulfilling phrase, that he would prefer to see his own sons return home on a bier rather than have them stay at home as cowards.[5] To underline his qualities of leadership and commitment, he promised to accompany the men into battle. 'I do not plead that you should go', he told a recruiting meeting at Holyhead,[6] 'I plead with you to come, for I am going'. Soon he was officially appointed the chief recruiting officer for the proposed Anglesey Battalion of 1,000 men.[7] But despite his best efforts, and the outward displays of enthusiasm, initial results in the county were extremely disappointing. Not more than 36 had signed up by the end of August.[8] At a meeting in Amlwch, they were only able to muster another fourteen volunteers.[9] After two months, it was conceded that the local recruiting initiative in Anglesey had been a dismal failure.[10]

Elsewhere in north Wales, the position was equally bleak. Only a dozen had joined up at Bethesda, where there was hostility to the presence of the quarry manager on the platform.[11] Indeed, ten days of recruiting in Caernarfonshire yielded only 60 volunteers by the beginning of September.[12] It was little wonder that Merioneth should emerge as the worst county in Wales for recruitment; at Harlech only Robert Graves and the local golf caddie had enlisted.[13] The response in Denbighshire also fell short of expectations. Total failure was the reckoning at Cerrigydrudion.[14] Large crowds gathered to hear the patriotic speeches, but as in the case of Abergele, Colwyn Bay and Ruthin, only a handful actually signed up.[15] Historically, it was redolent of the reception given to Gerald the Welshman and Baldwin, Archbishop of Canterbury, some seven hundred years earlier. When they undertook a preaching tour of Wales in 1188 to gather recruits for the third crusade, their abortive entreaties to the young men of north-west Wales, Anglesey especially, were likened to 'trying to extract blood from a stone'.[16]

Voluntary enlistment in Wales in the first months of the war revealed a distinct urban-rural divide. In populous, anglicized Glamorgan and Monmouthshire, Kitchener's appeal met with a magnificent response.[17] Thousands flocked to the recruiting stations opened in Cardiff, Newport and Swansea. No more ardent recruiters could be found than among the political and trade-union leadership of the south Wales miners. William Abraham, Thomas Richards, William Brace, Charles Stanton and D. Watts Morgan were in the forefront. Watts Morgan, the Rhondda miners' agent, set a personal example when he joined as a private on 4 August. Promoted to lieutenant, he helped raise the 1st Rhondda Battalion, composed almost entirely of working miners. Fulfilling his wish to join them at the front,[18] his was a distinguished military record. As the recruiting boom gathered pace, 22,500 Glamorgan men had enlisted by the end of September. War fever engulfed the mining valleys. Even at Tonypandy, a hotbed of socialism, and the scene of the working class riots of 1910–11 that led to the stationing of troops, hundreds were caught in the patriotic flow.[19]

A number of factors impeded recruiting in the predominantly Welsh-speaking rural communities of north-west Wales. Here was a region with a limited military tradition, usually linked to the former militia and volunteer corps. For decades, pacifism had been a feature of Welsh Nonconformist radicalism. Prior to his victory in the election of 1868, Henry Richard served as secretary of the Peace Society. Chapels continued to instil the Christian message of peace. Attitudes were reinforced a mere decade earlier by the powerful religious revival of 1904–5, inspired by Evan Roberts. Thousands of young men from working-class and lower middle-class backgrounds responded to its spiritual fervour as it swept through the agricultural and slate quarrying districts. Those who became 'soldiers of the Cross' in Roberts's 'army of Christ'[20] found it difficult to cast their principles aside. Public indifference prevailed. Most ordinary people remained ignorant of the issues at stake in 1914; the various continental crises would seem very remote. In any case, ambivalence towards the military often shaded into disapproval. Soldiering was for the few, the army a refuge for social pariahs; wars largely distant, imperialist events.[21] For the mass of labourers engaged in agriculture, harvest time meant a special bonus payment, and recruiters vied unsuccessfully with farmers. Caernarfonshire slate quarrymen had sound reason to detest the military. Troops were stationed in their communities at the time of the Penrhyn lock-out of 1900–3; but in direct contrast to the colliers, patriotism failed to eclipse their anti-militarism.[22] The North Wales Quarrymen's Union refused to give recruitment its official endorsement. Though thousands of quarrymen were placed on short-time work, only some 6 per cent of the labour force had enlisted by October 1914.[23] In the circumstances, it was even suggested that Welsh-speaking D. Watts Morgan be dispatched to north Wales to win over the working class.[24]

Opinion formers made a concerted effort to reshape attitudes. Some religious leaders, with no apparent damage to conscience, adopted the classic Christian justification of war as a 'just cause'.[25] The Revd John Williams, Professor T. A. Levi and other prominent Nonconformist leaders were to sign a manifesto to appeal for recruits.[26] Notables from political and academic life also lent their weight to increasingly hawkish press and platform propaganda, employing anti-German rhetoric to justify the war on moral grounds. Chief among them were the north Wales Liberal MPs – Ellis Jones Griffith, William Jones, Ellis W. Davies and Haydn Jones, and the eminent scholars – John Morris-Jones, O. M. Edwards, Sir Henry Jones and Sir Henry Lewis. Prussian militarism, they argued, threatened freedom, civilisation and religion. It was a righteous war, a war to end all wars. Nevertheless, it remained a challenge to nullify the indifference, misgivings and hostility encountered in the lower reaches of rural society, the main recruiting ground. Great powers of persuasion were needed to drum up sufficient patriotism in the ordinary man so that he would decide to enlist.

Owen Thomas, in the meantime, was also assisting in the recruiting efforts in Caernarfonshire. His audience at Porthmadog were assured that he did not ask them to do anything he had not done, or was not prepared to do.[27] He shared a platform with Margaret Lloyd George and the Revd John Williams at Pwllheli.[28] Both men had also addressed a meeting of quarrymen at Llanberis, but very few joined.[29] On 24 September, at a packed meeting in Cricieth town hall, he accompanied David Lloyd George to press home the message of recruitment.[30] Having transferred his sympathy from the Boers to the plight of 'little' Serbia and Belgium, and being in government as the Chancellor of the Exchequer, Lloyd

George was fully pledged to the war effort. But whilst encouraging others to enlist, he remained adamant that no son of his was to be put in harm's way.[31] Even his prestige and oratory over twenty-five minutes failed to budge the audience at Cricieth. One interested observer noted that 'no recruits tendered themselves'.[32]

For Lloyd George, personally, there was much more at stake. Only five days earlier in London, during the course of an inspirational speech to a gathering of Welsh dignitaries, presided by the Earl of Plymouth (of St Fagans, Cardiff), he had aired his 'poetic idea' of a 'Welsh Army'. Evoking an ancient warrior spirit, he felt that Wales, as a small nation, also had a crucial part to play.[33]

A provisional committee was formed on 21 September and a decision taken to officially launch the scheme at a national conference in Cardiff. Though sanctioned by Kitchener, he would later voice his reservations. Representatives of all sections of Welsh public life met at the Park Hotel, Cardiff, on 29 September.[34] Prominent political, religious, business and labour leaders heard Lloyd George again call for an entirely new Welsh Army Corps to supplement the three regular Welsh regiments, namely The Royal Welsh Fusiliers, The Welsh Regiment and The South Wales Borderers. By setting a target of 40–50,000 men, it was to be a most ambitious undertaking. To implement the scheme, a National Executive Committee under the Earl of Plymouth was named.[35]

Owen Thomas did not attend the inaugural conference in Cardiff, and only after a meeting of the National Executive Committee on 2 October was his name added to their number.[36] Naturally enough, as a director of the East African Estates Ltd, the Earl of Plymouth would be well acquainted with Thomas and also his military record. Lloyd George, for his part, had been given an insight into his character at the Cricieth meeting, to say nothing of the scale of the task that confronted him. At a time when the recruiting boom was at its height elsewhere in the land, following a second appeal by Kitchener, two months of campaigning in north-west Wales had achieved very little. Public opinion was yet to be convinced.

Lloyd George instinctively recognised Owen Thomas as the ideal figure to change local hearts and minds. He possessed all the essential qualities. As a military officer, who served with distinction in the Boer War, he had experience of raising troops. He was a highly regarded, Welsh-speaking Nonconformist, as well as a would-be Liberal politician, with deep-rooted connections in rural society. He understood the people and, by extension, the social, cultural and religious issues that undermined initial efforts to enrol volunteers. Moreover, he presented a reassuring presence, a father figure, who would elicit trust among parents. Owen Thomas, the archetypal 'Christian warrior',[37] was clearly the man with a popular identity uniquely fitted to overcome the formidable barriers in north-west Wales, and to galvanize the recruitment drive.

Logistical uncertainties coupled with opposition at the highest level seriously impeded the progress of the Welsh Army Corps.[38] Lloyd George faced a strong challenge as Kitchener, who questioned the reliability of Welsh units, raised objections to the creation of an 'all Welsh military formation'. Clashes between the Chancellor and the Secretary for War were partially resolved on 10 October, when the War Office gave official authorisation. Anger at reports of further anti-Welsh bias – Welsh recruits were forbidden from speaking Welsh on the parade ground or in their billets – flared into another 'royal row' in the Cabinet.[39] So it was not until 30 October that Lloyd George finally carried the day and the real work of raising the Welsh Army Corps could commence.

In the meantime, Owen Thomas had presented the Earl of Plymouth with a number of recommendations based on his previous military experiences.[40] To ensure the success of Lloyd George's grand design, he proposed that they frame their recruitment appeals around a blend of localism and Welsh patriotism. Following the third meeting of the National Executive Committee on 16 October, attended by Thomas, his views were incorporated into a draft scheme. Thomas believed that farmers and farm labourers, two classes hitherto largely untouched, would provide strong, healthy recruits of the best type. Upon enlistment, they should not be drafted to distant military depôts but trained locally, and every effort made to secure staff officers fluent in the Welsh language or else with Welsh connections. Emphasis was placed on local route marches as another incentive to recruitment. To boost the ranks, they could also appeal to the strong Welsh element exiled in London, Liverpool,

Manchester and other English cities. On 28 October, in a letter to Major-General Sir Ivor Herbert (Lord Treowen), another member of the National Executive Committee, he emphasised that a Welshman should be assigned to the post of brigadier-general.[41] Rumours that Colonel R. H. W. Dunn, an Englishman residing in Wrexham, was to be appointed, filled him with dread. Being 'quite unknown', he would have little influence on the classes they hoped to recruit.

Thomas need not have worried; Lloyd George clearly shared his concerns. As well as relenting on the matter of the Welsh Army Corps in the Cabinet showdown on 30 October, Kitchener also conceded to Lloyd George's choice of military leader in north Wales. At his manipulative best, he made sure that his protégé would be cast in the central role. Colonel Owen Thomas accompanied him to the War Office, and on the same day, on his commendation, Kitchener promoted Thomas to the rank of brigadier-general there and then.[42] Although he had previously fulfilled two significant assignments under his command during the course of the Boer War, it was a magnanimous gesture, for Kitchener must also have known that it was he who had briefed Lloyd George on the anti-Welsh bias within the War Office. It proved to be a dramatic moment. Aside from dropping his hat in amazement, Thomas became dumbstruck at the sudden elevation. It remained for Lloyd George to voice his acceptance.[43] Accordingly, Owen Thomas was gazetted brigadier-general on 31 October 1914.

Three infantry brigades of the 1st Division Welsh Army Corps (later officially designated as the 43rd (Welsh) Division) were created, and based respectively in the north Wales coastal resorts of Llandudno, Colwyn Bay and Rhyl. Each brigade was to consist of four battalions, each 1,100 strong. Llandudno became the centre for the 128th Brigade under Brigadier-General Owen Thomas, who arrived on 1 November to stay at the St George's Hotel, prior to setting up his headquarters at Maenan House in Lloyd Street.[44] In his new post, girded with status and authority, he was officially recognised as Lloyd George's principal recruiter in the three counties of Gwynedd – Anglesey, Caernarfonshire and Merioneth. Predictably, features of Thomas's command bore the imprint of the thinking revealed in his draft scheme. Determined to achieve a 'thumping success',[45] he proposed to visit every district in his area, to talk to men in their own language. As recruiting commenced, he already had a nucleus of 700 men from the Caernarvon and Anglesey Battalion of the Royal Welsh Fusiliers. He also received the authority to nominate his own officers, a freedom that allowed blatant military nepotism. From now on, in his graphic phrase, the two objects in his life were 'to wipe out the anti-military spirit that existed in Wales, and to wipe out the Germans'.[46]

As he began his daunting mission, he had to face petty jealousies within the higher military echelon. Not everyone appreciated the political nature of his meteoric promotion. Envy surfaced at Caernarfon on 3 November, in one of his first recruiting meetings,[47] Thomas touchily described all the officers who shared the platform with him, as being 'green with jealousy'.[48] Sir Ivor Herbert, who, it turned out, had recommended Colonel R. H. W. Dunn for the post, was particularly 'insulting' in that he referred to him as a general only once in his speech. Dunn, nevertheless, did receive promotion to brigadier-general and was given command of the 129th Brigade at Rhyl, while Brigadier-General Sir Ivor Philipps, MP, another of Lloyd George's nominees, commanded the 130th Brigade at Colwyn Bay.

From the beginning of November, Thomas headed a vigorous recruiting campaign in alliance with county recruiting committees and local recruiting officers, notably Lieutenant Hugh Pritchard in Anglesey and H. R. Davies, the second son of Richard Davies, MP, in Caernarfonshire. On the platform, Thomas blended the personal and the patriotic, spiced with a measure of humiliation, to assert considerable psychological pressure. He could claim that all three sons were now serving officers, and again he spoke of leading his men into battle. At Bethesda, he advised the young women present to be careful what type of husband they selected from among the quarrymen; those who chose to stay at home rather than bear arms would be found under the bed if a thief broke into the house.[49] Thomas was all too aware that he had very little time to stifle inbuilt resistance. To pave the way, he induced slate quarrymen to enlist by granting them army pay and allowances for attending evening drill instruction while they remained at work on full pay.[50] Every kind of recruiting tool was implemented. Newspaper notices gave details of how to enlist at local recruiting stations. Specially commissioned recruiting posters, in both English and Welsh, appeared on public buildings. Military recruiters trawled the hiring fairs distributing bilingual leaflets. Owen Thomas had emphasised the value of the route march in fostering interest; detachments of uniformed men accompanied by a military band made an impressive spectacle. Of many such events, the north Wales recruiting marches in early 1915 were the most ambitious, when 250 men visited the main towns of Caernarfonshire and Merioneth, and another force of 860 soldiers toured Llŷn.[51]

Just as Owen Thomas shrewdly recognised in 1887, when he overcame religious prejudice to raise the Cemaes Rifle Volunteers, Lloyd George was equally aware of the vital role Nonconformist ministers played in transforming public attitudes. The Reverends John Williams, Thomas Charles Williams and J. T. Job – remarkably, also the chief promoters of Evan Roberts's revivalist mission – were arch-jingoists from the outset. One of the most eloquent of pulpit orators, the Revd John Williams, Brynsiencyn, accompanied his old friend Owen Thomas to give recruitment his blessing in north Wales and Liverpool.[52] A close ally on Liberal hustings, prominent in the 1910–13 Welsh Disestablishment campaign, his qualities were well known to Lloyd George. To elevate his public status as the religious counterpart to the Brigadier-General, he expediently appointed him honorary chaplain to the Welsh Army, with the rank of colonel, in late November.[53] In military uniform and ministerial collar, Williams presented a haughty, unedifying spectacle. Despite evidence that his haranguing raised many shackles, the fervent appeals, and assurance that both he and Thomas would accompany them to France, persuaded hundreds to enlist.[54]

Recruits were promised military training under Welsh officers. The Caernarvon and Anglesey Battalion was placed under Colonel David Davies, scion of the distinguished Llandinam dynasty. With War Office approval, the London Welsh Battalion arrived at Llandudno in early December to raise numbers to almost 2,000.[55] Among their officers were two of Lloyd George's sons, Captain Richard Lloyd George and Lieutenant Gwilym Lloyd George.[56] By the end of the year, the four Royal Welsh Fusilier battalions of the 128th Brigade of the 43rd (Welsh) Division were numbered the 13th (1st North Wales 'Pals'), 14th (Caernarvon and Anglesey) and 15th (London Welsh), with the 16th taking the overspill from the 13th. All three of Owen Thomas's sons were attached to his brigade. Robert Newton was captain in the 15th Battalion, while both Owen Vincent and Trevor obtained a commission as lieutenants in the 13th and 16th.[57] Brought up in England, their fluency in Welsh is doubtful. To boost the number of Welsh-speaking officers, Thomas strongly urged R. Silyn Roberts, secretary of the University of Wales Appointments Board, to use his position to guide graduates towards the Officer Training Corps.[58] Eventually, he would claim that 150 out of 200 staff officers spoke Welsh; in one battalion alone all but two of the 30 officers were Welsh-speaking.[59] True to his own down-to-earth style he made a point of personally conversing with the monoglot young men under his command.[60]

Llandudno was divided into four sectors (based on county council electoral wards), with a battalion in each.[61] By good fortune, recruits in this popular tourist resort in the quiet winter season found themselves billeted in boarding houses and local hotels. For most, this was comparative luxury, complete with home-cooked meals – but no feather beds or intoxicants. Owners received an allowance of 3s-4^{1}/2d per man per day, later reduced to 2s-6d, to create a reported bonanza of £400,000 for the town.[62] Owen Thomas, who resided at the Wilton Hotel on south parade, took personal responsibility for the welfare of the young men in his charge. Strict rules were imposed as part of his moral and religious commitment to parents. They had to return to their billets by 9 p.m. (public houses in the district were ordered to close at this time), though the curfew was later extended to 10 p.m. Recruits were encouraged to attend a place of worship on Sunday.[63] Thomas set a personal example by worshipping at the Welsh Independent chapel in Deganwy Avenue. Later, he would expressly thank local Nonconformist ministers and Anglican clergy for offering pastoral support and spiritual guidance to his men.[64] That there were few complaints of misbehaviour – excepting the antics of the more worldly miscreants from the London Welsh Battalion[65] – was testament to his guiding hand and the standards he set.[66]

In the invigorating seaside air a military regime was in place to turn raw recruits into competent soldiers. Basic army training aimed to raise levels of physical fitness and instil discipline. Drill, parades and route marches put the men in shape, though a considerable number would be discharged on medical grounds.[67] Once again, Thomas returned to Morfa Conwy to witness his men at training and rifle practice, arrangements that had ruinous consequences for the local golf course. Skirmishes, or mock battles, were arranged to take advantage of the topography of the Little Orme. Actual battlefield exercise, however, was inadequate in that it lacked modern weapons, bayonet training or introduction to trench warfare. Patriotically, soldiers of the Welsh Army Corps were to be provided with uniforms made of *brethyn llwyd* (Welsh grey cloth). The clothing and equipment sub-committee discussed contracts at a meeting held at Carlton House, Regent Street, London, in November, when Thomas was called upon to proffer procurement advice as a 'businessman',[68] but supply failed to meet the growing demand. Ill-equipped soldiers often wore civilian clothes to complement the broom handles that substituted for rifles.

Provision for recreation was made in chapel schoolrooms and public libraries, with rooms set aside for reading and writing. Soccer and rugby matches, sports days, concerts and *eisteddfodau* created an *esprit de corps*. *Eisteddfodau* promoted the Welsh character of the brigade; and to emphasise pride in language and nationality, Owen Thomas addressed his men in Welsh, his preferred language.[69] In January 1915, a soldiers' *eisteddfod* was held in the pier pavilion, followed by another on St David's Day. Two detachments from the 16th and 17th Battalions competed in the male-voice choir competition at the National Eisteddfod in Bangor in August. Dressed in khaki, the choir of the 16th Battalion was awarded first prize.[70] War dominated the proceedings. Echoing the comments of *eisteddfod* luminaries, Thomas had earlier treated this moment of high culture as an occasion to stir fervent patriotism. Presiding on 'Lloyd George's day', he steered the young men swept along by the current of emotion towards recruiting officers stationed outside the pavilion. He even suggested that the *eisteddfod* itself lay on military style competitions such as target shooting.

Despite the persistent apathy in rural areas,[71] each of the four battalions was up to strength in January 1915. Thomas could be 'very well satisfied' with the 'remarkable growth' of his brigade; over 4,000 men had joined in a matter of ten weeks, to bring the total to 4,700.[72] Receiving War Office sanction, he then began to raise two more battalions in February and March: the 17th (or 2nd North Wales 'Pals') and a bantam battalion to incorporate men under the regulation height of 5ft 3ins. Again, he addressed county recruiting committee meetings and a series of public meetings. At Trefriw, the conflict was presented as a choice between 'Christ or Germany'.[73] Yet, difficulties persisted. In his opinion, there were 2,000 men in Anglesey still eligible for service.[74]

Sufficient progress had been made for Lloyd George, on Thomas's suggestion,[75] to visit Llandudno for a St David's Day review of the 128th Brigade. As 5,500 men marched along the promenade, each with a leek on his cap or shoulder strap, on the dais to take the salute were General Sir Henry Mackinnon, General Officer Commanding, Western Command, Major-General Sir Ivor Philipps, commander of the 43rd Division, and the Earl of Plymouth.[76] Thousands of onlookers braved the icy cold to wave their red dragon flag. On this impressive occasion, Lady Boston presented

128th Brigade marching along the promenade at Llandudno, 1 March 1915.

128th Brigade march past the reviewing stand, Llandudno, 1 March 1915.

Brigadier-General Owen Thomas with a ceremonial sword of honour on behalf of the Anglesey Ladies Recruiting Committee. It bore the Welsh inscription *'Oddi wrth Ferched Môn ... yn achos Cyfiawnder a Rhyddid, 1915'* (From the Women of Anglesey ... in the cause of Justice and Freedom, 1915). Later, at a luncheon in the St George's Hotel, tribute was paid to his unflagging energy and determination in overcoming all obstacles. He had played a fundamental part in realising Lloyd George's vision of 'a nation in arms'. A number of photographs captured the day – the parade, the presentation and the staff officers. Owen Thomas posed with his three sons in military uniform for what became an iconic image of a shared personal pride in patriotic duty – and what ended as the ultimate family sacrifice.

Inspired by events, Thomas stepped up the recruiting effort in March, concentrating on Caernarfonshire, where, according to H. R. Davies, only 4,200 had enlisted.[77] Thomas was particularly disappointed with the position in the south of the county and farmers in Llŷn were admonished for not releasing their labourers for military service.[78] As a farmer himself, he knew they could manage with fewer workers. To influence recruitment into the 17th Battalion, command was given to Colonel Henry Lloyd Mostyn, a surname synonymous with the civic development of Llandudno. Much was made of its Welsh-speaking officers and that military orders

Brigadier-General Owen Thomas receives a Sword of Honour from Lady Boston, Llandudno, 1 March 1915.

General Sir Henry Mackinnon, Rt Hon David Lloyd George and Brigadier-General Owen Thomas, Llandudno, 1 March 1915.

were posted in both English and Welsh. Though he claimed to be 'a better fighter than orator', willing to die for his country, this did not prevent him for fulminating against the Germans. If they were to arrive, he warned at Pwllheli, they would murder their women and children and burn their homes.[79] The Revd John Williams, resplendent in military uniform, added his amen by demonising the Germans as a 'Godless nation'. German barbarism became a recurrent theme. At Dolwyddelan, Thomas informed his audience that the cruelty of the 'wild beasts of Africa in their wild state' was 'nothing to that of the Hun'.[80] By May, he had also grasped the propaganda value of the recent supposed German atrocity – the crucifixion of a Canadian soldier – to add to the horrors.[81]

He soon found that the enemy was closer than expected. In August 1915 two German submarines, the U-27 and U-38, made a rendezvous off

Great Orme's Head, Llandudno, in a failed bid to pick up three German officers who had escaped from the Dyffryn Aled Prisoner of War Camp, Llansannan.[82] Besides the 'hundred and one things' that occupied him as brigade commander,[83] Thomas had to deploy men on search operations and step up security. Indeed, so it is claimed, a lieutenant in the 17th Battalion who collared a suspected 'spy' on Llandudno's West Shore would receive his personal congratulations.[84]

Despite the enthusiastic reception in Pwllheli, Blaenau Ffestiniog and other places where he spoke in Welsh, his campaign had faltered. Even the distribution of 30,000 leaflets at the hiring fairs failed to sway farm hands in Caernarfonshire. By the end of May, only 156 had enlisted; none at Sarn, though hundreds attended the hiring fair.[85] It was not only the labourers, the very class he had targeted, who let him down. Thomas was scathing of middle-class 'shirkers', the sons of farmers, merchants, shopkeepers and the like.[86] No matter how determined the effort, or how effective his talent as a communicator, he could sense from the steady downturn in recruitment that the voluntary system had run its course. By June 1915, he calculated that he had addressed about 150 meetings since the declaration of war.[87] While he firmly believed that one volunteer fired with genuine patriotism was worth two to three pressed men, the prospect of conscription, which he opposed, seemed to loom in his mind.

From 5 May, when the 43rd Division had been re-designated the 38th (Welsh) Division, the 128th Brigade became the 113th Infantry Brigade. Following a review that month of the six battalions by General H.E. Dickson, Inspector of Forces, Thomas reported a shortfall of only 400 men.[88] One final effort swelled the ranks and by the end of June, the 17th Battalion was also reported to be at full strength. Another intake of outsiders resulted in the formation of the 18th Battalion (2nd London Welsh), so that the Bantams, stationed at Deganwy, became the 19th Battalion. For Brigadier-General Owen Thomas, it was mission accomplished. Between 1 November 1914 and 30 June 1915, as the War Office officially recognised, he raised 10,500 men for the 'North Wales Brigade', nominating eight battalion commanders and 350 other officers.[89] This was a considerable personal achievement. The *Welsh Outlook* went so far as to declare that no man had done more to create the new Welsh Army.[90] The fundamental shift in attitudes within communities in north-west Wales, culminating in the improved recruitment levels, was in large measure due to his leadership and personal qualities. Upon closer analysis they were, in truth, but modest results, that fell short of expectations. Of course, many had joined units beyond their locality, such as the Cheshire Regiment and the King's Liverpool Regiment. As Thomas acknowledged in April 1915, only around half of the 7,000 men under his command at that time were Welsh.[91] To boost troop numbers, a substantial proportion, therefore, had been drafted from outside his military catchment area.

After almost nine months of preparation in Llandudno, ending with a civic farewell outside the railway station, the 113th Infantry Brigade began to transfer to their training centre at Winchester. Three battalions, the 13th, 14th, 15th, left in early June. To one admirer, Owen Thomas was 'their Wellington'.[92] Only this time the commander would not be leading his men into battle. He had been confidentially forewarned of his impending fate, well in advance it appears, by Lloyd George. It came as a devastating blow. For Owen Thomas, understandably, this was 'the greatest disappointment' of his life.[93] At a stroke the carefully constructed military

Brigadier-General Owen Thomas and his son Robin.

persona he had projected in north Wales would be tainted. Above all, he feared being 'openly cursed' by fellow Welshmen with whom he had 'broken faith'. The hundreds of parents who entrusted their sons to his care, and who accepted his assurances that they would go to the front under his personal command, had every reason to feel betrayed.

To the powers that be, Owen Thomas had served his prime military purpose as a recruiter. He was now expendable. Classed a 'dug-out' in army parlance – a retired officer recalled into service after years of absence – he was too old, at 57 years, for active service. Neither did they consider him effectively qualified to command his brigade in the field. This decision gained substance with a report submitted by Major-General Sir Ivor Philipps, commander of the 38th (Welsh) Division, in September[94] – a man whose own shortcomings would soon be exposed. Though possessing 'great energy', Thomas lacked military knowledge and training in the 'higher branches' of the profession. In other words, he personified a somewhat old-fashioned military style, rooted in the mindset of a cavalry officer of the Boer War. He was supposedly unfamiliar with new regulations and out of touch with the latest tactical thinking. Once the official communication arrived, Thomas did everything possible to get the decision reversed. Aggrieved, bitter, humiliated, he pleaded to be given an alternative overseas posting in East Africa, Serbia or elsewhere. According to the Revd John Williams, he travelled to London to argue his case fearlessly with the authorities at the War Office.[95] It amazed him how keen Owen Thomas was to go to the front.

Still officially in command, Thomas accompanied his brigade to Winchester to complete its final military training. Rifle practice on Salisbury plain was coupled with last-minute preparation for trench warfare. Having achieved its initial target of 40,000 men, the 38th (Welsh) Division was inspected and praised by none other than Lieutenant-General Sir Archibald Murray, Deputy Chief of the Imperial General Staff, in September. He judged them to have attained the required standard and to be ready for service in France. And as for the 113th Brigade, he publicly informed Owen Thomas that it was an honour to command such a unit.[96] A Welsh religious service was held in November attended by Thomas and the Revd John Williams,[97] who would also, on grounds of age, remain behind. Those whom they had recruited, and promised to accompany, were further reviewed by the Queen at the end of the month, when Thomas relinquished his command. In early December the 38th (Welsh) Division disembarked in France to become part of Kitchener's Fourth Army. Brigadier-General Llewelyn A. E. Price-Davies, 37 years old, awarded the Victoria Cross for heroism in the Boer War, would lead the 113th Brigade to the Western Front to be tested in combat.

For a time, Owen Thomas's fate remained a mystery, raising concerns in the Welsh press. The publication of two official letters, orchestrated in Whitehall, succeeded to mollify his disappointment and save his face in public.[98] On 28 October, Lord Derby, Director General of Recruiting, had urged him to continue with his recruiting work in north Wales. This was echoed by David Lloyd George on 2 November. He hoped that his invaluable service in Llandudno and Winchester would again be put to good effect in implementing Derby's scheme of voluntary enlistment. Single men between 18 and 41 were asked to attest themselves for military service through a process of canvassing. Scheduled to end on 30 November, the scheme was extended until 15 December. This positive spin on matters restored Thomas's reputation to a great degree. As presented in public, it was in response to a personal plea from Lord Derby and Lloyd George that he would set aside any personal ambition, to return to north Wales to serve in a new key post. On 5 November, he assumed command of the 14th (Reserve) Infantry Brigade at Kinmel Park Camp, near Abergele, Denbighshire. His mission statement was to raise, and subsequently train, more recruits.

Constructed by McAlpine in that

Brigadier-General Llewelyn A. Price-Davies, VC, in old age. [W. Alister Williams Collection] year, Kinmel Park Camp was a vast, purpose-built infantry training facility, the largest in Wales. Corrugated iron huts were erected as billets, together with a military hospital and garrison church. A rifle range and zig-zag practice trench system gave recruits the best possible preparation for warfare on the Western Front. (This same camp, in March 1919, became the scene of a two-day mutiny by war-weary Canadian troops awaiting demobilization.)

Failure on the day of the Llanfechell hiring fair on 1 November gave a good indication of the task that lay ahead.[99] Though Hugh Thomas, Carrog, had read a telegram of support from the Brigadier-General at the open-air recruiting rally, not one man responded to the call. In Anglesey alone at least a thousand eligible men had still not enlisted.[100] After a year of war, the carnage and stalemate on the Western Front considerably changed the public mood. High casualty rates, recorded with photographs of the fallen in local newspapers, became a telling obstacle to voluntary recruitment. Against this background, Owen Thomas issued a personal 'call to arms' on 20 November, phrased so as to fuse Welsh patriotism and religious sensibilities.[101] Young men were urged to answer the nation's call as they had done in the time of past heroes such as Llywelyn *Ein Llyw Olaf* and Owain Glyn Dŵr – albeit inspirational leaders who had fought for Welsh independence against the English. Two-thirds of the officers were Welsh and the Welsh language was the daily means of communication between officers and men. Once more, he sought to allay parental anxieties. Welsh-speaking chaplains, mainly from the Nonconformist denominations, were at hand to oversee the moral and spiritual welfare of recruits. Religious services, Sunday schools and prayer meetings met every need. To underline both the national and religious dimension, Thomas again turned to history.[102] This would be the first distinctive Welsh force since Rhys ap Thomas of Dinefwr led his men to support Henry Tudor at Bosworth in 1485, only this time they would be drawn from all parts of the country. For an army influenced by religious ideals, the closest parallel was Cromwell's New Model Army during the Puritan Commonwealth.

Spurred by such sentiments, an anonymous donor offered a prize of £5 for the best short poem, in either Welsh or English, to convey Brigadier-General Owen Thomas's 'call to arms' in verse.[103] Altogether 156 compositions were received, and adjudicated by John Morris-Jones, Professor of Welsh Language and Literature at the University College of North Wales, Bangor. He considered the winning entry *'Wŷr Ieuanc Cymru'* (Young Men of Wales) to be of the highest literary merit.[104] Not surprisingly, given that *'Y Gwyngyll'* was the pseudonym of the Revd J. G. Jenkins (*Gwili*), editor of *Seren Cymru* and a national eisteddfod crown bard. Sung to the rousing tune of 'Captain Morgan's March' it concisely expressed the nationalistic spirit of Thomas's appeal.

The days of the public recruiting meetings had passed, so Thomas came to rely on local recruiting committees to canvass those willing to attest. But patriotism, poems and persuasion were not sufficient for men to pledge themselves to the Derby scheme. Returns from the three county committees show that no more than 30 per cent of men of military age had attested in Gwynedd at this time.[105] Results in general indicated a failure of the voluntary system, making compulsion inevitable. Though the first Military Service Act of 27 January 1916 introduced conscription for single men between 18 and 41, the Derby scheme was further extended for a few more weeks to give voluntary enlistment a final opportunity. This allowed Owen Thomas time to issue his final 'more urgent' appeal from Kinmel Park Camp on 19 January, when he reiterated his strong belief in the voluntary system.[106] He implored single, unattested Welshmen to rally to the flag in 'the good name of the Welsh nation' so as to render the Military Service Act a 'dead letter' in the country. It merely prolonged the inevitable; on 25 May the second Military Service Act introduced conscription for all men aged 18–41.

In Kinmel, Owen Thomas set about organising and training the seven battalions of the 14th (Reserve) Infantry Brigade – the 12th, 14th, 18th, 20th, 21st, 22nd Battalions Royal Welsh Fusiliers and the 22nd Battalion The Welsh Regiment. His dedication to the task was such that he worked seven days a week, starting at 9–9.30 a.m. and was often at his post at 7 p.m. Over a period of 19 months, he only had four days leave. Training centred on physical drill, rifle practice, bayonet exercise and aspects of trench warfare with dummy and live bombs. Just half of the 20,000 or so men in the camp by March 1916 were drawn from Wales.[107] They came from every corner of the country, representing prevalent classes and occupation – farmers, labourers, quarrymen, colliers, bank clerks and students. Problems arose when other elements were added to the social mix. Within the billets, naïve rural recruits often came face to face with unsavoury characters, drawn from the dregs of the slums, among the London 'Welsh'.[108] Whether it helped to amend their ways or not, every soldier was under an obligation to attend one religious service on Sunday.[109] This aspect of life at the camp gained warm approval; the Union of Welsh Independents, with good reason, rejoiced in Thomas's achievements, and the number of recruits from their denomination who had rallied under his leadership.[110]

Very early in his new command, Owen Thomas was given a searing reminder of the ultimate price his men might have to pay on the battlefield. After completing further training in France, the 113th and 114th Brigades of the 38th (Welsh) Division had moved to take over the Neuve Chappelle sector on the Western Front. One of the first casualties in the opening weeks prior to the main offensive was his youngest son, Trevor, aged barely 18.[111] Educated at Wellington College, the exclusive public school with its strong military links (the only son to attend), he had passed the entrance examination to Trinity College, Cambridge. Among the first to enlist, he obtained his commission as a lieutenant in the 16th Battalion in November 1914. He fell in action near Béthune on 10 January 1916 and was buried in the St Vaast Post military cemetery close to the neighbouring village of Richebourg-L'Avoue.

The death of his son intensified his compassionate side. Within military circles he had based his authority on humanity and decency, a trait acknowledged by men who served under his command. One old soldier considered him 'the most kind-hearted officer in the British army'.[112] Consistent with this, Thomas soon threw himself into a humanitarian project. The sight of former soldiers begging for food and clothing on the streets of Cape Town and Johannesburg in the aftermath of the Boer War had left a lasting impression.[113] Fears that the authorities might not provide adequate care for Welsh military personnel heightened his concern for their welfare. Troops returning from the battlefield deserved to be treated with dignity. To this end, he convened a conference in Shrewsbury on 25 February to outline his 'National scheme for safeguarding the interests of Welsh soldiers, sailors and their dependents during and after the war'. A distinguished gathering of some 300 delegates from all parts of Wales heard Thomas deliver an inspiring address, among them Lord Aberdare, the Bishops of St Asaph and Llandaff and numerous MPs.[114] He aimed to establish a national body that would offer financial aid and advice in cases of hardship, assistance in securing new or former employment, and help for disabled servicemen to acquire new skills or trades.

A committee was formed, with W. J. Evans, Abergele, son of Beriah Gwynfe Evans, as secretary. In furtherance of the scheme, public meetings were held at Cardiff, Caernarfon and Wrexham during March and April.[115] Though it received warm approval, the financial appeal, set at an ambitious target of £125,000, came to little. A trickle of donations amounted to a fund of only £350 by June 1916.[116] By this time, Owen Thomas's laudable intentions had been overshadowed by events.

Other instances of his humane leadership related to those who opposed the war and who sought exemption from military service. Together with the Revd John Williams, who assisted at Kinmel Park Camp, he was instrumental in gaining War Office approval in January 1916 for the formation of a special ambulance unit for Welshmen within the Royal Army Medical Corps.[117] Non-combatants were given the opportunity to make a positive contribution tending to the wounded at the front without infringing their pacifist ideals. The Welsh company of the RAMC, up to 260 strong, consisted of ordained ministers, clergymen and teachers, but mainly theological students. Following their first parade, in February, the newly-formed 'Welsh Ministers' company was officially inspected by Brigadier-General Owen Thomas outside Rhyl Town Hall. One of their number, the poet and dramatist Albert Evans-Jones (Cynan) served with the field ambulance and later as chaplain. Remarkable, and uncommon, toleration was shown by Owen Thomas to the absolute pacifists who refused to undertake work of national importance. At one time, as many as 230 conscientious objectors were held at Kinmel, among whom, reportedly, was George M. Ll. Davies, later Christian Pacifist MP for the University of Wales.[118] As prison visitor, the Revd J. H. Howard of Colwyn Bay, himself a well-known pacifist and socialist, was especially

Brigadier-General Owen Thomas (centre left) with, on his left, Colonel Wynne-Edwards, Revd Canon Llewellyn Davies and Revd John Williams (Brynsiencyn) at the official inspection of the 'Welsh Ministers Company' outside Rhyl Town Hall, February 1916.

appreciative. Thomas not only eased his entry into the camp, but many times placed his car and driver at his disposal. Only subsequently, with Thomas's successor, did he encounter a 'hostile attitude'.

NOTES

1. *Y Clorianydd*, 29 Gorffennaf 1914.
2. This chapter has benefited from the following studies: Clive Hughes, 'Army Recruitment in Gwynedd 1914–1916' (unpublished MA thesis, University of Wales, Bangor, 1983); again 'The New Armies', in I. F. W. Beckett and K. Simpson (eds.) *A Nation in Arms. A Social Study of the British Army in the First World War* (Manchester, 1985), and further information in a letter to the author, 31 May 1987; Peter Simkins, *Kitchener's Army. The Raising of New Armies 1914–1916* (Manchester, 1988); Neil Evans, 'Loyalties: state, nation, community and military recruiting in Wales 1840–1918', op. cit.
3. *Y Genedl Gymreig*, 11 Awst 1914.

4. *Y Clorianydd*, 2 Medi 1914; *Holyhead Chronicle*, 4 & 11 September 1914.
5. *Y Clorianydd*, 9 Medi 1914.
6. *Holyhead Chronicle*, 11 September 1914.
7. *North Wales Observer & Express*, 18 September 1914.
8. *Y Clorianydd*, 2 Medi 1914.
9. Ibid, 16 Medi 1914.
10. *Y Genedl Gymreig*, 3 Tachwedd 1914.
11. Cyril Parry, 'Gwynedd and the Great War, 1914–1918', *Welsh History Review*, 14(1) June 1988, p.83, fn.24.
12. *North Wales Observer & Express*, 4 September 1914.
13. Ibid, 11 September 1914; Robert Graves, *Good-Bye to All That* (London, 1929), p.71.
14. *Yr Wythnos a'r Eryr*, 14 Hydref 1914.
15. *North Wales Weekly News*, 20 August 1914; *Caernarvon & Denbigh Herald*, 27 August 1914.
16. *Gerald of Wales. The Journey Through Wales and The Description of Wales*, Translated with an Introduction by Lewis Thorpe (Penguin Books, 2004), p.186.
17. See especially D. F. Quinn, 'Voluntary Recruiting in Glamorgan 1914–16' (unpublished MA thesis, Cardiff, 1994).
18. *Glamorgan Free Press*, 22 October 1914.
19. Ibid, 8 & 29 October 1914.
20. Cf, D. Ben Rees, *Mr Evan Roberts: The Revivalist in Anglesey 1905* (Caernarfon, 2005), p.52.
21. Cf. Ifan Gruffydd, *Gŵr o Baradwys* (Dinbych, 1963), p.115.
22. See Dafydd Roberts, 'Dros Ryddid a thros Ymerodraeth. Ymatebion yn Nyffryn Ogwen 1914–1918,' *Transactions of the Caernarfonshire Historical Society*, 1984.
23. *Llandudno Advertiser*, 3 October 1914.
24. *Western Mail*, 3 November 1914.
25. For an analysis of the Christian response in Wales, see Dewi Eurig Davies, *Byddin y Brenin. Cymru a'i chrefydd yn y Rhyfel Mawr* (Abertawe, 1988).
26. *Y Tyst*, 14 Hydref 1914.
27. *Holyhead Chronicle*, 2 October 1914.
28. *Yr Herald Cymraeg*, 15 Medi 1914.
29. Ibid, 8 Medi 1914.
30. Ibid, 29 Medi 1914.

31. John Grigg, *Lloyd George. From Peace to War 1912–1916* (London, 1985), p.169.
32. University of Bangor. Belmont MSS. Diary of Sir Henry Lewis, Bangor, 301: entry 24 September 1914.
33. *Western Mail*, 21 September 1914.
34. Ibid, 30 September 1914.
35. *Welsh Army Corps 1914–1919, Report of the Executive Committee* (Cardiff, 1921).
36. *Western Mail*, 3 October 1914.
37. Kenneth O. Morgan, *Rebirth of a Nation: Wales 1880–1980* (Oxford, 1981), p.161.
38. Peter Simkins, op. cit., pp.96–99.
39. Peter Rowland, *Lloyd George* (London, 1975), pp.289–90.
40. National Library of Wales, Welsh Army Corps Records, C12/20, memoranda and correspondence, October 1914; C12/34 Colonel Owen Thomas's Scheme and related correspondence, October 1914.
41. Ibid, C8/4, letter from Owen Thomas to Sir Ivor Herbert, 28 October 1914.
42. A. J. P. Taylor (ed.) op. cit., p.8, entry 2 November 1914; p.11, entry 16 November 1914; Kenneth O. Morgan (ed.), *Lloyd George: Family Letters 1885–1936* (Cardiff, 1973), p.174, entry, 30 October 1914.
43. *War Memoirs of David Lloyd George*, Vol.1 (London, 1938), p.452.
44. J. E. Munby (ed.), *A History of the 38th (Welsh) Division* (London, 1920), p.2.
45. National Library of Wales, Yale Collection, 4, letter from Owen Thomas to Sir Henry Lewis, 5 November 1914.
46. Cf. *North Wales Weekly News*, 11 March 1915.
47. *North Wales Observer & Express*, 6 November 1914.
48. Letter from Owen Thomas to Sir Henry Lewis, 5 November 1914, op. cit.
49. *Y Dinesydd Cymreig*, 2 Rhagfyr 1914.
50. Regimental Archives, The Royal Welch Fusiliers, Wrexham, Acc. No. 8471, T. A. Wynne Edwards Papers.
51. *Llandudno Advertiser*, 23 January 1915; *Y Genedl Gymreig*, 4 Mai 1915.
52. *Y Brython*, 26 Tachwedd 1914.
53. *Western Mail*, 24 November 1914.
54. R. R. Hughes, op. cit., p.228.
55. *Llandudno Advertiser*, 12 December 1914.
56. Ibid, 19 December 1914.
57. Ibid, 16 January 1915.
58. David Thomas, *Silyn (Robert Silyn Roberts) 1871–1930* (Lerpwl, 1956), p.107.

59. *Yr Herald Cymraeg*, 25 Mai 1915.
60. *Y Tyst*, 1 Medi 1915.
61. *Llandudno Advertiser*, 21 November, 1914.
62. Ibid, 31 July 1915.
63. *Y Tyst*, 1, 29 Medi 1915.
64. *Yr Herald Cymraeg*, 24 Awst 1915.
65. Clive Hughes, 'The New Armies', op. cit., p.117.
66. *Llandudno Advertiser*, 2 January 1915.
67. Clive Hughes, 'The New Armies', op. cit., pp.117–9.
68. *Western Mail*, 13 November 1914.
69. *Abergele Visitor*, 30 January 1915; *Yr Herald Cymraeg*, 2 Chwefror 1915.
70. *Y Genedl Gymreig*, 10 Awst 1915; also Alan Llwyd, *Prifysgol y Werin. Hanes Eisteddfod Genedlaethol Cymru 1900–1918* (Cyhoeddiadau Barddas, 2008), pp.264–7.
71. *Y Clorianydd*, 16 Rhagfyr 1914.
72. *Llandudno Advertiser*, 30 January, 6 February 1915.
73. *North Wales Weekly News*, 4 March 1915.
74. *Y Clorianydd*, 17 Chwefror 1915.
75. *Llandudno Advertiser*, 6 February 1915.
76. Ibid, 6 March 1915.
77. *Yr Herald Cymraeg*, 30 Mawrth 1915.
78. *Y Genedl Gymreig*, 4 Mai 1915.
79. *Yr Herald Cymraeg*, 4 Mai 1915.
80. *North Wales Weekly News*, 6 May 1915.
81. *Y Clorianydd*, 19 Mai 1915.
82. Ivor Wynne Jones, 'U-boat Rendezvous at Llandudno', *Maritime Wales*, No. 3 (March, 1978).
83. Letter from Owen Thomas to (?) Bulkeley, 2 February 1915 (kept at Brynddu).
84. Ivor Wynne Jones, op. cit., p.85.
85. *Yr Herald Cymraeg*, 1 Mehefin 1915.
86. *Llandudno Advertiser*, 5 June 1915.
87. *North Wales Chronicle*, 4 June 1915.
88. *Llandudno Advertiser*, 1 May, 5 June 1915.
89. House of Lords Record Office, Lloyd George Papers, E/6/3/1, Owen Thomas Case: Statement of Facts, 16 November 1916, p.5.
90. *Welsh Outlook*, January 1916, p.5.
91. *Yr Herald Cymraeg*, 13 Ebrill 1915.

92. *North Wales Weekly News*, 6 May 1915.
93. House of Lords Record Office, Lloyd George Papers, D/20/1/44, Owen Thomas to David Lloyd George, 9 July 1915.
94. Ibid, E/6/3/1, Owen Thomas Case, pp.5–7.
95. *Y Clorianydd*, 10 Tachwedd 1915.
96. House of Lords Record Office, Lloyd George Papers, E/6/3/1, Owen Thomas Case, p.5.
97. *Llandudno Advertiser*, 6 November 1915.
98. *North Wales Chronicle*, 5 November 1915.
99. *Y Clorianydd*, 3 Tachwedd 1915.
100. *Y Wyntyll*, 13 Ionawr 1916.
101. *Y Clorianydd*, 24 Tachwedd 1915.
102. Ibid, 15 Rhagfyr 1915.
103. *Y Tyst*, 15 Rhagfyr 1915.
104. Ibid, 2 Chwefror 1916. There were 92 English and 64 Welsh entries.
105. Clive Hughes, 'Army Recruitment in Gwynedd 1914–1916', op. cit., p.307.
106. *North Wales Chronicle*, 4 February 1916.
107. *Y Tyst*, 29 Mawrth 1916.
108. Ibid, 9 Chwefror 1916.
109. Ibid, 24 Mai 1916.
110. R. Tudur Jones, *Yr Undeb. Hanes Undeb yr Annibynwyr Cymraeg 1872–1972* (Abertawe, 1975), p.205.
111. *North Wales Chronicle*, 21 January 1916.
112. *North Wales Weekly News*, 13 July 1916.
113. *North Wales Chronicle*, 7 January 1916; *Abergele Visitor*, 17 June 1916.
114. *South Wales Daily News*, 25 & 26 February 1916.
115. *Holyhead Chronicle*, 24 March, 14, 20 April 1916.
116. *Y Goleuad*, 23 Mehefin 1916.
117. R. R. Williams, *Breuddwyd Cymro mewn Dillad Benthyg* (Lerpwl, 1964), pp.2–4; *Rhyl Record & Advertiser*, 5 February 1916.
118. Caernarfon Record Office, Ellis W. Davies Papers, XD 70/245, notes made by Owen Thomas (n.d.). J. H. Howard, *Winding Lanes* (Caernarvon, 1938), p.148 – where the number of conscientious objectors is put at 70.

6: Removal from Command

THEN CAME THE UNEXPECTED. On 2 May the first whisper of Owen Thomas's impending departure from Kinmel Park Camp appeared in the *Liverpool Daily Post*.[1] That the War Office had relieved him of his command in itself caused a shock, and for no apparent reason, even more so. The failure of the military authorities to provide an explanation only served to muddy the waters. Immediately, the whole of north Wales erupted in protest and, following the lead given by Anglesey County Council on 4 May, an array of public bodies and Nonconformist denominations voiced their outrage.[2] Caernarfonshire, Merioneth and Flintshire County Councils joined the Union of Welsh Independents and the Calvinistic Methodist General Assembly, Independent, Methodist and Baptist county organisations, various boards of guardians, even the Vale of Conwy Agricultural Society, in a chorus of condemnation. Resolutions described the dismissal as an 'insult', 'scandal' and 'shameful deed', while expressing appreciation of the services Thomas had rendered. Following a meeting in Rhyl, this groundswell of anger coalesced into a high-powered deputation that met Lieutenant-General W. Pitcairn Campbell, the General Officer Commanding, Western Command, in Chester, on 1 June.[3] Lord Boston, Lord Mostyn and various lord lieutenants accompanied the Revd John Williams, but all Campbell could say was that the decision originated at the War Office.

A similar reaction was registered in the local and Welsh language press, not to mention the *Manchester Guardian*, whose editorial considered Thomas's removal 'almost beyond belief'.[4] Soon a vigorous press campaign was being waged, masterminded, to a significant degree, by Beriah Gwynfe Evans, the doyen of Welsh journalists, vociferous in both his nationalist and Independent beliefs. As one of Thomas's greatest admirers, he made the most of his press contacts to work behind the scenes, to feed information as well as script all the articles and press

Officers 16th Battalion, Royal Welsh Fusiliers, 1916. Lieutenant-Colonel Thomas Wynne-Edwards of Nantglyn is seated in the centre. [RWF Archives]

releases that appeared. They reflected his familiar style and bore the same nationalistic message.[5] Readers were reminded of Thomas's contribution and legacy in north Wales; overcoming ingrained religious prejudices against the military, he had won the confidence of a generation to allow 'the children of the Sunday school to become soldiers'.[6] He was the only Welsh-speaking general in the British army; he had appointed Welsh-speaking officers and chaplains, and promoted the use of the Welsh language in military establishments. Beriah Gwynfe Evans presented the dismissal as an affront to Welsh nationality, an attempt by the War Office to undermine the concept of a 'Welsh Army'. These were listed as Owen Thomas's 'sins' and headlined '*Ai pechod yw bod yn Gymro*' (Is it a sin to be a Welshman).[7]

If not actually instigated by him, a disaffected Owen Thomas had every reason to actively encourage the campaign. Fellow officers in Kinmel, on the other hand, were said to condemn his actions in that they ran counter to all military discipline.[8] He had been most unwise, even childish, and was in danger of being open to ridicule. Thomas, on his part, could well thank Beriah Gwynfe Evans for taking up his cause and the debt was repaid in 1920 when he became treasurer of Evans's testimonial fund, personally contributing £50.[9] In Thomas's absence, Lloyd George agreed to make the presentation at the National Eisteddfod in Caernarfon the following year.

But the protests and press campaign were to be of no avail. Owen Thomas was compelled to relinquish his post in controversial circumstances on 21 June 1916. For the second time in a matter of months he had every reason to feel aggrieved at his treatment by the War Office, and how this led to a very public perception of failure. It brought his military career, in all but name, to an ignominious end.

Ironically, it was left to an English MP to raise the matter in the House of Commons, prompted by a separate military scandal. Sir Arthur Markham, Liberal member for Mansfield, had already proved to be a thorn in the flesh of the War Office. He led the campaign against the recruitment of 'boy soldiers' in October and November 1915, to expose the fact that thousands of underage recruits, some as young as fourteen, were serving on the front line in France. This new scandal involved Mrs

Cornwallis-West, wife of Colonel W. C. Cornwallis-West of Ruthin Castle, a wealthy landowner and former Liberal Unionist MP. Markham had sought an interview with Owen Thomas a few days following his departure from Kinmel Park Camp, to determine to what extent Mrs Cornwallis-West's connection with a member of the Army Council had acted to his detriment.[10] In an opening salvo, he brought the 'North Wales Brigade' to the attention of the Commons on 28 June when reference was made to the interview with Kitchener and Lloyd George on 31 October [sic] and the assurance that Welsh-speaking officers were to be appointed – yet Thomas had now been replaced by a Scotsman.[11]

Only after receiving notice of the question did Sir J. Herbert Roberts, Liberal member for Denbigh and chairman of the Welsh Parliamentary Party, asked a supplementary question, seeking assurance, given public feeling in Wales, that Thomas would be given another post with equal responsibility.[12] In his official answer, H. J. Tennant, Under Secretary of State for War, announced that Thomas, on the word of Lieutenant-General Sir Archibald Murray, now Chief of the Imperial General Staff, had been relieved of his command 'in the interests of efficiency'. He later made it known that Thomas turned down the offer of another recruiting post in Wales. Regardless of Sir J. Herbert Roberts's contribution, members of the Welsh Parliamentary Party were roundly condemned in the press for their dilatoriness.[13] Despite receiving copies of the resolutions passed by countless public and religious bodies they had remained largely silent. At a critical time in Ireland, following the Easter Rising, it was regretted that a leader of the calibre of Parnell or Redmond, the principal Irish nationalist figures, did not emerge to correct the injustice.[14] Criticism touched a nerve. Ellis W. Davies, Liberal MP for Eifion, and the Welsh Parliamentary Party whip, lamely excused their inaction by claiming that Thomas had supplied Markham, not them, with details.[15]

Tennant's parliamentary answer seriously disturbed Owen Thomas. No adverse report had been made on his professional competence whilst in Kinmel, yet the phrase 'in the interests of efficiency' called into question his abilities as a military leader. A semi-official request for a Court of Inquiry under the King's Regulations (Paragraph 666), on 1 July, was turned down by the War Office. On 4 July, the day Lloyd George replaced the deceased Kitchener as Secretary for War, Thomas confided that he did not wish him any embarrassment in his new post, knowing that Markham intended to table further questions in the Commons.[16] This was followed by an official letter to the War Office on 6 July seeking an official inquiry, and another on 17 July requesting to see the report of his immediate superior. Nothing less would satisfy Thomas in his determination to clear his name. Rather than make a parliamentary issue of the case, Lloyd George gave Markham an undertaking that he would sanction an inquiry. Notwithstanding Markham's premature death (from strain induced by his persistence) a few days earlier, Lloyd George kept his word. On 10 August, the House of Commons passed a special amendment to the Army Act to pave the way for the Army (Court of Inquiry) Act of 1916. This made provision for the summoning of civilian witnesses before a military court.

There could scarcely have been a more poignant coincidence than Thomas's personal predicament and the apocalyptic human tragedy that befell the 'Welsh Army'. Between 5–12 July, the 38th (Welsh) Division underwent its baptism of fire on the Somme. In their first major offensive they were deployed to capture Mametz Wood, a dense 220-acre woodland area heavily defended by crack troops of the *Lehr* Regiment of the Prussian Guard.[17] The initial frontal assault on entrenched German machine-gun positions on 7 July ended in bloody failure with heavy casualties. Major-General Sir Ivor Philipps – who had been critical of Thomas's military qualities – was blamed, and summarily removed from his command by Sir Douglas Haig, Commander-in-Chief of the British forces in France.

The second attack on 10 July involved men of the 113th Brigade, '*disgyblion*' Owen Thomas (literally, pupils) to quote Beriah Gwynfe Evans.[18] After three more days of savage fighting, they succeeded in capturing the wood. It came at a terrible cost. In all, almost 4,000 casualties had been sustained: 1,187 were killed or missing in action, 2,806 left wounded. Captain Ll. Wyn Griffith thought it a 'useless slaughter'.[19] The operation attracted both criticism and praise. The battle effectiveness of the 'Welsh Army' came under scrutiny; much was made of the failure of leadership, the panic and confusion among troops. Others interpreted

Brigadier-General Owen Thomas.

their performance more favourably, in that no amount of military training could have prepared them for the difficult task. Lloyd George, understandably, gave a positive verdict, ascribing their victory to the 'strengthening power of religion'.[20] War memorials in all parts of Wales were later inscribed with the names of those who fell at Mametz. A belated tribute to their heroism came in July 1987, when a memorial monument, topped by a bright red Welsh dragon, was unveiled on a hill overlooking the fateful wood.

As far as it is known, Owen Thomas made no public comment on the carnage at Mametz. His transition to civilian status became publicly evident when he presided at a concert in Pwllheli in aid of the Belgian wounded on 7 August.[21] The town mayor, lamenting that he did not appear in uniform that day, vented the voice of a nation when he spoke of their determination to reinstate him.

The Court of Inquiry constituted to investigate Owen Thomas's case, which was held in camera in the Westminster Guildhall during September and October under the presidency of Field Marshal W. G. Nicholson, who also served on the commission of inquiry into the failed Dardanelles military expedition of 1915. Though the official report was finalised on 16 November, it was not made public. On receiving his copy on 23 November, Thomas indicated that its findings had been 'very satisfactory'.[22] After incurring a 'heavy financial burden' to remove the stigma, he was also anxious that the War Office should issue a public statement.[23] Sir J. Herbert Roberts, followed later by Haydn Jones, Liberal member for Merioneth, began to exert parliamentary pressure for the report to be released.[24] It was eventually published as a Parliamentary Paper (Cd. 8435) on 2 January 1917.[25] The painful disclosures were subsequently given widespread press coverage under such headings as 'Welsh Army Scandal'.

As the origins of the scandal were laid bare, it became immediately clear that Owen Thomas had been the unwitting victim of an unfortunate sequence of events. His military reputation suffered on two counts. First, as a result of being ensnared in an unedifying social scandal involving Mrs Cornwallis-West and a young soldier. Second, following a failure by superior officers to disclose adverse reports, made worse by the ambiguous or inaccurate wording of official letters.

The Court of Inquiry had dealt with two separate, though overlapping, cases instigated by the actions of Mrs Cornwallis-West. Nicknamed 'Patsy', she was renowned in high society for both her beauty and reputation as *grande horizontale*.[26] A former mistress of Edward, Prince of Wales (the future King Edward VII), she was even described by her own son as a 'wicked woman'. Though now in her late fifties, she set out to seduce Sergeant Patrick Barrett, a vulnerable, shell-shocked 23-year-old soldier, convalescing at the home of Mr Birch, land agent to Colonel Cornwallis-West. As a sign of her affection, she had used her far-reaching influence to gain Barrett's commission in the Royal Welsh Fusiliers. Once he spurned her advances, Mrs Cornwallis-West reversed the situation to imply that he was guilty of inappropriate

Mrs 'Patsy' Cornwallis-West.
[W. Alister Williams Collection]

behaviour. When the complaint was referred to Lieutenant-Colonel Delme-Radcliffe, his commanding officer, Barrett felt unjustly censured and suffered a mental collapse. Mr and Mrs Birch then contacted Sir Arthur Markham, who took up the case.

Mrs Birch also involved Brigadier-General Owen Thomas and, following their meeting, he wrote to General Sir Henry Mackinnon, former GOC Western Command, to express his concern at the injustice Barrett suffered. Mrs Cornwallis-West, at the same time enlisted the support of Lieutenant-General Sir John Cowans, the Quartermaster General, an old family friend, who half-promising to intervene on her behalf, did arrange Barrett's transfer to another battalion.[27] Against this background, Mrs Birch had also suggested to Thomas that the 'malign influence' of Mrs Cornwallis-West and Sir John Cowans had worked against him at Kinmel. In the case of Patrick Barrett, the Court of Inquiry concluded that Mrs Cornwallis-West's actions had been highly discreditable. Lieutenant-Colonel Delme-Radcliffe, who acted hastily and harshly, would be removed from his command. In contrast, Sir John Cowans was let off with only a reprimand; his future services were deemed to be in the national interest.

Mrs Cornwallis-West's string pulling had certainly been at the root of the second case concerning Owen Thomas. This time, she had sought to advance the career of Lieutenant-Colonel T. A. Wynne-Edwards, an ambitious battalion commander seeking to oust a supposedly over-promoted general. An Anglican Tory landowner, and former Territorial Army officer, from Plas Nantglyn, Denbighshire, Wynne-Edwards, nevertheless, had a good working relationship with Thomas while serving as commander of the 16th battalion in the 113th Brigade. Like Thomas, he was disappointed that age barred him from service in France, but this was compounded by his failure to gain command of the 21st Reserve Battalion that formed part of the 14th (Reserve) Infantry Brigade at Kinmel Park Camp. As an old friend of the Ruthin Castle family, he wrote to Mrs Cornwallis-West expressing his desire to command a brigade, sprinkled with disparaging references to Owen Thomas. On his suggestion, she forwarded the letter to Cowans, with the postscript that Wynne Edwards 'certainly has taught General O. T. all he knows'. Cowans then sent the

Private.

Plas Nantglyn,
Denbigh.

You have always been so kind to me, that I am going to ask you and Colonel West to do me a favour. I hear that there are going to be changes in the higher commands at Kinmel, and they really ought to give me a Brigade. I do not mind telling you privately that I feel very keenly the way in which they have passed me over, although I do not say so. Old Owen Thomas and I are the best the best of friends, and I really like him very much but it is a little bit galling to hear him blowing his own trumpet as he is doing now, when I know perfectly well that it is I who have taught him the work which is making itself heard. If Colonel West is going to Shrewsbury to-morrow, he may see some-body with whom he could put in a good word for me. Or better still if he would write to Sir John Cowans the War Office authorities would be bound to take notice of what he said. Anyhow I shall be ever grateful for any help you can give.

My poor boy has come home from the front covered from head to foot with that terrible skin desease Scabies. He cannot sleep at night and his nerves are all gone.

He went before a medical Board yesterday, and I am thankful to say they are recommending a long rest for him.

It has been a terrible strain upon him, but he has already begun to mend under Dr. Jacksons good treatment.

With kindest regards,

Yours sincerely,
(Signed) L.A. Wynne Edwards.

letter to Lieutenant-General Sir W. Pitcairn Campbell, adding his own high opinion of Wynne-Edwards, which Mrs Cornwallis-West duly endorsed. Pitcairn Campbell, who ignored Cowans's letter, and who dealt judiciously with Mrs Cornwallis-West, was cleared of any misdoing. Wynne-Edwards, in an act of rank disloyalty, stood guilty of a serious error of judgement, clouded by jealousy.

Though Owen Thomas was right to suspect the hand of Mrs Cornwallis-West in his downfall, unbeknown to him, his command at Kinmel Park Camp had been the subject of adverse military comments by superior officers. Quite simply, it was on the basis of these official reports, and nothing else, that he was removed from his post.

Lieutenant-Colonel Thomas Wynne-Edwards [RWF Archives]

After Major-General Sir Ivor Philipps's unfavourable report in September 1915, another official assessment cast Thomas's leadership in poor light. In accordance with a War Office directive in December, an evaluation was made of all brigadiers commanding reserve brigades. General Sir Henry Mackinnon had recommended that Thomas should retain his command even though he was 'somewhat old fashioned'. Minor failings were later noted and reference made to the immaturity of the youth under his command. However, these misgivings had not been communicated to Owen Thomas. On the contrary, Inspecting Generals, including Lieutenant-General Sir Pitcairn Campbell, had expressed satisfaction with the 14th (Reserve) Infantry Brigade. On 8 April, after his meeting with Mrs Birch, Thomas became aware of Mrs Cornwallis-West's incriminating letters and Colonel Wynne Edwards's covert attempt to replace him as brigade commander. They were enough to ignite his suspicions.

Another War Office instruction in April centred on replacing retired

Facing: The letter from Wynne-Edwards which was forwarded to Lieutenant-General Sir John Cowans by Mrs Cornwallis-West. [Gwynedd Archives Service]

officers – the so-called 'dug-outs' – with those returning from duties on the Western Front. Officers still considered suitable would continue in their post, otherwise they had to be replaced as soon as the opportunity arose. Pitcairn Campbell, Mackinnon's successor, placed Thomas in the second category, and when he visited Kinmel Park Camp on 29 April he unofficially informed him of the possibility that he might be relieved of his command. Though this was tantamount to an adverse report, it had not been communicated as such at the time. Once the news was leaked to the *Liverpool Daily Post* on 2 May it prompted the public outcry. The Welsh press was deluged with articles. Thomas dug in his heels, and much to Pitcairn Campbell's irritation, would harp on the fact that he was the only Welsh-speaking general. Whereas Kitchener wished to retain Thomas's services on account of his influence in Wales, the War Office received a critical letter from Field Marshal Viscount French on 22 May that questioned his military capability. Evidence was later produced to cast doubt on Thomas's qualifications and his men's battle-readiness. Because they were not trained for warfare on the most modern lines, a high percentage of 'inefficients' had been sent from Kinmel Park Camp to France. Unfortunately, once again, he was not informed of this, and so he had every reason to feel badly treated when he received official notice to vacate his command on 12 June. He remained in Kinmel until Lieutenant-Colonel E. B. Cuthbertson, a young Scotsman invalided from the front and attached to the Western Command Staff HQ in Chester, took over on 21 June. Seven days later, H. J. Tennant, in answer to Sir Arthur Markham in the Commons, explained that he had been superseded 'in the interests of efficiency'.

Only when Owen Thomas entered into correspondence with the War Office on 1 July was he given sight of French's letter. Its contents were damning. Reference to 'ignorance and incompetence on the part of a Brigadier' was naturally judged to be a personal attack (though French would claim he was enunciating a general principle). Thomas then asked to see the report which formed the basis of his conclusions. The War Office reply of 29 July gave an inaccurate and misleading statement of facts that fed Thomas's suspicions. To him, they appeared to be a confirmation of a conspiracy hatched by Mrs Cornwallis-West and Lieutenant-General

Sir John Cowans, rumours of which circulated in north Wales. After sifting through the evidence, the Court of Inquiry concluded that Thomas's fears were unfounded. Though Mrs Cornwallis-West had tried, unsuccessfully, to interfere in military matters, she had little to do with the case. Owen Thomas had been the victim of administrative failures. That the whole tenor of military reports did highlight his shortcomings as 'a trainer of troops' has to be acknowledged. Thanks to official blunders, however, his position was made much worse. In not communicating their reports directly to Thomas, both Pitcairn Campbell and French had failed to follow the prescribed military procedure.

His reputation was sullied in this way and Owen Thomas was justifiably embittered. When Ellis W. Davies eventually came to his defence, Thomas, in confidential correspondence,[28] pitched his criticism at Field Marshal Viscount French, Commander-in-Chief of the Home Forces following his removal as C-in-C of the British Expeditionary Force. Though Thomas expressed pride in having served under French during the Boer War, once his 'scandalous behaviour' had been exposed, he became the villain of the piece. Pitcairn Campbell's written observations had provided no substance or justification for French's 'damnable lying report'. In a less than convincing explanation, French made reference to critical opinions vented during a conversation with Pitcairn Campbell, a claim denied by the latter. Thomas's efforts to refute the charges would reveal not only French's vindictive side, itself a measure of the 'Little Field Marshal', but also how the top brass regarded political appointees with disdain. The prejudice of professional soldiers towards 'civilian officers' was matched by their contempt for the 'dirty finger of Politics' that tainted the 'Welsh Army' from the outset.[29] Granted considerable autonomy under Lloyd George's patronage, its military commanders were being put to the test. Major-General Sir Ivor Philipps had already been sidelined.

It smacked of a personal vendetta. Whereas the evidence proved French to be 'crooked', Owen Thomas regretted that the most malicious facts remained unpublished, allowing him to get away with only a 'very mild' censure. By now, the damage was done, and it left a lingering sense of injustice. For French, in effect, had ended his time as a soldier.

At least the report of the Court of Inquiry restored his honour.

Moreover, to soothe his sense of ill-treatment, it called for a recognition of his services. Condemning the depravity in the upper reaches of society, and petty jealousies within the military, the Welsh press also welcomed the findings and demanded some form of reparation.[30] In due course, Thomas could feel well satisfied with the official gestures of atonement. In his parliamentary answer to Ellis W. Davies, J. I. Macpherson, Under Secretary of State for War, cleared him of any 'inefficiency'.[31] Lord Derby publicly thanked him for his work in recruiting Welsh regiments. Lloyd George, who became Prime Minister on 7 December, moved swiftly, and on his recommendation, in an *amende honourable*, Owen Thomas was bestowed with a knighthood on 13 February 1917 in the postponed New Year Honours List.[32] A military seal was placed on the matter on 10 April when the War Office granted him the honorary rank of Brigadier-General.[33] This conferred the right to wear uniform, but only on military duties. In August 1919, he would receive a gratuity from the War Office.

Sir Owen Thomas returned to north Wales in March. He received a rousing welcome at Cemaes when the Revd John Williams and other local worthies joined former members of the Cemaes Rifle Volunteers to praise their 'patriotic general' at a reception in the village hall.[34] Earlier, at a St David's Day concert in Llandudno, he had been presented with a solid silver cigar case in recognition of his service and appreciation of what he had done for the town.[35] In his acceptance speech, Thomas pointedly summed up his personal feelings in the wake of events. Forbidden to serve on the front, he had perhaps been in a worse position than the trenches; for, he exclaimed, he knew what it was to face 'poisonous gas', let alone (with Africa in mind) the 'poisoned arrows'. Two issues would continue to fester. It had cost him £1,500 in legal expenses to clear his name, though he claimed to have 'vanquished seven generals' in the process.[36] Nor was he allowed sight of the supposed evidence on which Field Marshall Viscount French had based his report. When he took advantage of his position as a backbench MP to question the Secretary of State for War directly in the Commons in April 1920, Winston Churchill refused to reopen the case.[37]

Once the report was published, Thomas resumed work with his 'National scheme for safeguarding the interests of Welsh soldiers, sailors and their dependents during and after the war'. At a meeting of the national executive in February, details were given of the monies subscribed and its distribution to a very large number of deserving cases.[38] As part of the war effort, Margaret Lloyd George, too, presided over a similar voluntary organisation, the 'National Fund for Welsh Troops', that provided 'comforts' in the form of clothing, writing material, cigarettes, etc. To avoid the overlapping financial and administrative aspect, representatives of Owen Thomas's scheme met Margaret Lloyd George at 10 Downing Street in October to pave the way for a merger of both funds. Accordingly, at a joint conference in Shrewsbury on 30 November, the two schemes were formally amalgamated,[39] and £4,000 transferred from Thomas's scheme.[40] Under Margaret Lloyd George, the 'Welsh National Fund for the welfare of the soldiers and sailors of Wales and their dependents' eventually raised more than £200,000.[41]

Owen Thomas's woes were hardly over when news came of the death of his son, Robert Newton.[42] As a captain in the 15th Battalion of the 113th Infantry Brigade, he had spent eleven months in France and been awarded the *Croix de Guerre* for gallantry in action on the Somme. Like many army officers, the two surviving sons subsequently volunteered for service in the fledgling Royal Flying Corps (RFC) – forerunner of the Royal Air Force – founded in 1912. They had both been granted their aviator's certificate flying the Maurice Farman biplane: Owen Vincent at the Military School, Farnborough, in January 1916, Robert Newton at the Military School, Birmingham, in May. The expansion of the RFC from July 1916 extended the opportunities for pilot training. At first, the planes were primarily

A brief letter written by Owen Thomas to his sisters informing them of the death of Robert Newton (Robin).
[Courtesy of Robert Williams]

engaged in reconnaissance, and given the nature of things, the casualty rates were high; roughly one RFC officer in six was killed. Posted to the Middle East as a member of 14 Squadron, Captain Robert Newton Thomas took part in the offensive against German and Turkish forces during the Palestine campaign. Engaged on the Sinai front, near Gaza, the two seater BE.2e., A1803, reconnaissance aircraft he shared with 2nd Lieutenant J. W. Howells was shot down into the sea by a German flak battery on 23 July 1917.[43] Their bodies were never recovered. Aged 26, Captain R. N. Thomas is commemorated on Panel 10 of the Jerusalem Memorial.

For Owen Thomas, there was more than one reason to mark the National Eisteddfod at Birkenhead as another 'war eisteddfod'. Inducted into the Gorsedd of Bards as *Owain o Fôn*, the death of his two sons added to the solemnity as two moving scenes were witnessed.[44] Because Ellis H. Evans (Hedd Wyn), the victorious bard, had been killed in France a few weeks earlier, the chair was draped in black. Then, Lance-Corporal Samuel Evans, said to be the sole surviving member of the 17th Battalion choir that competed at the National Eisteddfod two years earlier, was invited to the platform. As his former commanding officer, Brigadier-General Owen Thomas, with little formal ceremony but the 'silent flow of tears', pinned white and black rosettes (to symbolise honour and mourning) on the chest of the badly maimed soldier.[45] Hundreds in the audience also had personal reasons to weep for a 'lost generation', perhaps with a pang of guilt in the case of a trio of tearful armchair warmongers also present: the Revd John Williams, Sir Henry Jones and Professor John Morris-Jones.[46] Such sacrifices would continue to traumatise society. For the three counties of north-west Wales the most tragic consequence of the Great War was the human cost. By November 1918, the army death toll for the three counties of Gwynedd had reached 3,649.[47]

In December, Thomas left for Kenya to assess the effects of war on the holdings of the East African Estates Ltd. He would stay for a year, returning in late November after the armistice had been signed. On the outward voyage, he witnessed a naval engagement that resulted in the sinking of two ships.[48] No details of the vessels or the location was provided, but it had been an anxious time because his own ship was

Members of 32 Squadron, RFC, July 1916. Commanded by Major Gerald Allen (centre – he married Owen Thomas's daughter, Mina) who had just taken over command from Major Lionel Brabazon Rees, VC, MC of Caernarfon, Third from the right is Lieutenant Owen Vincent Thomas with his friend, Lieutenant Gwilym Lewis (whose family originated from Caernarfon), on his left. The pilots are standing in front of one of the squadron's DH2 single-seater fighter aircraft. [W. Alister Williams Collection]

perilously close. This was the nearest he came to the sound of battle in the Great War.

Being away in East Africa meant he was absent for the marriage of his only daughter, Mina Margaret, to Major Gerald Allen in London on 7 March 1918. Allen, from County Cork, Ireland, served alongside her brother, Owen Vincent, in 32 Squadron, and was later commanding officer of 39 Squadron. It was whilst he was in Africa that Owen Thomas received news of the death of his one remaining son.

A graduate of Jesus College, Cambridge, Owen Vincent first served in France as a lieutenant in the 13th Battalion, Royal Welsh Fusiliers. After initial training with the RFC, he served with 32 Squadron, one of the most feared fighter squadrons. Above the battlefields of the Somme in the summer of 1916, he made reconnaissance flights and was engaged in aerial dogfights with the 'Huns'.[49] To counter the growing menace of German air raids, he returned to Britain in June 1917, tasked with intercepting enemy Gotha bomber aircraft as a member of 39 (Home Defence) Squadron.[50] With two brothers already killed in action, an official order on 7 August stated that he was 'not to be sent overseas in any circumstances'.[51] What followed thus becomes even more tragic. By December, he was stationed at North Weald, Essex, an airfield crucial to the defence of London, piloting two-seater Bristol Fighter aircraft on both daylight and night sorties. On the night of 16/17 February 1918, he almost became the victim of so-called 'friendly fire' when his plane was attacked in error by a squadron colleague.[52] Having survived air combat, he tragically lost his life on 29 July when instructing 2nd Lieutenant A. J. Cairns in night observation. A freak accident caused his Bristol F2B (B1331) to crash in flames. Captain O. V. Thomas, aged 24, was buried in St Alban's churchyard, Coopersale, near Epping, Sussex.

Each individual death in the Great War became the cause of acute family grief and mourning. On occasion, the scale of the suffering is beyond comprehension. No greater sacrifice was made than that of two English families: of eight serving brothers from the Beechey family of Friesthorpe, Lincolnshire, five would not return[53] and five Souls brothers from Great Rissington, Gloucestershire, also perished.[54] In Wales, at least two families, Bartlett of Penarth and Lowry of Llandyfaelog, equalled the

Brigadier-General Owen Thomas and his three sons, March 1915. L–R: Trevor (killed in action, 10 January 1916); Robin (killed in action, 23 July 1917) and Owen Vincent (killed in a flying accident, 29 July 1918).

ultimate sacrifice made by Owen Thomas and his wife. Thomas, of course, was a prominent military figure, and all three sons were familiar with the army tradition from boyhood. Under his watchful eye, they had come within earshot of hostilities in the Boer War. As young men, they were better prepared for military service than most Welsh recruits. By the same token, Owen Thomas knew that the conflict might take its toll, little thinking that the extravagant words of September 1914 relating to his sons returning home on a bier would come back to haunt him. It is doubtful whether he ever came to terms with the loss, whilst what happened at Mametz must have weighed heavily on his mind. The very personal anguish he suffered visibly aged him over the last few years of his life. The names of the three brothers are commemorated on the Llanfechell war memorial as well as within St Bridget's church, Skenfrith, a church closely associated with their grandmother.[55] They provide a sombre reminder of the family's tragic destiny in the Great War.

Notes

1. *Liverpool Daily Post*, 2 May 1916.
2. *North Wales Chronicle*, 5 May, 2 & 30 June1916; *Y Genedl Gymreig*, 16 & 23 Mai, 6, 13 Mehefin 1916; *Y Goleuad*, 2 Mehefin 1916; *Y Tyst*, 10 Mai, 7 Mehefin 1916.
3. *North Wales Chronicle*, 2 June 1916.
4. *Manchester Guardian*, 5 May 1916.
5. National Library of Wales, Welsh Army Corps Records, C8/4, letter from Owen W. Owen (Secretary, Welsh Army Corps) to the Earl of Plymouth, n.d. enclosing press cuttings from various Welsh language newspapers.
6. *Y Genedl Gymreig*, 9 Mai 1916.
7. *Y Tyst*, 10 Mai 1916; *London Welshman*, 13 May 1916.
8. Letter from Owen W. Owen to the Earl of Plymouth, op.cit.
9. *Y Clorianydd*, 26 Mai 1920.
10. House of Lords Record Office, Lloyd George Papers, D/20/2/102, letter from Sir Arthur Markham to D. Lloyd George, 29 June 1916.
11. *Hansard*, 5th Series, Vol. 83, 28 June 1916.
12. Ibid, 28 June 1916.
13. *Y Tyst*, 5 Gorffennaf 1916.
14. *North Wales Weekly News*, 29 June 1916.
15. *Y Genedl Gymreig*, 11 & 18 Gorffennaf 1916.
16. House of Lords Record Office, Lloyd George Papers, D/20/2/103, letter from

Owen Thomas to D. Lloyd George, 4 July 1916.
17. See Colin Hughes, *Mametz* (Gliddon Books, 1990 edition), the standard work on the battle.
18. *Y Genedl Gymreig*, 25 Gorffennaf 1916.
19. Ll. W. Griffith, *Up to Mametz* (London, 1931), p.201.
20. *The Times*, 21 August 1916.
21. *Holyhead Chronicle*, 11 August 1916.
22. *North Wales Chronicle*, 15 December 1916.
23. The National Archives, WO 339/158715, letter from Owen Thomas to the War Office, 29 November 1916.
24. *Hansard*, 5th Series, Vol. 87, 23 November, 4 December 1916.
25. House of Lords Record Office, Lloyd George Papers, F/6/3/1, Owen Thomas Case, Report of the Army Court of Inquiry, 16 November 1916. Extracts from Cd. 8435 (cf. The National Archives, WO 141/63) were published in *The Times*, 4 January 1917. They form the basis of following paragraphs.
26. Eileen Quelch, *Perfect Darling. The Life and Times of George Cornwallis-West* (London, 1972); Tim Coates, *Patsy: The Story of Mary Cornwallis-West* (London, 2003), also A. J. P. Taylor (ed.) op. cit., pp.111, 113, 125.
27. For a defence of Cowans, see D. Chapman-Huston and O. Rutter, *General Sir John Cowans*, Vol. II (London, 1924), pp.144–157.
28. Caernarfon Record Office, Ellis W. Davies Papers, XD 70/245, letters from Owen Thomas, 5, 16 & 31 January, 2, 10 & 21 February, 10 & 21 March 1917.
29. Ibid, 'Recollections of some of Campbell and French's evidence' (notes made by Owen Thomas?), and letter from Major-General F. S. Robb (Military Secretary to Kitchener) to W. Pitcairn Campbell, 18 May 1916.
30. *Yr Herald Cymraeg*, 8 Ionawr 1917; *Baner ac Amserau Cymru*, 6 & 13 Ionawr 1917; *Y Tyst*, 10 Ionawr 1917.
31. *Hansard*, 5th Series, Vol. 95, 20 February 1917.
32. *The Times*, 13 February 1917.
33. The National Archives, WO 339/158715, Owen Thomas's Record of Service File.
34. *Y Clorianydd*, 21 Mawrth 1917.
35. *Holyhead Chronicle*, 8 March 1917.
36. *Y Clorianydd*, 4 Rhagfyr 1918.
37. *Hansard*, 5th Series, Vol. 128, 20 April 1920.
38. *Holyhead Chronicle*, 16 & 23 February 1917.
39. *The Times*, 1 December 1917.

40. *Holyhead Chronicle*, 1 March 1918.
41. Viscount Gwynedd (Richard Lloyd George), *Dame Margaret* (London, 1947), pp.161–2.
42. *Y Clorianydd*, 1 Awst 1917.
43. www.australianflyingcorps.org/2004_2002/feature/palestine1917.html. The Air Battle over Palestine as told in the *Kriegs-Chronik der Leipziger Neuesten Nachrichten*, January 1917–December 1917, entry 25 July 1917.
44. *Western Mail*, 7 September 1917.
45. *South Wales Daily News*, 7 September 1917.
46. Cf. Gerwyn Williams, *Y Rhwyg* (Llandysul, 1993), p.151.
47. Cyril Parry, op. cit., p.95.
48. Cf. *Y Clorianydd*, 4 Ionawr 1922.
49. Gwilym H. Lewis, *Wings over the Somme 1916–1918* (London, 1976), pp.50, 82.
50. For details of his operations between 5 June 1917–20 May 1918, see Christopher Cole and E. F. Cheeseman, *The Air Defence of Britain 1914–1918* (London, 1984).
51. Record of Service, information provided by Owen Cock.
52. Christopher Cole and E. F. Cheeseman, op. cit., p.400.
53. Michael Walsh, *Brothers in War* (London, 2006).
54. Ibid, 'The Lost Souls' in *Saga Magazine*, November 2001.
55. Her book, *Bygone Days in the March Wall of Wales*, op. cit. is dedicated to their memory.

7. Westminster

THE WAR REVIVED AGRICULTURE, greatly improving the lives of those who worked on the land. When German U-boat attacks on merchant shipping disrupted food imports, the government had to take decisive steps to increase home production and so avert a crisis. Under the Corn Production Act of 1917, farmers received guaranteed minimum prices, a gesture balanced by granting workers a minimum wage. District wages committees, which were set up to fix both the local rate and working hours, consisted of an equal number of farmers' and workers' representatives, together with independent members. This concession gave a significant fillip to the National Agricultural Labourers' and Rural Workers' Union as well as the agricultural section of the Workers' Union. The opportunity to further workers' interests stimulated recruitment efforts, and trade union membership among the farm labourers expanded at an unprecedented rate. For one localised union, its newly-found strength prepared the groundwork for a historic political achievement.

Undeb Gweithwyr Môn (Anglesey Workers' Union) was a rural, working-class organisation with a strong sense of county identity, unique in Welsh labour history.[1] Established in Llangefni in 1909, it has been officially registered as an independent trade union in 1911.[2] Its origins and early leadership were directly linked to the agricultural labourers' movement inspired by Ap Ffarmwr in the 1890s. The initial aim was to seek improved working and social conditions. While a number of middle-class Liberal sympathisers gave support, more

Badge of Undeb Gweithwyr Môn (Anglesey Workers' Union) bearing the motto Môn, Mam Cymru *(Anglesey, the mother of Wales).*

radical elements, veterans true to the spirit of Ap Ffarmwr, sought a political direction towards the emergent Labour Party. From the first, the union struggled to survive. An infusion of members followed the formation of a separate insurance section under the National Insurance Act of 1911. Compared to the *Undeb Gweithwyr Môn* Approved Society, that filed over 1,000 members and a fund of £6,000 in May 1917, the labour section languished with only 99 members and £20 to its name.

Wartime conditions dramatically changed this position. For working-class families, higher food prices meant extra hardship and suffering, and it was against this background that W. J. Jones (Brynfab) penned a series of articles entitled *'Yfory Llafur'* (Labour's Tomorrow), published in *Y Clorianydd* between 4 July and 19 September 1917. His avowed socialist convictions, earlier forged when working in the Dinorwic Slate Quarry, were now intensified, for as a shopkeeper in Brynsiencyn he had witnessed poverty at first-hand. In a perceptive analysis of the changed circumstances, Brynfab outlined the new opportunities offered to the rural working class, especially in the wake of the Corn Production Act. And in presenting the Labour Party programme, he prepared the trade union movement for a political role.

History repeated itself. As with Ap Ffarmwr's newspaper articles in *Y Werin*, Brynfab's message struck a responsive chord. Aided by activists from the labour section of *Undeb Gweithwyr Môn*, a series of public meetings were held, characterised by a fervour redolent of the religious revival of 1904–5. Anglesey was soon 'ablaze'.[3] Platform speakers enthusiastically invoked the memory of Ap Ffarmwr and by the end of January 1918, the number of branches had risen to 20, bringing the total membership of the resuscitated labour section up to almost 1,000.[4] It had three objectives in the name of the working class: improved wages and working hours, better housing, and representation on the county council and other public bodies. In a remarkable demonstration of collective solidarity, delegates from 33 branches, now representing over 2,000 members drawn from all sectors of workers, met at Llangefni on 21 May to celebrate its first *Gŵyl Lafur* (Labour Day).[5] Also present were delegates from the Holyhead Trades and Labour Council. Formed in 1913, it could trumpet recent gains; a further 2,000 workers in the port town belonged to six affiliated trade unions. The overall confidence and ambition was fully warranted. Already, the prospect of running a Labour parliamentary candidate, an aspiration aired during Ap Ffarmwr's crusade, had appeared on the agenda of *Undeb Gweithwyr Môn* branches.[6] With all in favour, the announcement that they would nominate a contender was greeted with loud cheers.

Trade unionists at Holyhead had aimed to adopt a Labour candidate as early as 1913–14, and were later in touch with Arthur Henderson, general secretary of the Labour Party, who pressed for the formation of a Divisional Labour Party in the constituency.[7] Instead, arrangements would be left to a Joint Election Committee, composed of representatives from both organisations. In all but name, this was the genesis of the Anglesey Labour Party, though it did not officially affiliate until 1923–4.[8] Hailed as a political 'revolution',[9] Brynfab elaborated on the socialist aims of the Labour Party, fundamental to which was the nationalisation of land and vital public services. All the while the emboldened labour section of *Undeb Gweithwyr Môn* grew in strength. By the summer, under a full-time organizer, it claimed 40 branches and over 2,500 members, who sported their distinctive union badge with defiant pride. Six branches had a membership of over 100; at Llannerch-y-medd the figure was almost 250. As a sign of the times, *Y Wyntyll* renounced its Liberal Party allegiance to become a mouthpiece for labour interests. Towards the end of the year, the main focus was on the forthcoming parliamentary election and with over 90 per cent of the town's workforce unionised, officials of the Holyhead Trades and Labour Council were in an equally assertive mood. Once the Joint Election Committee had taken the crucial decision to contest the election,[10] the names of the favoured contenders emerged. Among them stood Brynfab and G. Llywelyn Williams, secretary of the Holyhead Trades and Labour Council. But an empty campaign war chest meant there was little prospect of paying the £150 electoral deposit. Finance became a primary consideration.

A week after the snap election was called, the name of Brigadier-General Sir Owen Thomas appeared out of the blue to challenge Sir Ellis Jones Griffith the sitting member. It is not known who actually inspired the invitation, but no doubt the influence of Hugh Pritchard was instrumental. A former editor of *Y Wyntyll*, and erstwhile secretary of the Anglesey Liberal Association, he had identified himself with *Undeb Gweithwyr Môn* from the outset. Prominent as a military recruiter alongside Thomas in the first months of the war, he was subsequently granted a commission as a second-lieutenant in the 15th Battalion, Royal Welsh Fusiliers, of the 128th Brigade in Llandudno. Seeing that Owen Thomas was in East Africa at the time, a discreet approach had to be made, with his brother, Hugh Thomas, acting as intermediary. In his letter of reply to W. J. Pretty, vice-president of *Undeb Gweithwyr Môn*, dated 20 November, Thomas submitted a personal statement to outline his credentials and political views.[11] A day later, at a meeting of the union executive, other candidates having withdrawn, Sir Owen Thomas was unanimously adopted as the parliamentary candidate 'in the labour interest', a decision endorsed by the Holyhead Trades and Labour Council.[12] Thomas, who had only just returned to Britain, could not attend in person. For the rank and file, this was the first they knew of his candidature and in terms of personality, *Undeb Gweithwyr Môn* could have made no better choice, but it was also a choice dictated by financial necessity.[13] Patently well-off, Thomas agreed to pay the electoral deposit and fund his own campaign.

Owen Thomas's political life had come full circle. Since the 1880s, as a prominent member of the Anglesey Liberal Association, and his role in Ap Ffarmwr's movement, he was, by common consent, the ideal parliamentary candidate to represent both the farmers and workers of his native county. When the opportunity evaporated in 1894, it was in the Oswestry constituency that he first stood. Again outside Anglesey, there were those who marked him out as a worthy representative. Even during the war, when in Llandudno, his name emerged as a possible Liberal contender for the Arfon constituency following the untimely death in May 1915 of William Jones, MP. As a man of the people, in sympathy with labour, he had received the nomination of a number of branches in north Caernarfonshire. In his letter to the secretary of the Arfon Liberal Association, Thomas had explained that the exigencies of war meant he had 'no time for politics'.[14] Later, in December 1916 and September 1917, he was mentioned as a possible successor to Ellis Jones Griffith in the event of his elevation to

High Court judge.[15] Once his name had been cleared by the Military Court of Inquiry, a general feeling emerged that it could not be long before he would represent Anglesey at Westminster.[16]

If the hallmark of a true politician is his commitment to serve the people, then Owen Thomas was suitably qualified. His record of service to community, enriched by contacts with a wider world, made him a fitting advocate for Anglesey. In all main spheres of his life – farming, the military and politics – he had shown his mettle. Here, at last, was the opportunity to fulfil a long-held political aspiration that would crown his public career. Doubtless there were other reasons why he accepted the invitation of the Joint Election Committee and abandoned his natural political home in the Liberal Party. Thomas could challenge Ellis Jones Griffith with few qualms. It was Ellis W. Davies who gained his gratitude for the part he played in securing the Commons statement that restored his military reputation in February 1917; Griffith had kept aloof. The transition to politics offered a form of public salvation, the means of regaining personal honour and status following two humiliating military episodes that tainted his good name; perhaps he saw it as an opportunity to get even with the 'Establishment'. Privately, the prospect may also have offered some balm to ease personal grief. On the other hand, there is every reason to believe that he had agreed to stand without having fully grasped the true nature of the labour movement in Anglesey. Over the course of the year he spent in East Africa, the political terrain had undergone a radical change to expose the underlying class divisions in society.

Thomas opened his campaign in Llangefni on 28 November at a meeting chaired by Thomas Rowlands, president of *Undeb Gweithwyr Môn*.[17] Recalling his appearance on the same platform during the recruiting drive of 1914, he now appealed for 'an army of supporters'. What he sought was a broad consensus. Once aware of the changed circumstances in Anglesey, he did not intend floundering in the cross-currents. Deteriorating relations on the question of wages and hours of work heightened class awareness, leading to confrontational disputes between *Undeb Gweithwyr Môn* and the farmers' unions. The ill-feeling alarmed Thomas. Especially when the executive of the Anglesey Farmers'

Union, followed by the county branch of the National Farmers' Union, urged their members to vote for Ellis Jones Griffith.[18] Similarly, the Anglesey Conservative Association, in deciding not to enter the political fray, gave their support to his opponent.[19] To Brynfab, this was proof of class division. Rather than identify himself with sectional interest, Thomas's instinct for conciliation, and past record in this respect, favoured unity and co-operation among the agricultural classes, whose interests, he argued, were 'inseparably connected'. He had not returned to Anglesey to oppose the farmers.[20] On the contrary, if invited by the Anglesey Farmers' Union, he would have stood in its name.[21]

The 'coupon election' of December 1918 allowed a little over two weeks of campaigning. As well as all men over the age of 21, the vote to women aged over 30 meant a substantially enlarged electorate. Ellis Jones Griffith stood as the official Liberal Coalition candidate approved by Lloyd George; Owen Thomas ran as an independent labour candidate, outside the Labour Party proper.[22] He, too, pledged his support for the Lloyd George Coalition and the policy of peace and reconstruction. All the same, he was very much his own man, determined to exercise complete freedom in political matters. In his election address (dated 4 December), and further declarations, he set out his beliefs.[23] He trusted that pre-war government commitments to Wales and the trade unions would be upheld. He advocated a generous financial settlement in the saga of Welsh Church disestablishment. Women were entitled to equal rights. He opposed extending conscription into peacetime. Discharged soldiers and sailors deserved appropriate government provision. He stood for free trade. A measure of home rule for Wales was favoured; the country's natural wealth – mines, quarries, water power – could underpin a scheme of free education from nursery to university, along with help for the aged poor. Security of tenure, fair rents, compensation for improvements, land courts and low interest loans to farmers were well-recognized demands. Among the benefits to workers, he called for a minimum wage, maximum working hours, a public health plan, improved housing and free education.

While reflecting socialist values to a remarkable degree, representing labour did not extend to a commitment to the Labour Party programme of nationalisation. As Owen Thomas came to terms with electoral realities in Anglesey, he continually sought to reposition his political stance. Hence the contradictory statements that clouded the issue. At one stage, he announced he would sign the Labour pledge, though it seemed more of a promise to support the 'general policy' of the Labour Party.[24] A message backing him was issued by J. H. Thomas, secretary of the National Union of Railwaymen, one of the main unions affiliated to the Holyhead Trades and Labour Council. Yet, in another speech, he declared that he would never sign the Labour ticket, nor consort with such men as Ramsay MacDonald.[25] Ambivalence and pragmatism were to be effectively combined.

Thomas was certainly conscious of his personal limitations. As he would later confess, he did not have the skills of a political orator; adding, more tongue-in-cheek, that in Anglesey everyone knew him and it was of no great importance what he said or how he said it.[26] If only for this reason, he came to rely on the organisational strength of the twin trade union bodies. In contrast to other rural constituencies in Wales, they provided him with a solid power base; together, they had over 5,000 members. From the time of his nomination, when he was proposed and seconded by officials of the Holyhead Trades and Labour Council, to the choice of agent and sub-agents, his campaign was highly dependent on the labour movement. The ailing Anglesey Liberal Association could only muster five sub-agents; Owen Thomas had 37, at least 20 of whom can be identified as trade union activists.[27] They provided him with a 'perfected electioneering machine'[28] to cover the island and mobilize support. Furthermore, officials of both union bodies were his principal platform speakers. Stalwarts summoned Ap Ffarmwr's name as a rallying call, while the audience were also reminded of Thomas's part in improving the working conditions of farm labourers (though the depth of his commitment was called into question).[29]

As his campaign intensified, with three or four crowded meetings nightly, it generated widespread enthusiasm. In hustings speeches, Thomas alluded to his time as 'father' of the Welsh Army.[30] Not only in the care shown for Anglesey men, but also the welfare of Welsh soldiers and their families in connection with the National scheme he had launched. In a county well-known for its denominational allegiances, the Liberal-Methodist nexus still persisted. Even his military *compadre*, the Revd John

Williams, stood firm in the Liberal camp, loyal to a fellow Methodist. Owen Thomas's election agent was the Revd Richard Morris, Independent minister at Llannerch-y-medd, a committed labour man who gave up the ministry a year later to become trade union secretary. A number of Anglican clergymen had already come out in support of *Undeb Gweithwyr Môn* and Thomas's conciliatory statement on the disestablishment settlement no doubt greatly pleased church members. Denominationalism might no longer be a potent consideration, but there was no better opportunity for Independents, Baptists and Wesleyans to register an anti-Methodist vote.[31]

Ellis Jones Griffith suffered grave disadvantages that diminished his prospects from the start. From a position of strength at the general elections of 1910, the Anglesey Liberal Association was moribund, morale among its supporters at rock bottom. Two former secretaries had defected to the labour movement; in the case of Hugh Pritchard, he would offer his services as registration agent to *Undeb Gweithwyr Môn*. After twenty-three years of service, Ellis Jones Griffith appeared to take the constituency for granted, giving precedence to his more profitable legal work and ambitions at the Bar.[32] As a member of the 'Liberal War Committee' in the Commons, he had been in the vanguard of the campaign for compulsory military service since May 1915.[33] To members of the Association, and many others, conscription was alien to the traditional Liberal creed and it aroused widespread disapproval, in contrast to the position taken by Owen Thomas. Disestablishment, championed by Ellis Jones Griffith, was of no real concern to ordinary people, and disillusionment with the Liberal Party was compounded by his complete disregard for the working class.[34] He had remained silent during the passage of the Corn Production Act, unable to support the amendment for a 30 shillings minimum wage.[35] There could be no better indication of his unpopularity among the workers than the 'feeble cheers' which greeted his unexpected appearance at the *Gŵyl Lafur* in May.

For all that, Owen Thomas's election victory was unexpected. On a 69 per cent turnout, his 9,038 votes to 8,898 gave him a slim majority of 140 following a recount. It was a momentous result in the political history of Anglesey, where the Liberal Party had held the seat since the Reform Act of 1832. Ellis Jones Griffith took especial umbrage and refused to shake Thomas's hand.[36] He would alliteratively ascribe his defeat to 'Church, Conscription, Congregationalists (i.e. Independents), Calumny'[37] – curiously choosing to omit combination. Of course, various political issues had played a part, but, publicly, it was a contest fought around a dividing line based on personality. And Owen Thomas proved to have the most popular appeal. He had a strong personal story to add to the respect and trust he commanded over the years. His wartime role and constant reference to his immense family sacrifice aroused a considerable groundswell of sympathy. Appreciation was voiced for the care taken of young soldiers in Llandudno and Kinmel, whereas the loss of all three sons personified the human cost for islanders coming to terms with the death of over a thousand men in the Great War. Women who went to the polls in large numbers were said to be supportive.[38] Thomas also commanded a great preponderance of the postal returns from among the 3,473 absentee soldiers and sailors whose votes had to be counted between 14 December, the day of the election, and 28 December, when the final count was declared.

Despite the strong trade union presence, voters in Holyhead had reportedly tilted to Ellis Jones Griffith by a ratio of 3 to 1.[39] If this be the case, then it was the rural labour dynamic that enabled Owen Thomas to realise his political ambition. If not well-funded, *Undeb Gweithwyr Môn* was sufficiently well organized at grassroots level to harness solid support in strongholds such as Aberffraw, Brynsiencyn, Gwalchmai, Llannerch-y-medd and other outlying villages where the result was enthusiastically celebrated. Owen Thomas would acknowledge this crucial role

Press photograph of Owen Thomas meeting Crimean veteran Thomas Barton whilst canvassing in Holyhead.

with a donation of £50 to the union fund and a promise to become an annual subscriber.[40] Victory came at a hefty cost. Election expenses to the tune of £899-11s-1d were mainly paid out of his own pocket; voluntary donations raised by local union activists would not have amounted to much.[41]

Just as the 1868 election represented the triumph of the Nonconformist middle class, Owen Thomas's achievement in 1918 appeared to herald a further political transformation in the name of the *gwerin* (common people) of Anglesey.[42] What had been prophesied in 1890 came to pass. Brynfab certainly saw it as an end to the old order and a victory for the working class – a claim that received greater resonance when Thomas officially joined the Parliamentary Labour Party (PLP) in the House of Commons. In this respect, his return gained added significance, not only in Welsh, but British politics. R. T. Jones, secretary of the North Wales Quarrymen's Union, had won 8,145 votes on a labour and nationalist platform to come second in the Caernarfonshire constituency, yet elsewhere in rural Wales, notably Denbigh and Pembroke, the Labour Party challenge fared badly because of lack of organisation. Its showing in English rural seats was no better. Even though the National Agricultural Labourers' and Rural Workers' Union had laid a solid base in Norfolk, a county noted for its rural radicalism, two leading union figures, R. B. Walker and George Edwards, were defeated.[43] Only in the primarily agricultural constituency of Holland-with-Boston, Lincolnshire, could Labour claim a seat in rural England, where the victor, W. S. Royce, was a former Conservative. It was two years later that the Labour Party celebrated its first genuine parliamentary gain in the countryside following George Edwards's success in the South Norfolk by-election.

Owen Thomas took the Labour whip more from his indebtedness to the organized labour movement in Anglesey than from political conviction. He would admit to having no 'great knowledge' of the Labour Party in parliament.[44] Together with another two independent Labour MPs and a Co-operative Party member, he brought the PLP total to 61.[45] At first sight, Thomas appeared an unorthodox Labour MP: in terms of upbringing, social character and occupation, he hardly fitted the traditional working class mould.[46] By no means a typical trade union sponsored candidate, his close labour ties, nevertheless, gave him a common bond with party colleagues, 49 of whom were trade union nominees. Of the ten Labour MPs returned from Wales, nine were from industrial Glamorgan and Monmouth, with links to the South Wales Miners' Federation. Seven Scottish MPs also represented mining constituencies, including the fiery Neil Maclean. Following the defeat of Ramsay MacDonald, it was a Scottish miner, William Adamson, who initially became chairman of the PLP. How comfortable Owen Thomas felt on the Labour benches, and to what extent he genuinely embraced socialist ideas, with commitment to the state control of land, would soon be put to the test. Apart from William Abraham (Mabon), the embodiment of Nonconformist Lib-Labism, he would find a kindred spirit in D. Watts Morgan, the military recruiter and decorated war hero who had once served under him, and perhaps W. S. Royce, a supporter of farm workers' trade unionism with business interests in South Africa. None of the three could be classed as socialists.

Immediately following a landslide victory, the Lloyd George Coalition ran into difficulties. Postwar economic conditions presented serious problems as prices outstripped wages, leading to trade union militancy. Debates in the Commons in February 1919 focussed on the industrial unrest and possible solutions. For the most part, Owen Thomas proved to be a loyal Labour MP. He followed the party line to support a number of official motions and amendments. Despite his election pledge, it meant voting against various Coalition government proposals. When William Brace coupled better wages and working hours with the nationalisation of land, railways and mines, Thomas entered the lobbies alongside the likes of Adamson, Clynes, Hartshorn and Maclean.[47] As relations in the coal industry deteriorated, Lloyd George staved off the threat of a miners' national strike when he proposed the Sankey Commission to examine the whole industry. Both the Miners' Federation of Great Britain and the Labour Party demanded nationalisation. Though Thomas abstained in two divisions, he joined his Labour colleagues on 25 February to vote against ownership based on the principle of joint control.[48]

In March he supported the Prevention of Unemployment Bill presented by A. E. Waterson, the first Co-operative Party MP.[49] On 7 May, he voted against Coalition budget proposals that aimed to raise additional duties on foodstuffs.[50] Poor households already struggled with the burden of a 130 per cent rise in the cost of living. On the same day, he backed D. Watts Morgan's motion calling for the restoration of pre-war railway passenger fares. His firm stand on measures affecting the lot of the working class was proudly cited as evidence of his continued adherence to Labour principles.[51]

For his maiden speech on 13 March 1919, Thomas joined a debate singularly appropriate in the light of his own experiences. Not for nothing had he taken up the controversial case of Violet Douglas-Pennant, summarily dismissed from her post as commandant of the Women's Royal Air Force in August 1918 by the Secretary of State for War.[52] The sixth daughter of the slate magnate, the second Baron Penrhyn of Llandegai, she had shared a platform with Thomas in May 1917 in support of the proposed North Wales Heroes' Memorial.[53] Her callous treatment bore parallels with his own experience in Kinmel. Similarly, it generated considerable agitation in north Wales and calls for a public enquiry. In a letter to the *Daily Telegraph*, Thomas made it known that he was ready to raise the matter in the Commons.[54] His first move came in the form of a parliamentary question relating to a Court of Inquiry under the King's Regulations, a procedure he was all too familiar with.[55] During the debate that followed, he roundly condemned the way Douglas-Pennant had been 'cruelly treated'.[56] Despite strong pressure from several MPs, the government refused to grant a judicial enquiry. Even when the case was taken to the Upper House, the findings of the Select Committee of the House of Lords failed to clear her name. Indeed, the scandal of 'Britain's Dreyfus' was never resolved. Douglas-Pennant, it seems, had been dismissed not on the grounds of 'efficiency' but because of character defects that made her 'grossly unpopular'.[57]

True to his manifesto promise, Thomas voted against the Conscription Bill and its powers to prolong the period of military service.[58] Another specific election commitment would cause great consternation. In April, in alliance with Anglicans and Conservatives – most notably the High Churchman, Lord Robert Cecil – he signed a memorial seeking adequate reimbursement for the church in the final settlement of Welsh Disestablishment.[59] It was a controversial stance. As the only Nonconformist among the

27 signatories, he came in for rare criticism.[60] His own denomination, above all, was unable to accept that an 'enlightened Independent' could be capable of such a deed. At one time, *Y Tyst* refused to believe he had been a signatory.[61] To the dismay of Liberal Nonconformist opinion, Thomas honoured his election pledge by voting for the Welsh Church (Temporalities) Bill on its second reading on 6 August. At last, the long running disestablishment controversy was brought to an end.

More in keeping with his character was the concern shown for those facing problems in agriculture. No one knew better the circumstances of tenant farmers, and in a series of parliamentary questions he sought solutions to their plight. At a time of the break-up of great landed estates, he wished to see low interest loans being made available to tenants seeking to purchase their holdings.[62] Agricultural credit banks, he pointed out, had proved successful in Australia and other countries.[63] In view of the rising costs of labour, transport and agricultural implements, he favoured reducing the income tax paid by farmers to pre-war levels.[64] He also sought fair compensation for cattle slaughtered after contacting bovine tuberculosis.[65] When the deteriorating economic situation forced the government to repeal the Agricultural Act of 1920, that guaranteed minimum prices, Thomas voted to retain subsidies for farmers.[66]

Naturally enough, various military issues were addressed in keeping with personal concerns. He wished to see the pension scheme for war service extended to the dependents of military personnel.[67] Reflecting his own principled stand on the Welsh language, he advocated the appointment of Welsh-speaking members to war pensions tribunals, Welsh-speaking officers to command Welsh Territorial units, and official press advertisements, relating, for instance, to the war financing 'Victory Loans', translated into Welsh.[68] Of interest to his own constituency was the release of S.S. *St Trillo* from Admiralty service – it had served as a minesweeper during the war – and its return to the Liverpool & North Wales Steamship Company to resume passenger services between Liverpool, Llandudno and Menai Bridge.[69] MPs appointed to a select committee drew on their knowledge and experience. Thomas was well-fitted to serve on the Inter-Departmental Committee set up in April 1919 to consider the provision of residential treatment for ex-servicemen suffering from pulmonary tuberculosis, and their re-introduction into employment on the land.

Thomas was not above lobbying for his own business ends. A good number of parliamentary questions involved the economic troubles of British East Africa and aspects of post-war reconstruction. The release of government funds was an essential precondition for improving railway links and the transport of goods.[70] To facilitate further land settlement schemes, plantation owners and settlers had to be free of financial burdens. Mindful of the financial losses suffered by the East African Estates Ltd he sought adjustments in the rupee exchange rate, in the knowledge that lower production costs would be the spur to cotton and sisal cultivation.[71] Again in connection with his company's interests, he called for the reinstatement of offices at Carlton House in Regent Street, compulsorily vacated for government use during the war.[72]

Thomas's claim to be 'as loyal a supporter of the Labour Party in and out of the House of Commons as any man'[73] came under severe strain when he took exception to the behaviour of Neil Maclean. Though he admired moderate colleagues like J. R. Clynes, he had nothing in common with the hard-left forerunner of the 'Red Clydesiders'. Following Maclean's public avowal of Bolshevism in Soviet Russia at the Southport Labour Party conference on 27 June, Thomas handed a formal complaint to William Adamson. Things were made worse three days later when Maclean, a Labour whip, refused to rise in the Commons for the national anthem in celebration of the Peace Treaty signed at Versailles.[74] Thomas was greatly offended. Reacting to Maclean's 'gross disloyalty', he distanced himself from a party which tolerated a 'Bolshevik' whip. After explaining his stand, both *Undeb Gweithwyr Môn* and the Holyhead Trades and Labour Council unanimously signalled their approval, 'all Anglesey ... commend your action'.[75]

Not that they were in a position to dictate otherwise. The labour movement in the county had been shaken by two events. First, it was left weakened after a major setback in the county council elections. Buoyed by their parliamentary success, the concerted electoral challenge mounted in March, in a bid to gain influence in local government, ended in a humiliating rout. Only three of the twenty-two Labour candidates had been returned; Lewis Thomas, founder member of the Independent Labour Party in Anglesey, won the only contested seat.[76] Among the casualties were the Revd Richard Morris, Thomas Rowlands and W. J. Pretty. Their failure to topple the Liberal old guard not only severely dented working-class aspirations, but offered further evidence that the electorate had voted for the man in December 1918, rather than a party or political ideology. The labour movement had thus little choice but to rally behind their MP. Besides, *Undeb Gweithwyr Môn* was also embroiled in a controversial internal dispute. It had little future as a small, independent trade union. A majority of the executive committee favoured refuge within the powerful Workers' Union, the largest trade union in Britain. To Brynfab it looked more like a takeover than a merger. The National Agricultural Labourers' and Rural Workers' Union had been snubbed, and the decision made without an official ballot of *Undeb Gweithwyr Môn* membership. Undeterred, the 46 branches in the labour section were eventually transferred *en bloc* on 1 September.[77] Retitled the Anglesey Workers' Union, it kept a measure of autonomy with the Revd Richard Morris as full-time organising secretary. This amalgamation caused personal rifts, but the repercussions would be altogether more political in that the rebranded union became aligned, through the Workers' Union, with the Labour Party.

At a meeting of the PLP in July, Thomas had proposed that Maclean resign his post. When he refused, he announced that he was leaving the Labour benches and formally resigning from the Labour Party.[78] But as during his election campaign, his pronouncements cloaked a certain ambiguity. Still maintaining a threadbare allegiance to Labour,[79] he now gained what he had probably long sought, namely the freedom to act politically as he so wished. Henceforth, reverting to his colours in the 1918 election, he intended to sit as an independent labour member. Even so, the Joint Election Committee could take pride in his parliamentary record. He may have followed in the tradition of two previous 'silent members', Richard Davies and Thomas Lewis, in that he lacked the lustre of a Commons orator. Yet, by any standard, Owen Thomas had proved to be a conscientious MP, both in terms of parliamentary questions and his Commons voting record. Out of 74 divisions he voted against the

Coalition government on 57 occasions, a record no other Welsh Labour MP could claim.[80]

In July 1919, Thomas and his wife had moved to 'Penbryn', an imposing country mansion in the parish of Harpsden, Henley-on-Thames, Oxfordshire. After their terrible family loss they returned to an area of picturesque tranquillity not far from Fawley. In recognition of his service to his native county, he was appointed Deputy Lieutenant of Anglesey that summer.[81] Constituency ties were further maintained when he addressed the Holyhead Trades and Labour Council and members of *Undeb Gweithwyr Môn* at their second *Gŵyl Lafur* to give an account of his parliamentary work.[82] He vouched his commitment to the interests of the working class, while at pains to emphasise that he was in the Commons to serve both labourers and farmers. Further political meetings were held in Llangefni and Holyhead, but a recurrence of malarial fever later prevented him from holding a series of public meetings to explain his desertion from the PLP.[83]

Still, he left for Egypt at the end of November as a member of the special commission of inquiry under Lord Milner.[84] Representing the Commons and Labour Party, his longstanding acquaintance with Milner melded with his reputation as an authority on tropical agriculture. Investigation into the root causes of recent riots and demonstrations in the British Protectorate had to address the economic and agricultural issues. Following unprecedented price rises in food, clothing and fuel, the grievances of the *fellahin* (the Arab peasantry) were being fomented by political agitators. Almost half a million families had no land. Over three months, between December 1919 and March 1920, Thomas toured the country, also visiting Sudan with Sir J. Grenfell Maxwell. When the report was finally published in February 1921, its conclusions concentrated on the political aspects.[85] Demands for autonomy were acknowledged and sweeping proposals made for a radical political change, realised when Egypt was granted partial independence the following year.

Thomas would complain that political activists prevented the *fellahin* from having their say. Possibly because their conditions improved, and discontent had subsided, his views were not incorporated into the report of the Milner Commission. Instead, they are found in a confidential

The Milner Mission to Egypt. L–R: Back row: Arthur Lloyd, MP; Sir Cecil Hurst; Brigadier-General Owen Thomas; J. Spender; E. M. Ingram. Seated: Sir James Rennell Rodd; Rt Hon Viscount Milner; General Sir John Maxwell.

private report and an interview published in *The Times*.[86] To obviate the food shortages and land hunger that stoked the political unrest, he had submitted a series of recommendations that have a familiar ring. Security of tenure and fair rents again echoed solutions to the Welsh Land Question. He also advocated the sale of small plots to landless *fellahin* on which to grow crops and keep cattle, improved rural housing, and the establishment of agricultural credit banks. Because the food problem eclipsed all others, cereal growing had to take precedence over unrestricted cotton cultivation.

One surprising by-product of his membership of the Milner Commission was a later newspaper report of an invitation for him to visit Ireland to undertake an independent political investigation at a time of discussions to break the deadlock in the Anglo-Irish conflict.[87] It claimed that he had entered into correspondence with a number of prominent politicians from the main parties. Quite who invited him, or what they expected him to achieve, remains unknown, but at this time (July 1921) Lloyd George and De Valera agreed to a truce that preceded the Anglo-Irish Treaty at the end of the year.

Soon after returning from Egypt, Thomas had attended the 1920 *Gŵyl Lafur* – May Day celebrations at Holyhead, held jointly by the Anglesey Workers' Union and Holyhead Trades and Labour Council.[88] He accompanied Charles Duncan (a former Labour MP) and George Titt, two leading figures in the Workers' Union. *Undeb Gweithwyr Môn*'s merger with the Workers' Union had meant automatic affiliation to both the Trade Union Congress and Labour Party. In reaffirming his allegiance to the Labour Party, Thomas's withdrawal from the PLP proved to be short-lived. For him, it was a 'high honour' to represent Labour; indeed he regarded the Labour Party as an embodiment of the old Liberal values and principles he held so dearly. All this made for a more settled outcome in

The Anglesey Workers' Union officials, Holyhead, 1920. L–R. Front row: William Williams; George Titt; Charles Duncan, MP; W.J. Pretty; Thomas Rowlands; Lewis Thomas; H. Jones. Second row: H. Thomas; William Owen; W. Pritchard; John Evans; R. Hughes. Back row: D. Williams; Revd Morris; David Lloyd.

the constituency. In the Commons, Thomas continued to vote with Labour. In June, he supported a leftist motion that had favoured a special taxation on war fortunes.[89] By August, his record in the division lobbies showed only 17 votes in support of the Coalition government, and 98 against.[90]

Unsurprisingly, he intervened in a military row when news was leaked of the proposed disbandment of both the Irish and Welsh Guards on grounds of economy.[91] Formed in February 1915, the Welsh Guards had fought with valour at the battle of Loos the following September. Owen Thomas registered a robust protest, ahead even of Lieutenant-General Francis Lloyd, the officer originally charged with raising the unit. Leading the national outcry, he maintained, in a letter to *The Times*, that the Welsh nation would not tolerate such an insult.[92] If economies were to be made, he suggested, among other things, weeding out 'useless generals'. Such was the strength of feeling among Welsh MPs that Churchill, as Secretary of State for War, responding to Thomas's parliamentary question, had to give an assurance that neither the Irish nor Welsh Guards would be abolished.[93]

Predictable, too, were the parliamentary questions tabled in the wake of developments in East Africa. Kenya's transformation into a Crown Colony in June 1920 had left the coastal zone under the jurisdiction of the Sultan of Zanzibar. At a time of financial retrenchment, this would have a bearing on the business interests of the East African Estates Ltd. An anxious Owen Thomas drew attention to how commercial undertakings were penalised.[94] In the same vein, he tried to convince the government of the trade benefits that would accrue from the construction of a deep water wharf at Kilindini harbour, near Mombasa, and lower freight charges on the railways.[95] Very often, he seemed more concerned with East Africa than Anglesey.

More attention was being paid to his constituents at the end of the year.[96] At a time of severe unemployment, he raised the possibility of re-opening the Parys Mountain copper mine, once Anglesey's premier industry, and deepening the inner harbour at Holyhead so as to improve the trade link with Ireland.[97] He sought justice in the case of an 80-year-old monoglot Welshman from Pentraeth, drawn into a false declaration because of his inability to understand the official regulations relating to old-age pensions.[98] As the bitter four-month quarrymen's strike at Penmon seemed set to drag on, he called for government intervention when all attempts at arbitration had failed.[99]

From mid-December, he spent three months in Kenya attending to the company affairs of the East African Estates Ltd. He left behind a divided and damaged labour movement in Anglesey. The political bombshell had been dropped in October. In letters to the respective chairmen of the Anglesey Workers' Union and Holyhead Trades and Labour Council, he announced his resignation from the Labour Party.[100] Yet again, his political sensibilities had been grievously tested by Neil Maclean's indiscretions. At a time of class struggle, when workers occupied factories in the Italian cities of Milan and Turin, a national strike of coalminers inspired Maclean to advocate a similar Bolshevik style take-over of the mines as a prelude to a 'revolution' that would being socialism to power in Britain.[101] This was the last straw. Notwithstanding his admiration of Clynes, Brace and J. H. Thomas on the moderate wing of the party, he could not remain on the Labour benches when presented with the theories of the extreme socialist section. He now intended to become an Independent member, in support of Lloyd George's Coalition. Because of his earlier threat to relinquish the party whip, this final break could not have come as a complete surprise.

Owen Thomas's erratic behaviour within the PLP had strongly suggested that his political allegiance would not be a lasting commitment. Ostensibly accountable to a Joint Election Committee, the resignation not merely divided opinion within the labour movement, but also exposed fundamental differences. No joint meeting was called, so both bodies dealt with the crisis separately. Because the Holyhead Trades and Labour Council had not affiliated with the Labour Party, it could pass a vote of confidence with little difficulty.[102] Though urged to stay as an 'Independent Welsh Nationalist in sympathy with moderate Labour policy',[103] Thomas was given complete freedom of action to speak and vote according to his own political convictions as was agreed at the time of the 1918 election. The Anglesey Workers' Union, on the other hand, had been placed in an invidious position. Officially allied to the Labour Party, the executive committee was bound to accept his resignation.[104] Unhappy with the precipitate action of its counterpart, all it could do was ask Thomas to delay his decision for six months to allow time to find an alternative candidate. In the eyes of one possible contender, E. T. John, a view shared by Brynfab, the resignation was 'an act of utter disloyalty'.[105]

Despite a personal plea from the Revd Richard Morris, Thomas refused to consider even a nominal membership of the Labour Party. He was determined to leave the PLP and be his own man in the Commons. Subsequent joint meetings between the Anglesey Workers' Union and Holyhead Trades and Labour Council came to nothing.

Prior to sailing to East Africa, Thomas at least continued to vote with the Labour Party.[106] As the months passed, the stalemate continued. The Anglesey Workers' Union was unable to put forward an official Labour Party candidate; E. T. John, the former Liberal MP who switched to Labour, turned down repeated requests. All the while, the two labour bodies remained manacled to their MP. Invited to address the 1921 May Day rally, Thomas confirmed his departure from the PLP, adding that he had not crossed the floor of the House, nor joined another party.[107] Having gained his political independence, he still continued to vote against the government and consistently sided with the PLP on issues of benefit to workers.[108] In June, he opposed reductions in the rates of unemployment benefits paid under Unemployment Insurance Acts.[109]

This made the situation all the more palatable for the two labour bodies, now presenting a united front with the next general election in mind. The impecunious Joint Election Committee had little room to manoeuvre. Neither the Anglesey Workers' Union nor the Holyhead Trades and Labour Council held a political fund worth mention.[110] Precisely the same circumstances prevailed as in 1918. Sir Owen Thomas held the upper hand, not least because he would again be expected to finance his own election campaign, estimated at £700–£800.[111] Moreover, a strong challenge was anticipated as Sir Robert J. Thomas had decided to stand down as Coalition Liberal MP for Wrexham in order to fight Anglesey as a National Liberal. (At the time of his nomination by the Anglesey Liberal Association, Owen Thomas, curiously, received 3 votes to his 34.[112]) E. T. John, meantime, had opted to contest Brecon and Radnor. The labour movement in Anglesey bowed to the inevitable, so weak was their position. Owen Thomas received a mandate to stand as an Independent candidate with official Labour support.[113] This was the best electoral deal it could hope for. But the political sophistry incensed the minority left-wing element as represented by Brynfab.

Notes

1. For a detailed history of the union, see David A. Pretty, 'Undeb Gweithwyr Môn: Anglesey Workers' Union', *Transactions of the Anglesey Antiquarian Society*, 1988 (Part 1), 1989 (Part 2).
2. The National Archives, FS 11/133, Register N$^{o.}$ 1485, 17 August 1911.
3. *Y Wyntyll*, 6 Rhagfyr 1917.
4. Ibid, 30 Ionawr 1918.
5. Ibid, 23 Mai 1918.
6. Ibid, 9 Mai 1918.
7. *Holyhead Chronicle*, 17, 24 & 31 May 1918.
8. *Report of the 24th Annual Conference of the Labour Party* (1924), p.285.
9. *Y Wyntyll*, 13 Mehefin 1918.
10. Ibid, 5 Medi 1918.
11. Ibid, 28 Tachwedd 1918. In recollections entitled 'The Start of the Labour Party in Anglesey', William Long, Brynsiencyn, claims that it was he and William J. Pretty who took the initiative to contact Owen Thomas. Notes supplied by Emily Long (daughter) to the author, 13 August 1979.
12. *Holyhead Chronicle*, 29 November 1918.
13. Cf., *Y Clorianydd*, 8 Tachwedd 1922.
14. *North Wales Weekly News*, 3 June 1915.
15. *Y Goleuad*, 29 Rhagfyr 1916; *Y Clorianydd*, 26 Medi 1917.
16. *Y Clorianydd*, 14 Chwefror 1917.
17. Ibid, 4 Rhagfyr 1918.
18. Ibid, 11 Rhagfyr 1918; *Liverpool Daily Post*, 10 December 1918.
19. *Holyhead Chronicle*, 29 November 1918.
20. *Liverpool Daily Post*, 30 November 1918.
21. *Holyhead Chronicle*, 29 November 1918.
22. Cf. R. Douglas, 'A Classification of the Members of Parliament elected in 1918', *Bulletin of the Institute of Historical Research*, Vol. XLVII, 1974, p.93.
23. *Holyhead Chronicle*, 6 & 13 December 1918.

24. *Liverpool Daily Post*, 5 December 1918; *Holyhead Chronicle*, 6 December 1918.
25. *Holyhead Chronicle*, 13 December 1918.
26. Cf. *Y Clorianydd*, 26 Chwefror 1919.
27. *Y Wyntyll*, 12 Rhagfyr 1918.
28. *Liverpool Daily Post*, 2 December 1918.
29. *Y Wyntyll*, 12 Rhagfyr 1918.
30. *Y Clorianydd*, 4 Rhagfyr 1918.
31. *Y Wyntyll*, 19 Rhagfyr 1918.
32. T. I. Ellis, op.cit., Chap.VIII, and p.190 which also notes certain character defects.
33. M. Johnson, 'The Liberal War Committee and the Liberal advocacy of conscription in Britain 1914-1916', *The Historical Journal*, Vol. 51, N$^{o.}$ 2, June 2008.
34. *Holyhead Chronicle*, 23 August 1918.
35. *Y Wyntyll*, 25 Hydref, 1 & 8 Tachwedd 1917.
36. E. W. Rowlands, 'Etholiad Cyffredinol 1918 ym Môn', *Transactions of the Anglesey Antiquarian Society*, 1976–77, p.74.
37. T. I. Ellis, op. cit., p.188.
38. *Holyhead Chronicle*, 20 December 1918.
39. Ibid, 3 January 1919.
40. Ibid, 24 January 1919.
41. *Y Wyntyll*, 28 Tachwedd 1918. Four *Undeb Gweithwyr Môn* members at Aberffraw, for instance, were delegated to raise funds.
42. Ibid, 2 Ionawr 1919.
43. Alun Howkins, *Poor Labouring Men. Rural Radicalism in Norfolk 1870–1923* (London, 1985), p.126.
44. Cf. *Holyhead Chronicle*, 10 November 1922.
45. *Report of the 19th Annual Conference of the Labour Party* (1919), p.30.
46. W. L. Guttsman, *The British Political Elite* (London, 1968), p.236.
47. *Hansard*, 5th Series, Vol. 112, 13 February 1919.
48. Ibid, Vol. 112, 25 February 1919.
49. Ibid, Vol.114, 31 March 1919.
50. Ibid, Vol.114, 7 May 1919.
51. *Y Wyntyll*, 27 Chwefror, 15 Mai 1919.
52. Violet Douglas-Pennant, *Under the Searchlight. A Record of a Great Scandal* (London, 1922).
53. *The Times*, 17 May 1917.

54. *Y Wyntyll*, 23 Ionawr 1919.
55. *Hansard*, 5th Series, Vol. 112, 17 February, 20 February 1919.
56. Ibid, Vol.113, 13 March 1919.
57. *The Times*, 31 May 1919.
58. *Hansard*, 5th Series, Vol. 114, 25 March 1919; *Y Wyntyll*, 10 Ebrill 1919.
59. *Liverpool Daily Post*, 1 & 3 April 1919.
60. *Y Wyntyll*, 3 Ebrill 1919.
61. *Y Tyst*, 30 Ebrill 1919.
62. *Hansard*, 5th Series, Vol. 114, 7 April 1919.
63. Ibid, Vol. 120, 27 October 1919.
64. Ibid, Vol. 115, 5 May 1919.
65. Ibid, Vol. 115, 8 May 1919.
66. Ibid, Vol. 135, 25 November 1920.
67. Ibid, Vol. 114, 16 April 1919.
68. Ibid, Vol. 114, 16 April 1919; Vol. 120, 20 November 1919; Vol. 117, 7 July 1919.
69. Ibid, Vol. 118, 14 July 1919.
70. Ibid, Vol. 114, 2 April 1919.
71. Ibid, Vol. 119, 14 August 1919; Vol. 120, 30 October 1920.
72. Ibid, Vol. 118, 14 July 1919.
73. *Western Mail*, 9 July 1919.
74. *The Times*, 9 July 1919.
75. *Western Mail*, 25, 20 July 1919; *Y Clorianydd*, 30 Gorffennaf 1919.
76. *Y Wyntyll*, 13 Mawrth 1919.
77. Workers' Union, *Annual Report* 1919, p.21.
78. *Holyhead Chronicle*, 1 August 1919.
79. *Y Clorianydd*, 6 Awst 1919.
80. *Y Wyntyll*, 18 Medi 1919; *Holyhead Chronicle*, 26 September 1919.
81. *The Times*, 6 August 1919.
82. *Holyhead Chronicle*, 25 April 1919; *Y Clorianydd*, 11 Mehefin 1919.
83. *Y Clorianydd*, 24 Medi 1919.
84. J. Lee Thompson, *A Wider Patriotism: Alfred Milner and the British Empire* (London, 2007), pp.183–93.
85. *Report of the Special Mission to Egypt*, 1921 (Cmd.1131).
86. Bodleian Library, Oxford. Papers of Alfred, Viscount Milner, 447, fols. 211–48. Agricultural and Economic Position of Egypt, 20 April 1920; also *The Times*, 6 May 1920.
87. *Y Clorianydd*, 22 Mehefin 1921.

88. Ibid, 5 Mai 1920; *Holyhead Chronicle*, 7 May 1920.
89. *Hansard*, 5th Series, Vol. 130, 8 June 1920.
90. *Y Clorianydd*, 25 Awst 1920.
91. *The Times*, 5 June 1920.
92. Ibid, 7 June 1920.
93. *Hansard*, 5th Series, Vol. 130, 9 June 1920; *The Times*, 16 June 1920.
94. *Hansard*, 5th Series, Vol. 131, 12 July 1920; Vol. 132, 4 August 1920.
95. Ibid, Vol.131, 9 July 1920; Vol. 132, 4 August 1920.
96. *Y Clorianydd*, 8, 22 Rhagfyr 1920.
97. *Hansard*, 5th Series, Vol. 134, 17 November 1920; Vol. 135, 8 December 1920.
98. Ibid, Vol. 135, 30 November 1920.
99. Ibid, Vol. 135, 7 December 1920.
100. *Liverpool Daily Post*, 20 October 1920.
101. *The Times*, 18 October 1920.
102. *Liverpool Daily Post*, 22, 29, 30 October 1920.
103. *Holyhead Chronicle*, 12 November 1920.
104. *Liverpool Daily Post*, 8 & 10 November 1920.
105. National Library of Wales, E. T. John Papers, 2,722, E. T. John to Beriah Evans, 19 October 1920.
106. *Liverpool Daily Post*, 13 December 1920.
107. *Y Clorianydd*, 11 Mai 1921.
108. Ibid, 31 Awst, 14 Medi, 12 Hydref 1921.
109. *Hansard*, 5th Series, Vol. 143, 27 June 1921.
110. *Y Wyntyll*, 16 Ionawr 1922. The Holyhead Trades and Labour Council had only £3-0s.7d. in its political fund.
111. *Holyhead Chronicle*, 11 November 1921.
112. *Y Wyntyll*, 1 Rhagfyr 1921.
113. *Liverpool Daily Post*, 5 November 1921.

8. Final Years

WHEN OWEN THOMAS AGAIN EMBARKED ON HIS TRAVELS, the outlook for organised labour in Anglesey seemed rosier. He left for India in November 1921, calling at Bombay (Mumbai) to witness some of the devastation that followed violent political rioting sparked by the visit of the Prince of Wales. He went on to Zanzibar, and then East Africa on company business – a grand tour that covered over 17,000 miles.[1] On his return in February 1922, he received a warm welcome in Llangefni arranged by his supporters within the Joint Election Committee.[2] Since he did not reside in the constituency at this time, he maintained a high profile with his many public appearances, primarily in connection with military and cultural causes.

From 1920, he had taken part in acts of remembrance to acknowledge the sacrifices made during the Great War. In Llandudno, he paid tribute to the 3,000 casualties suffered by the battalions he had commanded when stationed in the town.[3] Medals were presented to the bereaved relatives of men killed in action. During 1921–2, Thomas was called upon to unveil a succession of local war memorials in Anglesey.[4] In Newborough, he recollected his recruiting campaign in the village; many of those who answered the call were now names written in stone.[5] While his presence at such ceremonies allowed him to honour the fallen, they also proved to be a painful reminder of his personal loss. Commemorating the 38 former pupils of Llangefni County School in October 1921, he almost broke down when he recalled seeing the names of his own three sons on the Llanfechell war memorial the previous day.[6]

As well as presiding at local concerts, his generosity to local *eisteddfodau* was greatly appreciated. He donated a prize for the best drama at the Min Menai Eisteddfod of 1920.[7] More especially, under the bardic name of 'Owain Carrog', he bore the cost of the resplendent regalia worn by the *Gorsedd* officials of Eisteddfod Môn that was to be held at

Cemaes in 1923.⁸ On such occasions, he never failed to extol the Welsh language and culture; nor the value of Sunday schools.⁹ All his life he had striven to embody the cultural and Christian values instilled in him from youth.

On one major political issue relating to Wales, however, his complete change of mind astounded many. In his 1918 election address, he had presented an explicit case for a measure of Welsh self-government. Deemed 'an ardent Welsh Nationalist',[10] he professed to share the aims of *Cymru Fydd*, the patriotic movement championed by Lloyd George in the 1890s, and the political aspirations of E. T. John, who helped inspire renewed interest in Welsh home rule in 1918–19. Enthusiasm waned; yet in a further push the proponents of home rule convened a conference in Shrewsbury on 31 March 1922. It attracted little support from the Welsh local authorities. Ignoring the portents, Sir Robert J. Thomas moved the second reading of the Government of Wales Bill in the Commons on 28 April.[11] It proposed a legislature with limited powers to manage Welsh domestic affairs, utilising a proportion of Westminster taxation.

Owen Thomas (third from left) at the unveiling of the Llangaffo War Memorial, 6 May 1921.

Owen Thomas had already expressed his intention of voting against the Bill.[12] In an overt political reversal, he intervened in the Commons debate – a rare occurrence in itself – to lead the opposition.[13] It was an uncompromising performance. Though he still favoured devolution in principle, he argued that there was no public demand in Wales for the measure at that time. In scathing references to the ill-attended Shrewsbury conference he cited north Wales fears of Glamorgan domination, and the inadequate financial provisions. In further exchanges, J. Hugh Edwards (Neath) condemned his fickleness. Thomas, he said, had delivered a speech worthy of Sir Frederick Banbury, the Conservative Unionist MP for the City of London, who, employing similar obstructionist tactics that defeated Gladstone's Irish Home Rule Bill of 1892, eventually 'talked out' the measure. Denounced as a political 'weathercock',[14] Owen Thomas's shift in attitude could be explained in the context of the forthcoming general election. He had subordinated his nationalist convictions to political expediency. Arguably, it was a deliberate stratagem to highlight the differences between himself and his political rival in Anglesey.

The political showdown came in the November election. Sir Robert J. Thomas was a formidable opponent. Bootle born, but with family roots in Anglesey, the Liverpool shipowner and shipbroking magnate became noted for his philanthropy. He gave generously to war charities, and from his mansion at Garreglwyd, Holyhead, he showered largesse on the port – £150,000 by his own account. A Calvinistic Methodist, and Liberal of the true faith, he was seen as the man to regain the seat.[15] There were good grounds for optimism. Unlike the previous round, the Labour Party had failed to mount an organized challenge in the county council elections in March. Moreover, he had the support of Brynfab, bitter since Owen Thomas's 'inexcusable betrayal'.[16] For him, Thomas had exploited *Undeb Gweithwyr Môn*'s financial poverty to his own advantage and divided organized labour in the constituency. Sharing the platform with Sir Robert J. Thomas in Holyhead, Brynfab urged the workers to follow his example in the absence of an official Labour Party candidate.

Sir Owen Thomas stood as Independent candidate. In contrast to 1918, he was no longer beholden to the labour movement. This time he had addressed and won the official support of the Anglesey Conservative Association to broaden his power base.[17] Conservatives figured prominently on the election committee as well as election agents.[18] Nominated by Sir W. B. Hughes-Hunter, Plas Coch, the son of his former mentor, central figures in trade unionism were conspicuously absent.[19] Never before had Anglesey witnessed such a topsy-turvy contest. Support for the rival candidates cut across traditional barriers. Apart from Brynfab, other trade union activists, including the secretary of the Sailors and Firemen's Union in Holyhead, backed Sir Robert J. Thomas. Within Sir Owen Thomas's camp, farm workers, labour movement loyalists, military officers and true blue Tories presented an eclectic *mélange*.

By remaining loyal to Lloyd George, Sir Robert J. Thomas represented traditional Liberal values. Sir Owen Thomas offered no clear political creed. Shifts in his party allegiance enabled opponents to mock his 'chameleon changes' and 'political coat of many colours'.[20] On the hustings they capitalised on his turnabout on the question of Welsh home rule. Accusatory letters in the press would also note his inconsistency over local option, whereby a district could veto alcohol licensing.[21] Sir Robert J. Thomas supported the temperance movement, whereas Owen Thomas appeared to change his tune in order to attract Tory votes. Previously condemning alcoholism and favouring temperance, he now professed to have an open mind on local option, while rejecting prohibition.

In many ways, it degenerated into a prickly contest with both candidates adopting an aggressive stance. Of particular interest was their business involvement. Accused of being a war profiteer, Sir Robert J. Thomas pointed to his charitable contributions.[22] Sir Owen Thomas faced criticism for exploiting native labour in East Africa by paying slave wages to workers on company plantations, a charge he refuted by claiming they received government rates of pay.[23] As expected, a great deal was made of their respective voting record in the House of Commons over the previous four years.[24] Their contrasting stand on matters such as conscription, import duties, war wealth, subsidies for farmers, reduction in tea duty and the level of unemployment benefits, placed Owen Thomas in a more favourable light. As a Coalition Liberal, his opponent invariably voted for the government, a course that often courted unpopularity. No local issues stood out. What appeared were allegations of 'organized hooliganism' – supposedly worse than could be found in the East End of London – perpetrated against supporters of Robert J. Thomas.[25] In this political rough and tumble, one Nonconformist minister was said to have been confined to bed after receiving a kick!

As in 1918, much more turned on personality and personal appeal. On the eve of the election a 6d booklet, entitled *Life in Pictures of Brig-Gen Sir Owen Thomas, Kt, MP, DL, JP* was published to chronicle his achievements and bolster his image. Photographs that illustrated various aspects of his life story as 'farmer and soldier' were prefaced with a potted bilingual biography by an unnamed editor. It outlined a career dedicated to public service, his motto being '*Eich Dyn*' (Your Man), a play on the German *Ich Dien* (I Serve) found on the Prince of Wales's feathers. One resonant observation, its barb undisguised, struck a devastating contrast: 'Others amassed great fortunes by business exploitations during the war; Sir Owen Thomas made sacrifices which should endear him to every heart'. The poignant photograph of the father and three sons in military uniform, captioned 'all three killed in action', was a powerful reminder of that sacrifice.

In a gruelling electioneering schedule, Owen Thomas addressed 57 public meetings over sixteen days.[26] By his own admission, he did not have a prepared speech.[27] For as he had confessed previously, he was so well-known it mattered little what he said. Something about his bearing enabled him to engage with his audience; here was a politician with a very human touch. More positive were the claims to have been a diligent MP who fulfilled his duties, answering each letter sent by a constituent.[28] Once again, he would carry the day. Securing 11,929 votes to 10,067, Sir Owen Thomas retained his seat with a comfortable majority of 1,862. On a high turnout of 80.5 per cent, his share of the poll rose from 50.4 to 54.2 per cent. It signalled a public vote of confidence, a continuation of popular trust and affection. Thanks to his philanthropy, Sir Robert J. Thomas polled heavily in Holyhead. Against this, Owen Thomas could rely on bedrock support in the rural heartlands. Besides ex-soldiers, he garnered the bulk of the Tory vote. He also benefited from the substantial number of Liberal abstentions, disgruntled Asquithian elements in a divided party who disapproved of Sir Robert J. Thomas's candidature as a National Liberal (the former Coalitionists) in support of Lloyd George.[29] Above all else, his success could be ascribed to his charismatic hold over the majority of Anglesey electors. Without doubt, it had the hallmark of another personal victory – that cost him £910-4s-10d in election expenses.[30]

In the new parliament at the close of the year, he voted against the Conservative government following a debate on the uncertain future of agriculture.[31] He also tabled two questions regarding Anglesey constituents that were a legacy of the Great War. First, compensation for the surviving crew members of HMS *Tara*, formerly SS *Hibernia*,[32] which had been requisitioned by the Admiralty for service as a patrol boat, before being sunk by a German U-boat in the Mediterranean in November 1915. Following their harrowing ordeal as prisoners of Turks and Arabs, the former crew were incapable of returning to civilian work, yet ineligible for war pensions. He then presented the case of an Anglesey soldier, blinded in both eyes, who had lost his maximum disability pension.[33] What turned out to be his last public engagements were two gatherings in Amlwch.[34] On 15 January 1923, he addressed a meeting of the Union of Post Office Workers, and two days later he presided at a local *eisteddfod*. Over the final weeks of his life, there had been a perceptible decline into ill-health. After the long tours abroad, the recurring bouts of malaria, the rigours of the election campaign took its toll. All the while there was the inner suffering. Since the death of his three sons, he had carried a heavy psychological burden. Early in February, before the new session of parliament, he was reported to be ill in a London hospital.[35] Following a cholecystectomy operation, he entered a nursing home in the capital, where he died, aged 64, on 6 March, after suffering a pulmonary embolism.[36]

For the final homecoming, the coffin was transported to Neuadd, prior to the funeral on 9 March. Acting on medical advice, Lady Thomas stayed in London, as did their daughter who was heavily pregnant at the time. After a brief service in the house, the two-mile-long cortège of some 200 motor cars and horse-drawn carriages, over 3,000 mourners in total, made its way to Ebenezer in Llanfechell, the chapel founded by his forefather.[37] People from all sections of society came to pay their respects. Among them representatives of the main spheres of Owen Thomas's career: ministers of religion, clergymen, military officers and ex-soldiers, county council officials, magistrates, masons, poor law guardians, and leading figures from the political parties and trade unions. Draped with the Union Jack, the coffin bore the brigadier-general's cap and sword. One particular aspect was missing. Many felt that he should have been accorded full military honours. But the British Army was not officially represented; there was no firing party or sounding of the Last Post over his grave as a final tribute.[38] If the War Office chose to ignore his past contribution, then Owen Thomas would be fully honoured by his own people.

A few days later, a memorial service was held in Holyhead, organized by ex-soldiers, ending with the playing of the Last Post. Soon, moves

Owen Thomas's coffin outside Neuadd.

were afoot to raise funds to perpetuate his memory.[39] It enabled the local committee to subsequently endow a hospital bed for former soldiers at the Bangor infirmary, and raise a memorial plaque inside Ebenezer chapel, unveiled on 31 October 1929.[40] A large Celtic cross now marked the grave.

Immediately after his death, the by-election of April 1923 had given another measure of his personal following as opposed to ideology. E. T. John, standing as the official Labour Party candidate, could only attract 6,368 votes in a three-cornered fight.[41] Anglesey reverted to traditional Liberalism. Investments in Holyhead had at last paid off for Sir Robert J. Thomas. However, the slump in the shipping industry during the trade depression of the late 1920s forced his political retirement before the 1929 election, and having lost £300,000, he was declared bankrupt. Sir Owen Thomas, according to his will dated 6 December 1919, had left an estate valued at £15,377 to his wife, the 'brave woman' who 'had been everything in the world to me'.[42] Set against this is the suggestion, or so the rumours go, of a strained relationship, exacerbated by his long absences, not to mention his perceived extravagance – with the steam launch cited as a case in point. Lady Thomas, her thoughts virtually unrecorded,[43] had remained in the background to cope with the desolation of a family torn apart by war. Having 'lost all my men folk,'[44] she found solace in travel. As a lady of independent means, her time was divided between Bournemouth, South Africa and Jersey – where the family papers were lost, and the ceremonial sword of honour of 1915 confiscated, during the wartime Nazi occupation of the island. She lived to the age of 92. Her burial in Inishannon, County Cork, Ireland, close to the home of her daughter, in January 1958, marked a century since Owen Thomas's birth. Separated in death, it was appropriate that he should lie in native soil. Though he had travelled far and wide, to move in elevated circles, he could claim to have remained at heart a true Anglesey man.

Memorial plaque in Ebenezer chapel, Llanfechell. The translated inscription reads:
IN LOVING MEMORY
OF THE BELOVED GENERAL SIR OWEN THOMAS, MP
FOR MANY YEARS A FAITHFUL DEACON IN THIS CHAPEL WHO TOOK A DEEP
INTEREST IN THE SUNDAY SCHOOL.
WE AS A CHAPEL CHERISH HIS MEMORY
HE DIED ON MARCH 6TH 1923.
BURIED IN THIS CEMETERY 9TH MARCH.
THIS MEMORIAL TOGETHER WITH THE ENDOWMENT OF A BED FOR SOLDIERS IN
BANGOR HOSPITAL WAS BESTOWED IN HIS MEMORY BY HIS MANY ADMIRERS.

The memorial cross on Owen Thomas's grave in Llanfechell.

Notes

1. *Y Clorianydd*, 8 Mawrth 1922.
2. *Holyhead Chronicle*, 31 March 1922.
3. *Y Clorianydd*, 2 Mehefin 1920.
4. E.g. at Pentraeth, Bryngwran, Llanddona, Pensarn, Talwrn, Marianglas, Benllech, Llangaffo, Llanbedrgoch.
5. *Y Clorianydd*, 18 Mai 1921.
6. *Y Wyntyll*, 13 Hydref 1921.
7. *Y Clorianydd*, 2 Mehefin 1920.
8. Ibid, 17 Mai 1922.
9. *Y Wyntyll*, 27 Ebrill 1922.
10. Cf., *Western Mail*, 7 March 1923.
11. *The Times*, 29 April 1922.
12. *South Wales News*, 27 April 1922.
13. *Hansard*, 5th Series, Vol. 153, 28 April 1922.
14. *Y Clorianydd*, 8 Tachwedd 1922.
15. Emlyn Richards, 'Syr Robert John Thomas, Y Garreglwyd', *Transactions of the Anglesey Antiquarian Society*, 1998, pp.64–5.
16. *Holyhead Chronicle*, 3 November 1922.
17. Ibid, 10 November 1922.
18. *Y Clorianydd*, 24 Mai 1922.
19. *Y Wyntyll*, 9 Tachwedd 1922.
20. *Holyhead Chronicle*, 12 May 1922.
21. *Y Wyntyll*, 30 Tachwedd, 14 Rhagfyr 1922, 4 Ionawr 1923.
22. Ibid, 2 Tachwedd 1922.
23. *Liverpool Daily Post*, 11 November 1922.
24. *Holyhead Chronicle*, 10 November 1922.
25. *Holyhead Mail*, 24 November 1922.
26. Ibid, 17 November 1922.
27. *Y Wyntyll*, 2 Tachwedd 1922.
28. *Y Clorianydd*, 1 Tachwedd 1922.
29. *Y Wyntyll*, 23 Tachwedd 1922.
30. *Y Clorianydd*, 27 Rhagfyr 1922.
31. *Hansard*, 5th Series, Vol. 159, 5 December 1922.
32. Ibid. Vol., 11 December 1922. See also Aled Eames, *Ships and Seamen of Anglesey 1558–1918* (Llangefni, 1973), pp.510–16.

33. *Hansard*, 5th Series, Vol. 159, 12 December 1922.
34. *Y Clorianydd*, 24 Ionawr 1923.
35. *Holyhead Chronicle*, 9 February 1923.
36. Death certificate (with 65 given as his age).
37. *Y Clorianydd*, 14 Mawrth 1923; *Y Wyntyll*, 15 Mawrth 1923; *Holyhead Mail*, 16 March 1923.
38. *Holyhead Chronicle*, 23 March 1923.
39. *Y Clorianydd*, 25 Gorffennaf, 1 Awst, 28 Tachwedd 1923.
40. Ibid, 6 Tachwedd 1929.
41. Sir Robert J. Thomas had 11,116 votes and R. O. Roberts (Conservative) 3,385.
42. *The Times*, 25 July 1923. The will had been drawn up while on SS *Malta* in the Mediterranean, bound for Egypt.
43. What information survives has been supplied by Audrey K. Allen in a letter to the author, 4 August 1987, supplemented by additional details from Bob Allen, 19 September 2010.
44. Letter from Frederica W. Thomas to Anthony John Arkell, 28 May 1928 (letter in the possession of Tom Arkell, and quoted with kind permission). A. J. Arkell, MC, was a close friend of Owen Vincent Thomas during their time as RFC pilots. The letter also recalls Owen Thomas discussing agriculture when dining with the Duke of Abercorn, and an (undated) visit to the Dublin Horse Show.

9. Conclusion

Few Welshmen of his generation led a life as diverse or as remarkable as that of Owen Thomas. His distinctive personal qualities were evident from the outset, and the challenges he embraced at an early age set the tone for an extraordinary personal journey. Defined by energy, courage and ambition, he was a man of many parts. Most certainly, his contribution and important achievements within three distinct aspects of his career can be considered worthy of greater historical recognition.

His mastery in farming methods and land management enabled him to progress from running the family farm to managing his landowner's 5,404-acre estate in Anglesey. Acknowledged by government, he established himself as an authority on agriculture. What is less well-known is his close affinity with Africa. Operations during the Boer War fitted him ideally for getting to know the new environment. At a time of aggressive British imperialism, driven by the likes of Rhodes and Milner, he literally surveyed the ground in far-flung parts of the continent to pave the way for further colonialist expansion and exploitation. Thomas's participation was a singular Welsh contribution to the economic initiatives that impelled empire building. His challenging assignments place him next to his explorer compatriot Henry Morton Stanley as one of the most widely travelled Welshmen in Africa. Like Stanley, his face would remain tanned by the tropical sun. Thomas's work was more specialised. In detailed analytical surveys he examined every aspect, from the quality of the soils and vegetation down to the matter of insects, assessing livestock and land values when advising various settlement and plantation companies. Ranked among the foremost specialists on tropical agriculture, he crowned his farming career as managing director of the East African Estates Ltd, responsible for 358,000 acres in Kenya, an area almost the size of Pembrokeshire. The reputation he made for himself justified his place in African history.

Perhaps the most controversial aspect of his military career was the role he undertook during the Great War. Moral judgements have to take account of the realities of the time, when traditional values, beliefs and liberties were challenged to the extreme. In contrast to stay-at-home persuaders who brought pressure upon young men to enlist, his military commitment was in line with his distinguished service in the Boer War. Placed at the heart of combat, Owen Thomas had first hand experience of battle and the brutality of war. As brigadier-general, he became chief recruiter for Lloyd George's Welsh Army and a household name throughout Wales. With single-minded determination, he sought to overturn the formidable obstacles to recruitment, injecting purpose and personal assurance. Allowing for the hyperbole, one verdict recognized a truth, 'under his magic hand, peace loving Wales had been converted into a huge camp'.[1] He could quite properly claim to be the 'father' of the Welsh Army Corps. Others saw things differently. Resentful of Owen Thomas's popularity, Colonel T. A. Wynne Edwards's behaviour increasingly verged on paranoia, so much so that, as late as 1919, he would attempt to inveigle him into reopening the Court of Inquiry case.[2] Notwithstanding the envy, rancour and bias generated among other high-ranking officers, no-one did more to initiate a change of attitude in the mainly Welsh-speaking, Nonconformist rural communities of north-west Wales. It had been a most difficult mission, and as he admitted, it could only be counted a partial success in terms of the actual number of soldiers recruited in the region. Not the least of his disappointments was the humiliation he endured when cast aside by the War Office. In many respects, he did lack the technical military experience for battlefield conditions in France but on the other hand, he was right to see himself as the victim of injustice, resentful of the manner he ended this phase of his life being dragged into scandal. Historically but one in a 'long line of British military commanders'[3] to challenge unjust officialdom, this brigadier-general (a rank soon to be abolished) would at least emerge with his honour restored.

His political ideas were based on traditional Liberal Nonconformist values, bolstered by an instinctive concern for social justice. Fulfilling his personal ambitions, victory in the 1918 election made political history in that it was one of the first constituencies in rural Britain claimed by the Labour Party. Its advance in the countryside relied heavily on the farm workers' unions. Thomas's alignment with the organized labour movement in Anglesey dated back to Ap Ffarmwr's crusade; but as events were to prove, he set strict limits to his political radicalism. In supporting the rights of labour, his belief in compromise rather than class confrontation, and rejection of full-blooded socialist ideology, he was more a rural variant of Lib-Labism, holding much in common with William Abraham, the south Wales miners' leader. Electoral success reflected the high esteem in which he was held; after all, his opponents, Sir Ellis Jones Griffith and Sir Robert J. Thomas, were two able, experienced politicians. Personal popularity, in turn, allowed him to act as a maverick parliamentarian, changing path at Westminster as he so wished. Consequently, this limited his political legacy. Thomas's period as a member of parliament marked no great change, and any hope of Labour supplanting the Liberal Party proved premature. It would be 1951 before Anglesey returned its first genuine Labour MP, when Cledwyn Hughes snatched victory at his third attempt.

Undeniably, Owen Thomas had his faults. Accomplished in raising troops he may have been, but there were shortcomings in his military make-up, sufficient to raise official doubts in 1915–16. Failure to adjust to the combat needs of the day reduced the war-fighting qualities of some trainees, allowing top commanders to contrive his downfall. In political life, relationships with natural supporters were to be marred by his changes of loyalty. With some justification it could be said that he had exploited, and subsequently betrayed, the labour movement in Anglesey. Other factors accounted for the decline of rural trade unionism, yet those who had chiefly guaranteed his electoral moment in 1918 were effectively deprived of an authoritative figure in not an entirely honourable way. Both his parliamentary performance and political inconsistencies prompted criticism; readily ditching his avowed nationalism to oppose Welsh home rule laid bare his shallow convictions.

Both word and deed exposed personal flaws. Racial antipathy in the context of Africa. Though inspired by the Independent faith of his forefathers, his strong Christian conviction was disfigured by prejudice against the native black people. His treatment of them was no better than that usually meted out to 'lesser' races by the white European. With at least one eye to his public image, he enhanced his own standing by resorting to boastful embellishments or dubious claims. The size of the African 'farm' in his charge would be inflated to 600,000 acres.[4] Military colleagues remarked how he was fond of blowing his own trumpet, basking in his claim to be the only Welsh-speaking general in the British Army. The nearest thing to a personal memoir was the revelatory interview published in *Y Clorianydd* in March 1915.[5] Even then, he peddled at least two falsehoods: his capture of Jan Christiaan Smuts, and the high sales of his book on South Africa.

Against all this were the solid qualities. Fortitude in the face of tragedies that stalked his personal life: the early death of his father, the shattering loss of all four sons, three on active duty in the Great War. Generosity of spirit as shown by his support for the less fortunate in Welsh rural society, and the concern he felt for the young recruits under his command that extended to the care of ex-servicemen. Owen Thomas was a man of great personal warmth who gained respect and public affection. Notable for his ability to engage with people of all classes, he never lost the common touch. He was equally at ease with the farm labourer and private soldier as with landlords, generals, politicians, peers and religious leaders. A young Anglesey recruit, whom he knew, retained a memory of being pointedly singled out for a friendly chat whilst on military parade at Winchester in 1915.[6] Among fellow members of the Milner Commission to Egypt, the British diplomat Sir J. Rennell Rodd fondly recalled 'the genial member for Anglesey'.[7] Even Colonel T. A. Wynne Edwards, despite his disloyalty, admitted to a grudging admiration for 'old Owen Thomas'.[8] Newspaper tributes at the time of his death attested to his dignity and widespread popularity. Wales lost one of its foremost public figures. '*Yr hen gadfridog annwyl*' (the dear old general) had left a deep impression on those who knew him; in the eyes of many, he was a hero.

Notes

1. *North Wales Chronicle*, 30 June 1916.
2. Eric Griffiths, *Squire of Nantglyn* (Wrexham, 2004), pp.98–105. His denial of jealousy, and his assertion that Thomas sought a command in East Africa – thus creating a vacancy for him at Kinmel – carried little conviction (Regimental Archives, Royal Welch Fusiliers, Wrexham, Acc. N$^{o.}$ 8471, T. A. Wynne Edwards Papers, Confidential Statement, nd).
3. A. D. Harvey, 'Generals in Defence of their Honour', *RUSI Journal*, Vol. 152, N$^{o.}$ 4, August 2007, pp.74–7.
4. *Y Clorianydd*, 11 Mai 1921.
5. Ibid, 3 Mawrth 1915.
6. William Owen, *Codi Canol Cefn* (Dinbych, 1974), p.73.
7. www.net.lib.byu.edu/estu/wwi/memoir/Rodd/Rodd15.htm. Sir J. Rennell Rodd, *Social and Diplomatic Memories, 1902–1919*, Chapter XV.
8. House of Lords Record Office, Lloyd George Papers, E/6/3/1, p.12.

Appendix 1: Nominal Roll of the Prince of Wales' Light Horse, 1899–1902

Compiled from WO 127 at the National Archives with additional data from *South African Field Force Casualty List, 1899–1902* (1972 reprint).

Abbreviations:

Lieut-Col – Lieutenant-Colonel
Capt – Captain
Lieut – Lieutenant
RSM – Regimental Sergeant Major
Sgt Mjr – Sergeant Major
SSM – Squadron Sergeant Major
QMS – Quartermaster Sergeant
Sgt – Sergeant
L/Cpl – Lance Corporal
Cpl – Corporal

D – Died
DoD – Died of Disease
DoW – Died of Wounds
Dr – Drowned
I – Invalided
M – Missing
PoW – Prisoner of War
R – Rejoined
W – Wounded

Commissioned Officers
Adamson, William, Lieut
Alletson, George Coventry, Lieut
Anderson, Rupert Leonard, Lieut
Attwell, Wilten William, Lieut
Berry, Charles Frederick, Lieut, Cyclist, KIA
Blaine, Alfred Edmund B., Capt
Boase, John Tregartha, Lieut
Bramley, A. Jennings, Major
Budgen, Thomas Alexander, Lieut
Chinn, Alfred Arthur, Capt
Chittenden, Edgar Darlington, Capt, W
Clark, Campbell John, Lieut
Clark, J. Dalrymple, Capt
Clarke, Julian Wilfred Shaw D., Capt
Crosby, Arthur James, Capt
Davies, James G., Lieut
Davies, Richard Lloyd, Lieut/ Capt
Edward, William, Lieut
Elson, De Vere, Capt
Evans, O. T., Lieut
Fairclough, R., Lieut

Featherstone, William Henry, Lieut
Fielden, Harold, Major
Gray, Alfred Edward, Lieut
Haddock, L. B., Capt
Hamer, Charles A., Lieut
Hanson, Daniel Henry, Lieut, I
Harris, Evelyn Clarkson, Cpl/Lieut, 20342
Heaney, George Harris, Lieut
Henry, Arthur Douglas, Lieut/Capt
Hopkins, George Mitchell, Lieut
Hopkins, William James, Lieut
Hopper, John Dickson, Lieut
Hughes, Frederick Bolton, Capt
Ingles, J., Lieut
Irons, Alfred Percy, Lieut
Jones, Alfred Fuller, Lieut
Jones, James, Capt/Paymaster
Kennedy, Lord Charles, Capt
Lewis, C. A. Owen, Major
Lewis, Franklin Charles, Lieut
Lloyd, Frank Lewis, Lieut
Lockart, C. F., Lieut

MacAdams, Hugh Crawford Vickers, Lieut
Matcham, Wiltshire E., Capt/Major
McGuffin, Hugh James, Lieut
Meyrick, Griffith William, Lieut
Miller, Arthur Cecil, Lieut
Miller, Lancelot D. Cyncourt, Lieut/Capt
Morris, Edward Wynne, Lieut
Nelson, Jacobus Adrian, Lieut
Oldham, Philip, Capt, W
Parsons, Forrest Gale, Lieut
Penberthy, Frederick Julius, Lieut/Capt
Pershouse, William Bradney, Lieut
Rayner, John Henry P., Lieut/Capt
Robson, Wilfred Mounsey, Lieut
Rosser, Thomas Pryce, Lieut
Rynhardt, Henry John, Lieut
Sedgewick, Harold Jennings, Cpl/Lieut, 20333
Sharpe, Robert Wilfred, Lieut
Shaw, Theodore Livingston, Lieut
Smith, James Knight, Lieut
Temple, Charles Henry, Lieut
Thomas, Hubert DeBurgh, Lieut
Thomas, Owen, Major/Lt-Col
Thomas, W., Lieut
Thomas, W., Surgeon Capt
Thomas, William Henry, Capt
Thompson, Henry Charles, Lieut
Tice, George Percy, Lieut/Capt
Van der Byl, Paul Andrew, Lieut
Vizard, Arthur, Lieut
Voysey, William Aming, Lieut/Capt
Willcox, I. Dean, Lieut
Williams, John Owen, Lieut

Non-commissioned Officers
Alberlyn, Jacob, Sgt Sadler, 20448, W
Anderson, Rupert Leonard, Cpl, 20335
Anderson, William, Sgt Mjr, 26999
Applebee, Morris, QMS, 20403
Archer, John William, SSM, 26880
Armitage, James Barnett, Cpl, 34540
Armstrong, Francis, L/Cpl, 34501
Baudinet, George William, QMS, 26002
Beachmore, William, Cpl, 34544
Bean, George Thomas, Cpl, 34541
Berry, Eustace, Cpl, 27794
Bevan, Edward Kearn, Cpl, 34364
Blackwell, Harold, Cpl, 20330
Blake, Frederick John, Sgt, 25801
Bosman, Hermanus Francis, L/Cpl, 25953
Brand, John D., Sgt, 26000
Brand, William, SSM, 25816
Broadfoot, John Maxwell, Cpl, 27155
Broadfoot, Tom Jones, Sgt, 30549
Brough, George G., Cpl, 30536
Bryce, William Henry, Sgt Mjr, 30319, DoW
Burton, A. J., L/Cpl, 34239
Carney, Thomas, Cpl, 31792
Carter, Thomas Robert, Sgt Mjr, 25647
Catton, Lewis, Cpl, 26011
Chalmars, Patrick Allen, Sgt, 34502
Chave, Arthur Frederick, Cpl, 27081
Christensen, Albert George, Cpl, 26754
Clarke, Stephen William, Sgt, 27148
Cleir, William, Cpl, 30331, W
Cohen, David, S. Sgt, 20424
Conroy, William Patrick, Cpl, 34465
Cowan, James, RSM, 20279
Coward, Gerald, Sgt, 32792
Custance, Dennis, Cpl, 20456
Davies, Clement C., Cpl, 20455
Davies, Thomas, SSM, 26301, M/R
Desmond, Annesley R., QMS, 27636
Dixon, John, QMS, 25712
Dixon, Joseph Nicholas R., Sgt, 34506
Doveton, Percy, Sgt, 27019
Dowell, Charles Henry, Sgt, 30302, PoW
Duggan, Dennis, SSM, 34532
Dumas, Allan Russell, L/Cpl, 30305
Dunlap, James Lafayette, L/Cpl, 31812
Ellaby, Charles Edward, Sgt, 25625
Elliott, William, Cpl, 27843, M/R
Elmer, Robert, Sgt, 27077, M/R
English, James Henry, QMS, 30313
Evans, Edward Thomas, QMS, 25638
Eyre, Edmund, Cpl, 26879
Fairleigh, Robert, SSM, 26284
Ferguson, Alexander, Sgt, 25745
Foreman, Thomas Alfred Benjamin, L/Cpl, 26944
Fox, Alfred, L/Cpl, 26906
Fraser, Alexander Bowie, L/Cpl, 27759
Fraser, John, L/Cpl, 30477

Gale, George Henry, Cpl, 21462, DoD
Gall, John, Sgt Mjr, 20207
George, James, Cpl, 32717, DoD
Godfrey, Whybert, Sgt, 20487
Grace, Gerald, Sgt, 34552, W
Gray, Robert Hamilton, Sgt, 27790
Gros, Eugene, Sgt, 25649
Hairs, William John, Sgt, 30220
Halls, Herbert John, Sgt, 30478
Harney, John, L/Cpl, 26942
Harris, Alexander James, Sgt, 20453
Hartley, John Holmes, Cpl, 26793
Harvey, Frederick John, L/Cpl, 31485, Dr
Hawkins, Ockwell, Cpl, 32770
Heineman, John Henry, Cpl, 25749
Henry, John McLavish, L/Cpl, 36789
Hewstone, Harry, QMS, 25952
Hicks, George Bertram, Sgt Mjr, 20393
Holmes, Thompson, SSM, 26865
Hook, Edward, Sgt, 25624, DoW
Howell, Thomas Morgan, Sgt, 27766
Hughes, William, Sgt, 30669
Hughes, William Matthew, Sgt, 25633
Hunt, Edward, Sgt, 25535
Hutchinson, James, Sgt, 26828
Imlack, George A., Sgt, 31396
Ireland, William Rupert, Cpl, 26784
James, Harry, L/Sgt, 26841
Jardan, Robert Joseph Henry, RSM, 31487
Jarvis, Edward, L/Cpl, 31815, K
Jennings, Thomas, Sgt, 26909
Jones, William Ernest, L/Sgt, 26019
Keeling, William D. M., Sgt, 26740
Kelleher, John, L/Cpl, 27211
Kent, George Henry, SSM, 3633
Keyes, Edward John, Sgt, 26822
Keys, Edmund John, Sgt, 3385
Kincey, Arthur Henry, Sgt, 34538
King, Frank Herbert, Sgt, 20452
Knoble, Adolf, Cpl, 25680
Knoutzs, Frederick, Sgt, 31497
Kros, Gaston, Sgt, 20400
Lancaster, Henry, Sgt Mjr, 26875
Lemon, James, Sgt Mjr, 27797
Lewis, Evan, Sgt, 31459
Lewis, Wynne Hill, Sgt, 30304
Lingard, John Edward, L/Cpl, 30617, KIA
Lodwick, William, Cpl, 27795, W, PoW

McDarneale, Patrick, Sgt, 27197
McGlone, John, Cpl, 27676
McIntyre, Colin, L/Cpl, 30483
McMillan, Eric Cape, Cpl, 26811
Magie, Hugh, Cpl, 26996
Marlowe, Leopold Conway, Sgt, 25810
Matthews, John, Cpl, 25661
Matthews, William, Sgt, 26780
Maugan, Michael, Cpl, 31440, PoW
Menlove, Arthur, SSM, 34489
Merrick, William Thomas, Cpl, 27641
Michell, Frederick George, Sgt, 27009
Mills, Edmond James, Cpl, 34507
Minchinton, Bertie, Sgt, 26994
Moggridge, John Willoughbly, Sgt, 30277, W
Moore, James, Cpl, 31437
Morrison, John George, Cpl, 25691
Morrison, William, SSM, 25739
Moss, Clarence Edward, Sgt, 32318
Munro, Andrew, Sgt, 27187
Munro, John Augustine, Sgt, 30306, W (accident
Murray, Charles, Cpl, 26857
Murray, Charles, Cpl, 39222
Murray, Gilbert Ramsay, Cpl, 25988
Namkervio, Robert Henry, Cpl, 30520
Nicolson, James, Cpl, 30312, DoD
O'Connell, James David, Sgt, 27214
O'Donoghue, William, L/Cpl, 26753
O'Hara, Ernest Michael, Cpl, 30324
Orme, Charles, Sgt Mjr, 27762
Pailthorpe, Edwin Percy, Cpl, 30278
Parker, Francis Edgar, Sgt, 25725
Patrick, Thomas Wylie, Sgt Mjr, 34472
Peak, Leonard Preston, Cpl, 20454
Pemberton, Douglas James, Sgt, 27062
Phillips, James, Sgt, 26015
Pitt, Frederick Arthur, Cpl, 25662
Polyblank, Charles, Pay Sgt, 25655
Powell, Frank, L/Cpl, 27653
Pownceby, Alfred, Sgt, 33798
Ray, Frederick Dent, Cpl, 20485
Reynhardt, Henry James, Sgt, 30550
Reynolds, Harry, RSM, 20461
Riddle, James, Cpl, 26923
Ridgard, Herbert Helivin, Cpl, 26785
Riley, Edward, Sgt, 27035
Roberts, Arthur Howard, Sgt, 30509
Roberts, Daniel, SSM, 26972

Roberts, James William, Sgt, 26858
Roberts, Joseph Thomas Goodman, Sgt, 26732
Ryan, Richard James, Cpl, 20395
Ryder, Thomas Jerome, Cpl, 25813
Roberts, Robert Owen, Sgt, 26297
Robertson, Alexander, Sgt, 27001
Robinson, James, Sgt, 30503
Rooke, George Leiman, Sgt Mjr, 30219
Rose, John, Sgt Mjr, 27073
Rundle, Samuel John, Cpl, 32791
Sallertz, Frederick, Cpl, 25664
Schauder, Adolph, Cpl, 26290
Scott, Oliver, Sgt, 30545
Servaes, Alfred James, QMS, 20423
Simpson, Leslie, Cpl, 26829
Sinclair, John, Cpl, 27638
Skipworth, Edward Leonard, QMS, 20341
Smyley, John Neville, Sgt, 32709
Step, William, Cpl, 26292
Stirling, James, Cpl, 30527
Stivers, Seward J., Cpl, 31809
Sully, William Horace, Sgt, 31451
Sutton, Harry Lockley, Cpl, 27784, DoD
Swanston, David, Cpl, 26930
Tait, Joseph, RSM, 30482
Taylor, Arthur John, Sgt, 34490
Taylor, Harry James Charles, Sgt, 30518

Thomas, George Brown, Cpl, 30638, PoW
Thomas, William H., QMS, 36195, KIA
Thomas, William Hugh, RSM, 25692
Towler, Joseph Robert, Cpl, 33726
Tully, William Joseph, L/Cpl, 33519
Ungless, William Laton, Cpl, 27146
Uye, John James, Sgt, 27141
Van Staaden, John, Sgt, 26786
Vickers, Joseph Dashwood, Sgt, 27765
Vogan, Arthur James, Sgt, 36219
Waite, Henry Cambridge, QMS, 30359
Walker, Charles George, SSM, 20418
Walsh, Ambrose Patrick, Sgt., 34491
Warren, Bertram, Sgt, 32727
West, Hugh, Cpl, 26958
West, William Croucher, QMS, 20386
Wilkinson, Reginald, Cpl, 20334
Wilson, Arthur George, Cpl, 36196
Wilson, John, Cpl, 30367, W/M/R
Wilson, Thomas, Cpl, 27160
Winfield, Emanuel Henry, Sgt, 25819
Wood, James Henry, Cpl, 30548
Wood, Walter Beverley, Sgt, 26963
Woodford, Herbert Kiesall, SSM, 34535
Wragg, Alfred Henry, QMS, 25721
Yorath, L., Sgt, 20474
Yule, W., L/Cpl, 26995

Other ranks (all Troopers unless otherwise shown)
Abel, Arthur Henry, 30326
Abel, August, Cyclist, 27052
Abraham, J. H., 36227
Adams, Edward Richard, 27059
Adams, James Berman, 25724
Aderhold, James Blount
Agassiz, Cecil Traymor, 32722
Aikon, William, 26888
Aitchison, Hugh Francis Charles, 36201
Allen, Frank William, Tpr/ Bugler, 26293
Allen, Frederick Albert, 26895
Allen, John Wynne, 27219
Allen, Oliver Charles, 25986
Ambler, William David, 25955
Anderson, David Ford, 30280
Andrews, Benjamin, 27760
Andrews, James, Shoeing Smith, 30320

Andrews, Robert Alexander, 27199
Antonius, Michael, 25790
Aperios, Efstratios, 26775
Apps, Walter, 34496
Arbuckle, William, 20445
Armstrong, George Allman, 20391
Armstrong, Jock Kingsley, 20388
Arnall, William Gregory, 25744
Arnett, John, 27845
Arnold, Charles Albert, 32950
Artz, Michael, 32970
Ashdown, William, 31416
Aston, John, 39145
Aston, John, 32858
Aubrey, Thomas, 36226
Auchinleck, Daniel, 30498
Ayliffe, William Henry, 34493
Ayres, Charles Ellacote, 31432
Bacon, Frank William, 27646

Bailey, George Mitchell, 30310
Bailey, Harvey, 27196
Baines, George Victor, 34508
Baiso, Herbert David, 34467
Baker, Arthur Henry, 20484
Baker, William, 33688
Ballantine, James Gordon, 32710
Ballenger, F., 34514
Bancroft, Earl William, 31410, PoW
Banforth, Arthur, 30380
Bannerman, Kenneth M., 27782
Barbier, Robert, 30504
Barcroft, Henry Walter, 25669
Barends, Arthur John, 27056
Barends, John Maittand, Cyclist, 26953
Barker, Walter William, 26778
Barnes, Charles, 27143
Barnes, George Herbert, 26783, W
Barnes, John, 27190
Barnes, John Joseph, 37807
Barnes, Joseph, 26886
Barnett, James, 25684
Barnett, John, 25683
Barr, Benjamin John, 34543
Bartlett, Harry Edward, 32718
Barwise, Thomas, 26295
Batchelder, Walter, 26749, DoD
Bates, Edwin Charles, 27000
Batts, Jescy Thomas, 31454
Batts, William Hawkins, 31424
Baxter, Edward, 31447
Beach, George Jeffrey, 36202
Beale, Leonard, 34468
Beanchia, Frederick Charles, 20480
Beck, James Revboon, 25752
Bedford, Albert, 32733
Beer, Arthur, 27158
Begg, Henry Kelly, 27042
Bennett, James Gordon, 25774
Bennett, William, 27097
Berry, Charles Frederick, 27043
Berryman, William Edward, 26289, M/R
Biddlecombe, Charles
Biggs, Charles, 26752
Billett, William, 27083
Bingham, Edward Josh, 30308
Binns, Frank William, 30364
Bivor, Charles, 31818

Blackmore, Francis, 20407
Blake, Joseph Henry, 34477
Blake, Thomas, 31810
Blakeway, Alfred, 31434
Blanckenberg, Henry, 26964
Bloomberg, Bernard, 26777
Blossman, Jesse, 36189
Blyth, George, 31425
Boden, John, 20419
Booker, John Richard, 34474
Boon, Arthur Rundle, 25964
Booth, Rodney Carl, 27644
Boswell, Benjamin, 30363
Bourke, Patrick, 26937
Bowsan, Robert, 31419
Boyer, Samuel, 26871
Boyle, James, 31804
Boys, Charles Herbert, 26943
Bradley, B., 36203
Bramham, William, 30360
Bramley, Thomas, 31368
Brant, James Henry, 31446
Brasher, George, 33685
Bray, John Henry, 25793
Bray, John Henry, 36045
Breicher, George, 32940
Brimacombe, Austin Claude, 26946
Broadhurst, Mark, 34545
Brocon, William, 36229
Brodie, A. Gardiner, 26287
Brodin, William, 32915
Bronkhorst, William, 30499
Brown, Benjamin Bartte, 31442
Brown, Charles George, 25956
Brown, Edward, 31790
Brown, Edward John, 32736
Brown, Frederick Adolphus, 36204
Brown, George, 32916
Brown, James Douglas, 26971
Brown, Robert, 27783
Brown, Samuel, 31490
Brown, Thomas, 27695
Brown, Thomas Samuel, 31409
Brown, William, 25795
Brown, William, 33680
Brown, William, 34466
Browne, Robert William, 30303
Bryne, Harry Edward, 30311

Buckingham, Frederick, 26744
Buckingham, William George, 25657
Budrick, Stephen, 25687
Budrick, Stephen, 35917
Bunday, William, 25818
Burgess, Edward William, 27640
Burnes, J. H., 36205
Burnett, Charles Alexander, 34546
Burney, James Edward, 31458
Burns, James, 26755
Burton, Edward, 30283
Burton, Frank
Bush, James Richard, 27200, W
Calling, Joseph Lambert, 30279
Camm, Francis Robert Henry, 31431
Campbell, John, 30505
Cape, Sidney Scarwell, 36207
Capel, William, 20458
Carey, P. J., 36222
Carlton, F. W., 36177
Carroll, Phillip Joseph, 36200
Carroll, William, 27010
Carter, George, 34500
Carter, George Gilbert, 20486
Chambers, Arthur William, 20479
Chambers, Thomas, 26300
Chambers, William, 26904
Chandler, Walter, 32728
Chandler, William, 20389
Chapman, Frederick, 30273
Chareton, Arthur James, 31408, PoW
Cheeseman, William Henry, 25679
Cherry, James, 26726
Chitty, William, 32943
Chrisholm, Robert, 36206
Christian, George Miller, 26725
Clarence, George Phillip, 20494
Clark, Hugh, 31787
Clark, William, 30522, PoW
Clarke, Frederick, 27212
Clarke, John, 33738
Clarke, William Goodfellow, 26827
Clentworth, John, 24423
Cocklin, James, 31426
Colley, Howard, 34547
Connoley, John, 30636
Connor, David, 25995
Conroy, Lewis Frank, 33739

Cook, David, 31456
Cook, Oscar Harvey, 34513
Cooke, Charles, 25738
Cooke, John, 27157
Cooper, Sydney, 31401
Cordjohn, Charles Edward, 34537
Cornish, Charles Henry, 20457
Coster, James, 30531
Costin, Joseph, 27635, M/R
Counter, Albert Walter, 30381
Courtemay, Benjamin Charles, 25811
Cox, Albert Seward, 30362
Cox, George Henry Fredrick, 34515
Craig, Alfred, 34510
Crawford, John, 26018
Criticos, George, 31498
Cross, Sydney Herbert, 26887
Crosthwaite, Legacy, 20491
Crowson, George, 30698
Cruickshank, Harry, 34475
Cubine, Robert, 26733
Cubitt, Edward, 26794
Cunningham, Thomas, 26730
Cunningham, William Frederick, 25693
Curtis, Edwin Charles, 31465, DoD
Daley, Peter, 27645
Daly, James, 20410
Daly, Patrick, 26926
Damarell, Charles Henry, 27650
Daniel, George Vigo, 34548, KIA
Daniel, Norman B.
Darlington, T., 25785
Darnley, Richard, 34485
Davey, William, 37939
David, Matthew John, 25800
Davidge, Edward James, 25792
Davidson, George, 27060
Davidson, George, 27064
Davies, Albert, 20405
Davies, Albert, 26791
Davies, D. Daniel, 25678
Davies, David John, 31414
Davies, Thomas, 25947
Davies, Thomas Henry, 31428
Davies, Thomas John, 31415
Davis, Charles, 26816
Davis, George Richard, 26884
Dawson, Andrew Nelson, 30530

Day, Harry, 26917
De Villiers, Cornelius Flacon, Cyclist, 26965
De Villiers, George Daniel, 20412
Dean, Harry Hill, 27058
Dearlove, Frank Avery, 34497
Dengate, Herbert James, 26861
Dengate, Herbert James, 37806
Denniston, Reynold, 34549
Dermody, Benjamin, 34575
Desmond, Charles, 27677
Deumead, Percy Lofttime, 34505
Dickson, Angus Crawford, 26743
Dickson, Edward, 27800
Dimiao, Frank Avery, 27792
Dimmig, George, 27704
Dixon, John, 27037
Dobinson, Arthur, 26761
Dolan, James Patrick, 26546
Donnelly, Hugh, 26296
Donnelly, Hugh, 37671
Doran, Daniel, 26867
Dougherty, Thomas, 26868
Douglas, John, 31788
Dowdall, Henry Milton, 25814
Dowdle, George, 34498
Downes, James Henry, 36232
Doyle, Andrew, 32738
Drake, Patrick, 27206
Drew, Allan Richard, 25771
Driscoll, Edward, 26927, W (accident)
Driscoll, James, 27142
Drymen, Charles, 26843
Dubois, Percy, 27220
Duckitt, Charles Walter, 26840
Duff, Donald McDonald, 32805
Dunlop, Benjamin George, 30272
Dunn, James, 32971
Durkin, Joseph, 32938
Durton, Cyril Gorman, 20472
Duston, James, 25637
Dyer, George Henry, 36068
Dykman, George Henry, 20298
Earle, William, 34345
Eaton, Samuel, 25998
Eatwell, Thomas Edward, Cyclist, 27046
Eck, Henry John, 31399
Eddey, Lawrence Charles, 34523
Edmondson, Willaim, 25676

Edwards, John, 34469
Elliott, H., 36223
Ellis, Arhtur Wyatt, 20490
Elmes, John Frederick, 32793, M/R
Endean, Thomas, 36233
Evans, Albert Wakely, 27011
Evans, David, 31429
Evans, James, 27098
Evans, Samuel, 30309
Evans, Thomas, 27007
Evans, Thomas Kelly, 20206
Evans, William John, 25968
Fairhurst, John, 26898
Falk, Charles William, 36340
Fargerstraum, Kum Felix, 30274
Ferguson, George Neil, 31417
Ferguson, James, 25741
Ferguson, James Arnold, 26931
Ferguson, Ronald William, 27696
Ferns, John Montrose, 26017
Fienburg, Ernest Standley, 25997
Finch, William, 25711
Finch, William, 35991
Findlay, David, 32806
Finn, Joseph George, 30500
Fitzgerald, Edward, 31433
Fitzgerald, Richard Reginald, 31445
Fitzgerald, Thomas, 36225
Fitzpatrick, Arthur
Fitzpatrick, George Thomas, 26960
Flanders, James Erskine, 31381
Flannigan, Daniel Thomas, 32735
Foley, Jerimiah, 32844
Forbes, William, 26842
Ford, James, 27191
Ford, Joseph, 20428
Ford, Thomas, 33679
Forrester, Robert, 32946
Fose, Alec, 33797
Foster, Thomas, 36176
Fothergill, Kenneth Graham, 25961
Franklin, James Edmund, 27637
Franks, Peter, 26862
Fraser, Alexander, 27781
Fraser, James Wiley, 31795
Frederickson, Valdermar, 27063
Freebairie, Robert, 34487
Freeman, Albert, 39502

181

Freeman, Charles, 31455
Freeman, James, 32771
Fulton, James Michael, 20488
Furlong, Thomas Bernard, 34483
Furze, William John, 26924
Gabites, Albert George, 34550
Gamble, Thomas, 27642
Gambrell, Horace Sydney, 26817
Gardiner, Samuel Thomas, 27689
Garlick, Lawerence Albert, 34551
Garrison, Elmo Joseph, 26016
Garrity, William, 27154
Garshom, Jack, 34509
Gates, Edwin Charles, 20489
Geller, Charles Edward, 32737
Gent, Charles A., 36198
George, William, 20421
Gibbs, Herbert Thomas, 33716
Gilfillan, Alexander, 25764
Gill, Alfred Edward, 27151
Gill, George, 31411
Gill, John Blackett, 30475, W
Gill, Thomas, 27844
Gilles, Julius, 27649
Girke, Frederick, 31400
Gleave, James, 32860
Glover, Thomas John, 34521
Goldman, William Basil, 31801
Gontos, Dionisle, 25789
Goodwin, David Winsler, 27691
Gould, William John, 25812
Grace, John, 26905
Graham, Joseph Lionel, 34542
Granliese, James Thomas, 31884
Grant, Charles Edward, 25658
Grant, Robert George, 31423
Grant, William, 33683
Gray, Carl Edward, 34553
Gray, William, 34554
Gregg, James, 27647
Gregor, John, 30474
Greig, John, 32731
Griffen, Patrick Gerald, 27023
Griffiths, George, 34528
Griffiths, John Samuel, 25671
Griggs, Henry, 20415
Grint, Wallace, 26989
Gromquist, Bernard, 26948

Grose, Walter, 31363
Hackney, Albert, 34499
Haines, Henry, 30281
Hale, Horace, 31443
Haley, Harvey Hayden, 37630
Hall, William Christopher, 34555
Hallett, Henry William Percy, 32783
Hallewell, John William, 25773
Hallick, Clarence Francis, 20446
Hamilton, Albert Thomas, 31817
Hamilton, Thomas, 25760, DoD
Hammond, Charles, 30949
Hammond, Ralph, 25743
Hammond, Thomas Robin, 36208
Hanks, Herbert Winston, 25767
Hannah, Richard, 31364
Hannan, Dom, 26179
Hannan, Edmund, 27186
Hannan, John Alfred, 25770
Hansen, Bernard, 26741
Hansson, Bernard, 30213
Hanton, Alexander, 31480
Harmen, Henry, 27008
Harper, John, 20422
Harrell, Frederick, 37867
Harrill, Frederick Pettington, 25694
Harrington, John Henry, Bugler, 25736
Harris, Sydney Herbert, 36228
Harrison, George, 27070
Hartley, Charles Raven, 30282
Haskell, Joseph, 34524
Hawley, William Robert, 27152
Hayes, Thomas, 26998
Heaney, Roderick Henry, Trumpeter, 34862
Heaven, George Edward, 26899
Hegenbarth, Samuel Thomason, 30402
Henderson, Alexander, 31807, PoW
Henning, Frederick, Cyclist, 26966
Henning, Samuel Thomason, 26962
Herbert, Frank, 31379
Hex, Walter, 26286
Heyne, Albert Edward, 27067
Hickey, James
Higgins, John, 27217
Hill, Frederick William, 26216
Hill, Hugh, 20396
Hill, William Andrew, 26781
Hilliard, Leonard Herbert,

Hilson, John Willis, 20477
Hilson, John Willis, 37695
Hing, Alfred Ernest, 27192
Hinshelwood, James, 20392
Hinshelwood, Thomas, 20390, W
Hodgson, Charles
Holding, Thomas Albert, 25768
Holloway, Frank W.
Holme, George, 34557
Honey, Ernest, 26945
Hopkins, Henry, 34556
Hopkins, John, 30490
Horne, Cornelius J., 36178
Hoskins, George, 27697
Howard, James, 34534
Howell, Fred, 31466
Howell, Harry, 27057
Howes, George, 26815
Hubbard, William, 26814, M/R
Hudson, Edward Charles, 20464
Hudson, Lewis, 26968
Hughes, Alexander Edward Lloyd, 26008, W
Hughes, Arthur, 32712, W
Hughes, Owen, 26298
Hugo, Victor, 27048
Humphrey, Edmund, 36078
Humphries, Peter A., 30525
Hurle, Oliver James, 25667
Husk, Jesse, 25791
Hutcherson, George, 34480
Hyland, Harold Augustine, 25994
Hyland, Thomas, 27185
Irvine, Oliver Henry Johnstone, 36210
Ivers, Joseph, 34482
Jack, James Kendrick, 34558
Jackson, George, 27633
Jackson, William, 26182
James, Charles, 32937
James, John, 25644
Jamieson, David, 27201
Jatho, Rudolph, 20462
Jenkins, J., 36230
Jenkins, William Harry, 27692
Jennings, Edwin Norton, 30232
Jensen, Haus, 25724
Jensen, Victor Cornelius, 25654
Johansson, Alfred, 30226
Johnson, Alexander, 20478

Johnson, Arthur John, 26882
Johnson, Arthur William, 30307
Johnson, Charles, 26288
Johnson, George Herbert, 32739
Johnson, Harry, 30333, PoW
Johnson, William, 27694
Johnston, Arthur Patrick, 24473
Johnston, David, 30682
Johnston, John, 26869
Johnstone, John Edward Bernard, 27761
Jones, Frederick Chambers, 33622
Jones, Harvey Davis, 26747
Jones, Lon, 31468
Jones, Robert, 27210
Jones, Tom, 20394
Jones, William Percival, 30318
Jordan, Daniel, 34463
Jordan, Gerald Smith, 25751
Jost, Otto, 26742
Joyce, James, 34414
Joyce, William, 26821
Joynes, Waller, 27643
Kaminsky, Jacob, 32701
Kane, Michael Angelo, 26940
Kane, William, 31806
Kannegiesser, Eugene, 30696, Dr
Kaplin, Thurstan, 25665
Keddie, David
Keenan, William, 34536
Keeping, Thomas Jones, 20406
Kehoe, William, 27682
Keighy, John, 25623
Kelhan, Edgar, 32931
Kelleher, Charles, 25723
Kelly, John, 32782
Kemp, William Dunstan, 25653
Kennedy, James, 36230
Kennedy, Richard, 32668
Kenney, Henry Francis, 27049
Kenny, Henry John, 30270
Kent, Henry James, 27029
Kerlin, Patrick, 32859
Keverne, James, 20465
Kimber, Ein Frederick, 20427
Kincannon, Frank Locke, 31814
King, Frank Wells, 31407
King, John, 30382
Kinred, Herbert Cowley, 36211

Knight, William Ashton, 32681
Knowles, J., 34486
Knowles, John
Kohler, J., 36192
Korting, William
Krocnke, Gustave, 27218
Krous, Henry, 30325
Kuhl, Frederick, 25750
Laing, Henry James, 27026
Lake, Edward G.
LaPierre, George, 31808
Latlam, Robert Jenkins, 30383
Laurick, Frederick, 31791
Lavender, Alexander John, 30494, DoD
Lavine, Jacob, 25716
Lawson, Thomas Herbert, 26855
Lawton, William
Lazarus, Maurice, 36042
Lazarus, Morris, 20492
Leaman, Edward Charles, 34512
Learoyd, William Kelso, 26722
Leavy, James Henry, 36212
Lee, George, 36199
Lees, Frederick William, 31811
Lefebour, Wilfred, 27154
Lemke, Martin, 31441
Lennon, Joseph James, 25993
Lennox, Charles Percy, 34559
Lensner, Sam, 30322
Leonard, J. W. S.
Lewis, C., 36179
Lewis, Franklin Charles, 27680
Lewis, Samuel Hill, 20315
Lifset, Bernard, 25632
Lindsay, Alexander, 27209
Lindsay, Samuel, 32804
Linnecar, Leonard Archibald, 26789
Little, William, 25695
Llancastle, Sydney, 31412
Lloyd, Ben, 31450
Lloyd, Fredrick, 33675
Lloyd, Henry, 33684, DoD
Lloyd, Thomas, 32862
Lloyd, Walter Thomas, 33676
Lockhart, Frederick Charles, 27780
Long, Alfred James, Tpr / Cyclist, 27053
Lord, John Hayworth, 30495
Lowe, George, 33681

Lucas, Reginald George, 26746
Luddington, Daniel, 30534
Lumley, Arthur William Henry, 32732
Lumsden, William
Luyt, Frederick Matthew Stephen, 26818
Lynham, Thomas, 20447
Lyons, Charles Edward, 31799
Lyons, George, 32711
Macfarlane, James, 26874
Mackie, John Campbell, 26902
Mackley, Arden Floyd, 31418
MacNiel, Edward, 27005
McBain, Adam, 33686
McCallum, Alexander Henry, 32715
McCameron, James Henderson, 32730
McCann, George, 26866
McCarthy, Frank, 30491
McCarthy, George Desmond Richard, 31488
McClelland, Alfred James, 32721
McCormack, John, 31786
McCrystal, Patrick James, 27189
McCubbin, Hugh James,
McDermott, John, 30496
McDonald, John, 26922
McDonald, Thomas, 36184
McDoniard, John
McDowall, John H., 32942
McFarlane, Ernest Arthur, 26885
McGafferty, Peter, 26918
McGee, William John, 26731
McGivern, Hugh, 34471
McGreat, Michael Henry, 31405
McKay, Donald, 26774
McKenzie, Alexander, 33714
McKinney, William Herbert, 25082
McLaren, Peter, 32948
McLennan, Hugh, 32852
McLoughlin, John, 31448
McMorrin, Robert Jenkins, 20439
McNeill, Donald Robertson, 26925
McNiece, Joseph James, 25769
McPherson, George Jeffries, 30535, W
McVeigh, H., 36182
McVeigh, James, 31464
Madden, Patrick Faunt, 36221
Maher, Edward Joseph, 26788
Mallandam, Alfred, 31453
Mallett, Charles, 31444

Mapp, Robert William, 25966
Marguilies, David, 25710
Markham, William, 27208
Marks, Harry, 26967
Marr, Harry Jackson, 31395
Martin, Albert, 24271
Martin, John, 31802, PoW
Martin, Perry Trisham, 26299, W
Martin, Robert, 27017
Mason, Finch Arthur, 20463
Masterman, Charles, 31491
Masuriek, Rubin Francis, 31785
Mathis, Charles John, 27144
Matthew, Charles, 36063
Matthews, A. Edward, 36213
Meade, James Garfield, 31486
Meek, William, 26839
Melly, Montaque, 26891
Michich, Romano, 27145
Midmer, George David, 26883
Miller, Edward, 30315
Miller, Edward Woodman, 34484
Miller, Gustavz, 36191
Miller, John, 27025
Miller, William, 33687
Mills, Cecil James, 26859
Mills, William, 32917
Mills, William, 36181
Mitchell, George, 34503
Mitchell, James Henry, 20402
Mitchell, John Hamilton, 25742
Monkham, William
Montgomery, Charles, 30508
Moon, James, 27681
Moon, James Herbert, 31430
Moore, Alfred, 27193
Moorhouse, Ernest, 34560
Morgan, Charles, 27096
Moriarty, Patrick, 32795
Morris, George, 25788, DoD
Morris, Owen Richard, 36239
Morris, Wilfred, 20397
Morrison, Charles, 25713
Morrissey, Thomas Francis, 32716, DoD
Morrissey, William, 36180
Muirhead, Alexander, 25794
Mullarney, Richard Henry, 20460
Munro, Peter Stewart, 25746

Murdock, Alfred Edwin, 31793
Murdock, Donald Brady, 31796
Murphy, Arthur, 34527
Murphy, Henry, 34526
Murphy, James Francis, 26901
Murphy, John, 31798
Murray, Samuel, 27634
Mutch, Thomas, 27050
Mytinger, Hinton James, 31816
Neilson, Carl Ludwig, 30385
Naylor, John Henry, 36217, W
Nelson, Charles, 32725
Nelson, George, 31382
Neson, William Conrad, 26970
Nette, Henry, 20483
Neville, James Francis, 31800
Newman, Robert Thomas, 34481
Newton, Samuel Reginald,
Nicholson, Herbert, 33766
Nickel, Carl, 27140
Nicolson, Thomas Scott, 31406
Niece, William, 30532
Noble, Thomas Scott, 33677
Noowan, John
Norton, Henry, 26907
Nowack, Frederick, 27076
Nowack, Frederick, 37632
Nunn, Robert, 31789
Nunneley, Harold William, 34561
Nyborg, Arthur, 31439
Oak, Arthur Charles, 27213
O'Brien, Harry Herbert, 30529, PoW
O'Brien, James, 32319
O'Brien, John Charles William, 30501, PoW
O'Brien, Michael Joseph, 26872
O'Brien, Michael Joseph, 36062
O'Brien, Thomas Scott, 27648
O'Leary, John, 36183
October, Peter P., 30113, KIA
Olley, Albert
Ollson, Charles, 25737
O'Neil, William, 34530
O'Neill, Fitzpatrick
O'Neill, Thomas Scott, 25962
O'Toole, John, 27188
Owen, Hugh, 26908
Owens, William Michael, 27675
Palmer, Alfred William, 34504

Pando, Evarist, 26792
Parker, Nirthmon Eden, 31797
Parker, Robert, 32825
Parkinson, John Robin, 33767
Parry, Henry, 25999
Parsonage, James, 30269
Paull, Samuel Thomas, 25784, DoD
Payne, Frederick, 34518
Payne, William Penton, 33733
Peacock, Ernest William, 33703
Peacock, Percy Gavin, 27159
Peake, Herbert John, 25991
Pedersen, James Carl Frederick, 20449
Pedlar, Henry C., 32933
Pedlar, Joshua, 31436
Pedley, Dyer Berry, 32823
Peebles, John Kidd, 30643, PoW
Pelteret, Edward, 26961
Pemberton, Rae, 27075, M/R
Penfold, Robert Henry, 32667
Pennock, Henry, 26896
Perkins, Duncombe Steele, 27793
Peterson, John, 34520
Phillips, Ernest Michael, 25759
Pollecutt, Arthur Henry, 31452
Pollos, John, 25820
Pols, William, 26833
Poole, Albert, 25709
Poole, Arthur Hamilton, 26864
Porker, Leonard, 36193
Porteous, George Marshall, 36714
Poulson, James, 20398
Poulter, Frederick Charley, 25809
Power, Thomas
Prendergast, John, 27207
Prescott, Thomas Leonard, 25987
Price, David, 20413
Priest, Joseph, 30507
Priest, Lesle, 26723
Pritchard, William George, 26012
Puffer, Maurice Lyon, 32729
Purdie, David, 26845
Pyne, Richard, 27071
Quint, Samuel Tyers, 25666
Rae, Colin, 27015
Rae, Thomas, 27065
Raine, Robert Henry, 27045
Ralph, Alexander Watson, 32828

Randall, Robert George, 27150
Ratcliffe, Charles, 27687
Ratcliffe, Charles, 37631
Reed, Bertram John, 25959
Reed, Frederick Alvin, 32723
Rees, Charles Albert, 27018
Rees, Charles Stevenson, 30497
Reid, Thomas Lowden, 35857
Rence, Samuel, 30403
Rendle, Harry, 30334, PoW
Rennison, Albert
Renwick, Frederick, 27036
Revington, William George, 27022
Reypert, James William Frank, 30526
Richards, Fred, Bugler, 25948
Richards, John, 26900
Richards, Richard
Richardson, Clyde Speake, 31420
Ridley, Clement Archie, 36224
Riep, Walter, 27021
Rigden, James William, Cyclist, 30227
Riley, Charles George, 26955
Rivers, Joseph, 27069
Rix, Frederick, 26860
Roberston, James, 27156
Roberts, Archibald, 27182
Roberts, John Edward, 26758
Roberts, John Theodore, 27651
Roberts, Walter, 25726, DoD
Roberts, William, 20459
Robertson, John Lumsden, 27156, M/R
Robertson, Thomas Peter, 30533
Robinson, Alfred, 30506
Robinson, Alfred James, 27024
Robinson, Henry, 27184
Robinson, James, 34531
Robinson, John, 25740
Robinson, John, 32724
Robson, Robert, Cyclist, 26837
Robson, Wilfred Mounsey, 27679
Rodway, Gilbert, 26952
Rodwell, Arthur, 20387
Rodwell, Charles, 27014
Roe, Claude, 30212
Rofe, Wallace, 33715
Rogers, George Robert, 36215
Rogers, Toney, 25681
Rogerson, Thomas Miller, 36216

Roland, George Frederick, 27041
Roland, Isaac, 27040
Rollins, Henry, 26776
Rollins, James Carmichael, 25783
Rooney, Thomas John Valentine, 30493
Roper, James Henry Leslie, 33707
Rorke, Michael
Rose, Frederick Alexander, 34399
Rose, Nelson, 32713
Rosen, Harry, 30523, PoW
Rosewell, James Samuel, 34517
Ross, Daniel, 25967
Ross, Joseph William Douglas, 25765
Roughton, Walter Douglas, 32822
Roussis, George, 25787
Ryan, George Ernest, 25673
Ryan, Hugh Alexander, 27216, M/R
Ryan, John, 31457
Ryder, Thomas Jerome, 37716
Salisbury, James Arthur, 32794
Salkeld, Albert Edward, 30528
Samson, Jacob, 34529
Sandy, Ernest Edward, 30524
Sargent, Arthur William, 30697
Saunders, Albert Edward, 26889
Saunders, Gervase, 26748, W
Saunders, Neilson, 26873
Saunders, Robert Dudley, 26285
Saxon, John Preston, 27198
Scharffenvoth, Ferdinand, 26813
Scheller, Walker Joseph, 26967
Schmidt, Nicolas, 26294, M/R
Scholtz, Jacobus James, 26959
Schwartz, Bernard Oscar, 25996
Scott, George, 20411
Sears, Charles, 32338
Sexton, Dennis, 32720
Sharman, Thomas Arthur, 25766
Sharpe, David Goutts
Shaw, Oswald Robert, 33651
Shaw, Richard Westall, 33786
Sheard, William, 20476
Sheedy, Richard Patrick, 32714
Sheldon, Larsh Adolph, 31421
Shennan, Joseph, 31438
Shine, John, 26757
Sibley, Joseph Edward, 30365
Siddall, Thomas Rhodes, 26890

Simpkiss, Victor Edmund John, 27055
Simpson, John Mercer, Cyclist, 26957
Sinclaire, David, 31805
Single, Reginald Blackman, 32719
Slater, Peter, 31461, PoW
Slavin, Thomas, 31803
Small, James Francis, 27044
Small, Peter Frederick, 25989
Smith, David Elder, 32829
Smith, Edward, 30225
Smith, John Henry, 30519
Smith, Robert George, 26894
Smith, William Patrick, 26724
Smitheram, Nicholes, 32734
Smulian, Adolph, Saddler
Somerville, John, 30366
Soulsby, Frderick James, 30476
Soulsby, Robert, 26939
Southam, Walter, 26010
Speechley, John Ernest
Spence, John, 34494
Spencer, Clifton, 26870
Spencer, Walter
Spiers, Hallie, 26291, M/R
Spooner, John, 33763
Spriggs, George Henry, 31882
Stableford, James Albert, 27012
Stace, Albert Henry, 26969
Stacey, Frederick, 32780
Stadler, Joseph, 26721
Staite, John, 36149
Stanley, John Valentine, 26916, DoD
Stansfield, Craven, 26013
Stapleton, Patrick, 31813
Steer, Philip Morsey, 26020
Stefferson, Hans Oscar, 26756
Stephens, Edward Joseph, 25786
Stephens, Richard Edward, 31380
Stephens, William, 25762, DoD
Sternslow, Andrew James, 26790
Stevehens, John, 31494
Stevens, J., 31483
Stevenson, George Ingram, 32824
Stockman, Frederick, 31463
Stockman, H., 36185
Stoll, Frederick Henry, 27020
Stone, Lewis, 27194
Stonnell, James, 31794

Storan, Thomas, 32945
Storm, Jacob
Stricking, Thomas
Strong, Albert Marshall
Stuart, James, 26938
Stuart, John, 20414
Sullivan, James, 25992
Sullivan, James, 26014
Sullivan, Michael John, 34488
Swartz, Alfred Charles, 31499
Symons, Frederick Henry, 36194
Tait, Peter, 27788
Tait, Robert, 31369
Tatham, Robert Jenkins, 30383
Taylor, John James, 26729
Taylor, Peter, 32968
Taylor, William, 25796
Temant, Andrew Leon, 25797
Templeton, John, 31484
Terry, Thomas
Tew, Ernest Jones, 36218
Theesson, Dugnet, 27789
Thickins, William Herbert, 32726
Thielen, Charles Joseph, 25960
Thomas, Arthur, 34464
Thomas, David, 25727
Thomas, George, 30332, M/R
Thomas, Harry Pritchard, 31427
Thomas, John, 20404
Thomas, John, 25761
Thomas, John Crickton Stewart, 34470
Thomas, Joseph, 27013, W/D
Thomas, Owen Vincent, 27147
Thomas, Robert Newton, 36236
Thomas, Stricken, 27698
Thompson, Alexander, 31422
Thompson, Alfred Frederick Porter, 27639
Thompson, Frank, 26761
Thompson, James, 36186
Thompson, Joseph
Thompson, William, 30637
Thorne, Charles Ernest, 30386
Thorne, John, 36187
Thress, Frederick William, 30368
Tiernan, Lawrence, 34479
Titmas, Thomas William Langley Patrick, Bugler, 25636
Todhunter, James Andrew, 25674
Toerien, Simon M., 27066
Tomlin, Benjamin Stephen, 25949
Trendwith, Philip, 27690
Tripp, Edward, 26893
Trujillo, Ferdinand
Tucker, Alfred Percival, 26759
Tufnell, Herbert Thomas, 34511
Tuohy, Charles Patrick, 27688
Turnbull, John, 34516
Turner, Frank, 20399
Van der Byl, Paul Andrew, 26009
Van Neikerk, Christian, 27072
Van Neikerk, James Abraham George, Cyclist, 3040
Van Zyl, James, 33745
Vickerman, William Albert, 25675
Villet, William James, 25648
Visser, George, 25763
Vivian, Charles Ernest, 31460
Voysey, Sydney, 26302
Wahl, Louis, 26956
Walder, Albert Edward Walter, 31413
Wale, John Henry, 25950
Wallace, Patrick, 25722
Wallis, Robert Edward, 34478
Walmsley, George, 27785
Walters, Albert, 27153
Walton, Alfred, 30271
Ward, Frederick Johann, 32698
Ward, James, 25677
Ward, William, 31467
Warlock, Herbert, 25772
Warner, Richard, 30316
Warrington, Sydney Rutherford, 36856
Wass, John Arthur, 25965
Waters, Bertam, 27149
Waters, Dudley
Wathen, Henry, 33696
Watkins, Samuel, 34462
Watson, William Thomas, 30521, PoW
Webb, Alfred Ernest, 27004
Webb, James, 26844
Webber, Vincent Paul, 34522
Webster, John, 26881
Weir, Owen, 27787
Weldon, C., 36188
Wells, Hurlestone Vesey, 25689
Wells, James, 36220
Werner, W., 36190

Werra, Emile, 31449
West, Henry, 25817
West, Samuel James, 20426
Weston, Edward
Wexler, Abraham, 33736
Weymouth, Samuel, 26920
Wheeler, William James, 25958
Whelsley, John J., 25798
Whilkie, Johnnie, 20373
Whisken, Derrick Cameron, 25990
White, Charles Lewis, 26863
White, Edgar Richard Henry, 31507
White, John David, 27693
Whitlock, William, 34533
Whyte, James Johnston, 25808
Wibberley, Percy Towers, 20343
Wiggett, Archibald Douglas, 26954
Wilcher, Joseph, 36197
Wilde, S., 35856
Wilde, Sidney, 36237
Wilkinson, Henry, Cyclist, 30314
Williams, Bertram Frederick, 20408
Williams, Frank, 25634
Williams, Frederick, 20473
Williams, George Owen, 33652, W
Williams, Harry, 26745
Williams, John, 26838
Williams, John, 27002
Williams, John, 27003
Williams, Lewis, 34495
Williams, Thomas Henry Alfred, 20482
Williams, William Broadhead, 36238

Williams, William Griffith, 31435
Williamson, Herbert Reginald, 27047
Williamson, John, 34492
Wilson, Frederick, 25747
Wilson, George, 27038
Wilson, George, 37703
Wilson, John, 26903
Wilson, John, 27006
Wilson, John, 27215
Wilson, John, 36043
Wilson, John Henry, 26819
Wilson, Robert, Bugler, 26727
Wilson, William, 26728
Winchuttle, Sidney, 34476
Winn, Frederick Francis David,
Winn, Henry Leicester Jarvis, 26915
Winstansky, Mark, 32861
Winstone, Joseph Walter, 33678
Wojciechowski, August Raphael, 25717
Wolitsky, Simon, 26892
Wood, Charles, 32781
Woodford, Frederick Morgan, Cyclist, 27051
Woodrow, William Henry, 30492, PoW
Woods, Ernest, 27082
Woolf, Martin Nicolia, 30625
Woollard, Francis Joseph, 26751, DoD
Wrist, Christopher, 26928
Wyburd, Alfred, 25815
Wylie, Moses Dodds, 27786
Wylie, Robert, 30321
Wyman, Harry Henry, 20416

Appendix 2: 113th Infantry Brigade 1914–18

3 September 1914, the War Office sanctioned the raising of a North Wales 'Pals' Battalion (later designated 13th Battalion, RWF) which began forming at Rhyl on 2 October (moved to Llandudno 18 November).

28 September 1914, at Cardiff, Chancellor of the Exchequer, David Lloyd George announced the aim of forming a Welsh Army Corps.

10 October 1914 the Army Council instructed the formation of a Welsh Army Corps to be made up of two divisions. The brigades for the 1st Division Welsh Army Corps (43rd Division) were designated as 128th, 129th and 130th Brigades.

29 October 1914, the War Office sanctioned the formation of 1st London Welsh Battalion (later designated 15th Battalion, RWF) at Gray's Inn, London (moved to Llandudno 12 December).

30 October Lieutenant-Colonel Owen Thomas was appointed to command the 128th Brigade.

2 November Lieutenant-Colonel Owen Thomas commenced forming a Carnarvon & Anglesey Battalion (later designated 14th (Service) Battalion, RWF) at Llandudno. He remained in command until November 1915.

November 1914, the War Office sanctioned the formation of an additional battalion from men who were surplus to the needs of the 13th Battalion RWF. This became 16th Battalion, RWF.

Brigadier-Generals	Owen Thomas	October 1914
	Llewelyn A. E. Price-Davies, VC	November 1915
	H. E. ap Rhys Pryce	November 1917
	Adrian Carton de Wiart, VC	November 1918
Brigade Majors	Major C. S. Flower	September 1914
	Captain R. Bently	October 1915
	Captain J. C. M. Stewart	August 1916

Captain L. B. Brierley   May 1917
Captain M. G. Richards   January 1918

13th (Service) Battalion, Royal Welsh Fusiliers
Lieutenant-Colonel R. H. Dunn   October 1914
Lieutenant-Colonel Willes   December 1914
Lieutenant-Colonel Flower   October 1915
Lieutenant-Colonel Campbell   July 1916
Lieutenant-Colonel Leman   November 1917

14th Battalion, Royal Welsh Fusiliers
Lieutenant-Colonel David Davies   November 1914
Lieutenant-Colonel H. V. R. Hodson   July 1916
Lieutenant-Colonel E. W. P. Unlacke   June 1917
Lieutenant-Colonel B. W. Collier   March 1918
Lieutenant-Colonel C. C. Norman   November 1918

15th Battalion, Royal Welsh Fusiliers (1st London Welsh)
Lieutenant-Colonel Fox-Pitt   November 1914
Lieutenant-Colonel J. C. Bell
Lieutenant-Colonel C. C. Norman
Lieutenant-Colonel R. H. Montgomery

16th Battalion, Royal Welsh Fusiliers
Lieutenant-Colonel T. A. Wynne-Edwards   December 1915
Lieutenant-Colonel R. J. Carden   November 1915
Lieutenant-Colonel A. N. G. Jones   July 1916
Lieutenant-Colonel H. F. N. Jourdain   June 1917
Lieutenant-Colonel E. J. de P. O'Kelly   November 1917
Lieutenant-Colonel C. E. Davies   July 1918

Appendix 3: 38th (Welsh) Division, 1915–18

Divisional Commanders
    Major-General Sir Ivor Philipps   January 1915
    Major-General C. G. Blackader   July 1916
    Major-General T. A. Cubitt   May 1918

D Squadron, Wiltshire Yeomanry   November 1914–May 1916
119th Brigade, Royal Field Artillery   Withdrawn January 1917
120th Brigade, Royal Field Artillery   Disbanded October 1916
121st Brigade, Royal Field Artillery
122nd Brigade, Royal Field Artillery
38th Heavy Battery, Royal Artillery   Withdrawn November 1914

Divisional Ammunition Column   Organised January 1916

123rd Field Company, Royal Engineers
124th Field Company, Royal Engineers
151st Field Company, Royal Engineers

Divisional Signal Company

113th Infantry Brigade
    13th Battalion, Royal Welsh Fusiliers
    14th Battalion, Royal Welsh Fusiliers
    15th Battalion, Royal Welsh Fusiliers
    16th Battalion, Royal Welsh Fusiliers
    113th Machine Gun Company   Organised April 1916
    113th Light Trench Mortar Battery   Formed May 1915

114th Infantry Brigade
    10th Battalion, The Welsh Regiment
    13th Battalion, The Welsh Regiment

14th Battalion, The Welsh Regiment	
15th Battalion, The Welsh Regiment	
114th Machine Gun Company	Organised April 1916
114th Light Trench Mortar Battery	Formed May 1915

115th Infantry Brigade

2nd Battalion, Royal Welsh Fusiliers	Joined February 1918
17th Battalion, Royal welsh Fusiliers	
10th Battalion, South Wales Borderers	
11th Battalion, South Wales Borderers	Disbanded February 1918
16th Battalion, The Welsh Regiment	Disbanded February 1918
115th Machine Gun Company	Organised April 1915
115th Light Trench Mortar Battery	Formed May 1915

115th (Glamorgan Pioneer) Battalion, The Welsh Regiment	
Divisional Cyclist Company	Withdrawn May 1917
Machine Gun Battalion	Organised March 1918
176th Machine Gun Company	Joined March 1917
Divisional Train, 330–333 Companies, Army Service Corps	
129th Field Ambulance	
130th (St John) Field Ambulance	
131st Field Ambulance	
N[o.] 5 Mobile Bacteriological Section	Withdrawn December 1915
49th Mobile Veterinary Section	
235th Divisional Employment Company	Formed March 1917
38th Divisional Mechanical Transport Company	Joined December 1915

Sources & Bibliography

MANUSCRIPT SOURCES

BANGOR UNIVERSITY
Bangor General MSS. 15,237; 27,002; 27,007; 27,026–30.
Belmont MSS.
Plas Coch MSS.

BODLEIAN LIBRARY, OXFORD
Papers of Alfred, Viscount Milner.

BRYNDDU PAPERS (Privately owned)
Letters from Owen Thomas.
Plas Coch Estate Account.

CAERNARFON RECORD OFFICE
Ellis W. Davies Papers.

COMPANIES HOUSE, CARDIFF
Company File 87,739: Uplands of East Africa Syndicate Ltd/East African Estates Ltd.

DERBYSHIRE RECORD OFFICE
Papers of the Gell Family of Hopton.

HOUSE OF LORDS RECORD OFFICE
Lloyd George Papers.

NATIONAL LIBRARY OF WALES, ABERYSTWYTH
E. T. John Papers.
Welsh Army Corps Records 1914–25.
Yale Collection.

THE NATIONAL ARCHIVES
Colonial Office Papers (CO).
Records of the Registrar of Friendly Societies (FS).
Records of the Supreme Court of Judicature (J).
War Office Papers (WO).

REGIMENTAL ARCHIVES, THE ROYAL WELCH FUSILIERS, WREXHAM
T. A. Wynne Edwards Papers.

OFFICIAL PAPERS
Army (Courts of Inquiry) Act 1916, Report of the Court of Inquiry (Cd.8435),
Census returns for 1861, 1871, 1881, 1891, 1901 and 1911.
Hansard, Parliamentary Debates, Third Series.
Kenya, Returns Showing Crown Grants of Land of over 5,000 acres in Extent, 1926 (Cmd.2747).
Reports on the East African Protectorate, 1905–6 (Cd.3285–6); *1906–7* (Cd.3729–21); *1907–8* (Cd.4448–1); *1908–9* (Cd.4964–9); *1909–10* (Cd.5467–5); *1910–11* (Cd.6007–5); *1912–13* (Cd.7050–32); *1915–16* (Cd.8434–8); *1917–18* (Cmd.1–36).
Report of the Special Commission to Egypt, 1921 (Cmd.1131).
Royal Commission on Agricultural Depression, Second Report, 1896 (Cd.7981).
Royal Commission on Labour, The Agricultural Labourer, 1893, Vol. II (C.6894).

REPORTS
Report of the 19th Annual Conference of the Labour Party, 1919; 23rd Annual Conference, 1923; 24th Annual Conference, 1924.
Report of the Executive Committee of the Welsh Army Corps, 1914–1919, Cardiff, 1921.
Thomas, Owen, *Report to the Chairman and Directors of the Transvaal Consolidated Land and Exploration Co. Ltd, 30 January 1903.*
Thomas, Owen, *Report on the British East Africa and Uganda Protectorates for the Uplands of East Africa Syndicate, 1907.*
Welsh Army Corps, 1914–1919. Report of the Executive Committee (Cardiff, 1921).
Workers' Union, Annual Report, 1919.

WORKS OF REFERENCE

Burke's Landed Gentry, 1894.

Davies, J., Jenkins, N., Baines, Menna and Lynch, Peredur I (eds.), *The Welsh Academy Encyclopaedia of Wales* (Cardiff, 2008).

Dictionary of Welsh Biography down to 1940 (London, 1959).

Griffith, J. E., *Pedigrees of Anglesey and Carnarvonshire Families* (Horncastle, 1914).

Oxford Dictionary of National Biography.

Slater's Directory of North and Mid Wales, 1895.

Stenton, M. and Lees, S., *Who's Who of British Members of Parliament*, Vol. III 1919–45 (Harvester Press, 1979).

Who's Who, 1923.

Who's Who in Wales, 1920.

Wills, Walter H. (ed.), *The Anglo-African Who's Who and Biographical Sketchbook*, 1907 (reprinted by Jeepstown Press, London, 2006).

NEWSPAPERS AND PERIODICALS

Abergele Visitor
Baner ac Amserau Cymru
Y Brython
Caernarvon and Denbigh Herald
Cape Times
Y Celt
Y Clorianydd
Y Dysgedydd
Dysgedydd y Plant
East African Standard
Y Genedl Gymreig
Glamorgan Free Press
Y Goleuad
Yr Herald Cymraeg
Holyhead Chronicle
Holyhead (Weekly) Mail and Anglesey Herald
Liverpool Daily Post
Llandudno Advertiser
Manchester Guardian
Monmouthshire Beacon
Montgomery County Times
North Wales Chronicle
North Wales Observer & Express
North Wales Weekly News

Oswestry and Border Counties Advertiser
Shrewsbury Chronicle
South Wales (Daily) News
The Times
Times Literary Supplement
Y Tyst
Welsh Outlook
Y Werin
Western Mail
Y Wyntyll
Yr Wythnos a'r Eryr

SECONDARY WORKS

Amery, L. S. (ed.), *The Times History of the War in South Africa* (London, 7 vols. 1900–09).

Anglesey, The Marquess of, *A History of the British Cavalry 1816–1919*, Vol. IV (London, 1986).

Beckett, I. F. W., *Riflemen Form. A Study of the Rifle Volunteer Movement 1859–1908* (The Ogilby Trusts, 1982).

Beckett, I. F. W. and Simpson, K. (eds.), *A Nation in Arms. A Social Study of the British Army in the First World War* (Manchester U.P., 1985).

Benkovitz, M. J., *Frederick Rolfe: Baron Corvo – a Biography* (London, 1972).

Bennett, W., *Absent-minded Beggars. Volunteers in the Boer War* (Barnsley, 1999).

Chapman-Huston, D. and Rutter, O., *General Sir John Cowans* (London, 1924).

Churchill, Winston, *My African Journey* (London, 1908).

Clayton, Anthony and Savage, Donald C., *Government and Labour in Kenya 1895–1963* (London, 1974).

Coates, Tim, *Patsy: the Story of Mary Cornwallis-West* (London, 2003).

Cole, Christopher and Cheeseman, E. F., *The Air Defence of Britain 1914–1918* (London, 1984).

Crafford, F. S., *Jan Smuts: A Biography* (London, 1945).

Cragoe, M. and Williams, C. (eds.), *Wales and War* (Cardiff, 2007).

Cranworth, Lord, *A Colony in the Making* (London, 1912).

Creswick, Louis, *South Africa and the Transvaal War*, Vol. 7 (Manchester, 1902).

Davies, Dewi Eirug, *Byddin y Brenin. Cymru a'i chrefydd yn y Rhyfel Mawr* (Abertawe, 1988).

Douglas-Pennant, Violet, *Under the Search-Light. A Record of a Great Scandal* (London, 1922).

Eames, Aled, *Ships and Seamen of Anglesey 1558–1918* (Llangefni, 1973).

Ellis, T. I., *Ellis Jones Griffith* (Llandybie, 1969).
George, David Lloyd, *War Memoirs* (London, 1938).
Glyn, Ifor ap, *Lleisiau'r Rhyfel Mawr* (Llanrwst, 2008).
Goldman, C. S. (ed.), *The Empire and the Century. A Series of Essays on Imperial Problems and Possibilities* (London, 1905).
Graves, Robert, *Good-Bye to All That* (London, 1929).
Griffith, Ll. Wyn, *Up to Mametz* (London, 1931).
Griffith, W., *Methodistiaeth Fore Môn 1740–1751* (Caernarfon, 1955).
Griffith, W. P., *Power, Politics and County Government in Wales. Anglesey 1780–1914* (Llangefni, 2006).
Griffiths, Eric, *Squire of Nantglyn* (Wrexham, 2004).
Grigg, John, *Lloyd George: From Peace to War 1912–1916* (London, 1985).
Gruffydd, Ifan, *Gŵr o Baradwys* (Dinbych, 1963).
Guttsman, W. L., *The British Political Elite* (London, 1968).
Gwynedd, Viscount, *Dame Margaret* (London, 1947).
Holmes, Richard, *The Little Field Marshal: A Life of Sir John French* (London, 2004.)
Howard, J. H., *Winding Lanes* (Caernarvon, 1938).
Howell, David W., *Land and People in Nineteenth-Century Wales* (London, 1978).
Howkins, Alun, *Poor Labouring Men: Rural Radicalism in Norfolk 1872–1923* (London, 1985).
Hughes, Colin, *Mametz* (Gliddon Books, 1990).
Hughes, M., *Anglesey 1900* (Llanrwst, 2002).
Hughes, R., *Enwogion Môn 1850–1912* (Dolgellau, 1913).
Hughes, R. R., *Y Parchedig John Williams, DD, Brynsiencyn* (Caernarfon, 1929).
Humphreys, E. Morgan, *David Lloyd George* (Llandybie, 1943).
Hyman, Richard, *The Workers' Union* (Oxford, 1971).
Jeal, Tim, *Stanley. The Impossible Life of Africa's Greatest Explorer* (London, 2007).
Jones, D. and Thomas, Glyndŵr (eds.), *Nabod Môn* (Llanrwst, 2003).
Jones, R. Tudur, *Yr Undeb. Hanes Undeb yr Annibynwyr Cymraeg 1872–1972* (Abertawe, 1975).
Lewis, Gwilym H., *Wings over the Somme 1916–1918* (London, 1976).
Life in Pictures of Brig-Gen Sir Owen Thomas (London, nd., but 1922).
Llwyd, Alan, *Prifysgol y Werin. Hanes Eisteddfod Genedlaethol Cymru 1900–1918* (Cyhoeddiadau Barddas, 2008).
Marks, Shula, 'Southern and Central Africa 1886-1910. The Construction of the Modern South African State' in *The Cambridge History of Africa*, Vol. 6 (Cambridge U.P., 1985).
Marlowe, John, *Milner, 'Apostle of Empire'* (London, 1976).
Maurice, F and Grant, M. H., *Official History of the War in South Africa*

1899–1902 (London, 4 Vols. 1906-10).
McKibbin, Ross, *The Evolution of the Labour Party 1910–1924* (Oxford, 1974).
Middlemas, R. Keith, *The Clydesiders* (London, 1965).
M. N. J. (Jackson), *Bygone Days in the March Wall of Wales* (London, 1926).
Morgan, Kenneth O., *Wales in British Politics, 1868–1922* (Cardiff, 1963).
Morgan, Kenneth O., (ed.), *Lloyd George: Family Letters 1885–1936* (Cardiff, 1973).
Morgan, Kenneth O., *Rebirth of a Nation: Wales 1880–1980* (Oxford, 1981).
Morgan, Kenneth O., *Modern Wales: Politics, Places and People* (Cardiff, 1995).
Munby, J. E. (ed.), *A History of the 38th (Welsh) Division* (London, 1920).
Nicholson, I. and Lloyd-Williams, T., (eds.), *Wales: Its Part in the War* (London, 1919).
Owen, Bryn, *Welsh Militia and Volunteer Corps 1757–1908, 1: Anglesey and Caernarfonshire* (Caernarfon, 1989).
Owen, Bryn, *Owen Roscomyl and the Welsh Horse* (Caernarfon, 1990).
Owen, G. Dyfnallt, *Crisis in Chubut. A Chapter in the history of the Welsh Colony in Patagonia* (Swansea, 1977).
Owen, William, *Codi Canol Cefn* (Dinbych, 1974).
Paice, Edward, *Lost Lion of Empire. The Life of 'Cape-to-Cairo' Grogan* (London, 2001).
Pakenham, T., *The Boer War* (London, 1979).
Parry, Cyril, *The Radical Tradition in Welsh Politics* (Hull, 1970).
Pretty, David A., *Rhyfelwr Môn* (Dinbych, 1989).
Pretty, David A., *The Rural Revolt That Failed. Farm Workers' Trade Unions in Wales 1889–1950* (Cardiff, 1989).
Pretty, David A., *Anglesey. The Concise History* (Cardiff, 2005).
Quelch, Eileen, *Perfect Darling. The Life and Times of George Cornwallis-West* (London, 1972).
Quigley, Carroll, *The Anglo-American Establishment* (New York, 1981).
Rees, D. Ben, *Mr Evan Roberts. The Revivalist in Anglesey 1905* (Caernarfon, 2005).
Rees, T. and Thomas, J., *Hanes Eglwysi Annibynnol Cymru*, Cyf. II (Liverpool, 1872).
Richards, Emlyn, B*ywyd Gŵr Bonheddig* (Caernarfon, 2002).
Rowland, Peter, *Lloyd George* (London, 1975).
Simkins, Peter, *Kitchener's Army. The Raising of the New Armies 1914–1916* (Manchester U.P., 1988).
Sorrenson, M. P. K., *Origins of European Settlement in Kenya* (Oxford, 1968).
Stirling, John, *The Colonials in South Africa 1899–1902* (Edinburgh, 1907).
Symons, A. J. A., *The Quest for Corvo* (London, 1934).
Tanner, D., Williams, C. and Hopkin, D. (eds.), *The Labour Party in Wales 1900–2000* (Cardiff, 2000).
Taylor, A. J. P. (ed.), *Lloyd George: A Diary by Frances Stevenson* (London, 1971).

Thomas, David, *Silyn (Robert Silyn Roberts) 1871–1930* (Lerpwl, 1956).
Thomas, Owen, *Agricultural and Pastoral Prospects of South Africa* (London, 1904).
Thomas, Owen, *Stray Leaves from My East African Diary* (London, 1920).
Thompson, J. Lee, *A Wider Patriotism: Alfred Milner and the British Empire* (London, 2007).
Thorpe, Lewis, *Gerald of Wales. The Journey Through Wales and the Description of Wales* (Penguin Books, 2004).
Treves, Frederick, *Uganda for a Holiday* (London, 1910).
Walsh, Michael, *Brothers in War* (London, 2006).
Weeks, D., *Corvo* (London, 1971).
Westlake, Ray, *The Rifle Volunteers. The History of the Rifle Volunteers 1859–1908* (Chippenham, 1982).
Winter, J. M., *The Great War and the British People* (London, 1985).
Woolf, C., *A Bibliography of Frederick Rolfe, Baron Corvo* (London, 1972).
Williams, E. A., *The Day Before Yesterday. Anglesey in the Nineteenth Century*, Trans G. Wynne Griffith (Beaumaris, 1988).
Williams, Gerwyn, *Y Rhwyg* (Llandysul, 1993).
Williams, Glyn, *The Desert and the Dream: A Study of Welsh Colonization in Chubut, 1865–1915* (Cardiff, 1975).
Williams, R. Môn, *Enwogion Môn 1850–1912* (Bangor, 1913).
Williams, R. R., *Breuddwyd Cymro mewn Dillad Benthyg* (Lerpwl, 1964).
Wrigley, C. C., 'Kenya: the Patterns of Economic Life, 1902–45' in *History of East Africa* Vol. 2 (Oxford, 1965).

ARTICLES

Douglas, R., 'A Classification of the Members of Parliament elected in 1918', *Bulletin of the Institute of Historical Research*, Vol. XLVII, 1974.
Eurig, Aled, 'Agweddau ar y Gwrthwynebiad i'r Rhyfel Byd Cyntaf yng Nghymru', *Llafur*, Vol. 4, N°· 4.
Harvey, A.D., 'Generals in Defence of their Honour', *RUSI (Royal United Services Institution) Journal*, Vol. 152, N°· 4, August 2007.
Johnson, M., 'The Liberal War Committee and the Liberal advocacy of conscription in Britain 1914-1916', *The Historical Journal*, Vol. 51, N°· 2, June 2008.
Jones, Ivor Wynne, 'U-boat Rendezvous at Llandudno', *Maritime Wales*, N°· 3, (March, 1978).
Jones, R., 'The Anglesey Trading Company, Llanfechell 1896–1899', *Môn*, Cyf. IV, Rhif 2, Haf 1971.
Parry, Cyril, 'Gwynedd Politics, 1900–1920: The Rise of a Labour Party', *Welsh History Review* 6(3) June 1973.
Parry, Cyril, 'Gwynedd and the Great War, 1914–1918', *Welsh History Review*, 14 (1) June 1988.

Pretty, David A., 'The Political Career of Richard Davies, Treborth, 1868–1892', *Transactions of the Anglesey Antiquarian Society*, 1979.
Pretty, David A., 'Undeb Gweithwyr Môn: Anglesey Workers' Union', *Transactions of the Anglesey Antiquarian Society*, 1988 (Part I), 1989 (Part II).
Pretty, David A., 'Y Cyrnol Owen Thomas a'r Barwn Corvo', *Transactions of the Anglesey Antiquarian Society*, 1990.
Pretty, David A., 'Y Cyrnol Owen Thomas a Charles Sydney Goldman', *Transactions of the Anglesey Antiquarian Society*, 1991.
Richards, Emlyn, 'Syr Robert John Thomas, Y Garreglwyd', *Transactions of the Anglesey Antiquarian Society*, 1998.
Roberts, Dafydd, 'Dros Ryddid a Thros Ymerodraeth. Ymatebion yn Nyffryn Ogwen 1914–1918', *Transactions of the Caernarfonshire Historical Society*, 1984.
Rowlands, Eryl Wyn, 'Etholiad Cyffredinol 1918 ym Môn', *Transactions of the Anglesey Antiquarian Society*, 1976–77.
Rowlands, Eryl Wyn, 'Agweddau gwleidyddol ym Môn 1885–95', *Transactions of the Anglesey Antiquarian Society*, 1983.
Thomas, Owen, 'The Commercial Future of Rhodesia', *Magazine of Commerce*, April 1904.
Trapido, Stanley, 'Landlord and Tenant in a Colonial Economy: the Transvaal 1880-1910', *Journal of Southern African Studies*, Vol. 5, N° 1. October, 1978.
Walsh, Michael, 'The Lost Souls', *Saga Magazine*, November 2001.

UNPUBLISHED THESES
Edwards, J. E., 'Beriah Gwynfe Evans. Ei fywyd a'i waith', PhD, University of Wales, Aberystwyth, 1989.
Hughes, C., 'Army Recruitment in Gwynedd 1914–1916', MA, University of Wales, Bangor, 1983.
Owen, A., 'The port and town of Holyhead during the Depression of the 1930s', MA, University of Wales, Bangor, 1987.
Quinn, D. F., 'Voluntary Recruiting in Glamorgan 1914–16', MA, Cardiff, 1994.

Index

Aberffraw 26, 141
Abercorn, Duke of 64
Aberdare, Lord 106
Abergele 15, 85, 102, 106
Abraham, William (Mabon) 86, 143, 171
Adamson, MP, William 143, 146
Agricultural Act, 1920 145
Alival North 48, 57
Allen, Maj Gerald *127*, 128
Amlwch 11, 12, 16, 18, 20, 23, 26, 85, 163
Anglesey, Marquess of 11, 25
Anglesey Agricultural Labourers' Union
  35, 36
Anglesey Agricultural Society 12, 17, 18
Anglesey Agricultural Union 36
Anglesey Board of Guardians 22
Anglesey Conservative Association
  36, 138, 160
Anglesey County Council 32, 112, 146–8, 160
Anglesey Farmers' Union 137, 138
Anglesey Labour Party 135
Anglesey Ladies Recruiting Committee 97
Anglesey Liberal Association 13, 31–3, 37, 39,
  44, 136, 139, 140, 153
Anglesey Trading Company 40
Anglesey Workers' Union (see *Undeb
  Gweithwyr Môn*)
Ap Ffarmwr 33–6, *35*, 133–5, 136, 139, 171
ap Iwan, Llwyd 66
Arch, Joseph 36
Argentina 16, 52, 56
Army
  14th (Reserve) Infantry Brigade 102, 104,
    119, 121
  38th (Welsh) Division 99, 101, 102, 103, 105,
    116
  43rd (Welsh) Division 90, 93, 95, 99
  113th Infantry Brigade 99–102, 105, 116, 119,
    125
  114th Infantry Brigade 105
  128th Infantry Brigade 90, 93, *95*, *96*, 136
  129th Infantry Brigade 91
  130th Infantry Brigade 91
  Anglesey Militia 25
  Anglesey Volunteer Rifle Corps 25
  Brabant's Horse 46–50, *47*, *48*, 52
  Cape Mounted Rifles 41
  Cemaes Rifle Volunteers 26, 40, 47, 49, 92,
    124
  Cheshire Regiment 100
  Essex Regiment 44
  Frontier Mounted Rifles 47
  Irish Guards 151
  Kaffrarian Rifles 47
  King's Liverpool Regiment 100
  Manchester Regiment 25
  Prince of Wales' Light Horse 50–6, 50, 51,
    68, 84, Appendix 1
  Rimington's Guides 53, 55
  Royal Anglesey Engineers Militia 26
  Royal Army Medical Corps
    (Welsh Ambulance) 10
  Royal Flying Corps 125–8
    14 Squadron 126
    32 Squadron 127–8, *127*
    39 Squadron 128
  Royal Welsh Fusiliers 26, 88, 91, 118–9
    2nd Volunteer Bn 24, 25–6, *25*, 27
    3rd Volunteer Bn 28
    12th (Reserve) Bn 104
    13th (Service) Bn (1st N Wales) 93,100, 128
    14th (Service) Bn (C&A) 92, 93, 100, 104
    15th (Service) Bn (1st London Welsh)
      92, 93, 100, 125, 136
    16th (Service) Bn 93, 94, 105, *113*, 119
    17th (Service) Bn (2nd N Wales)

202

	94, 95, 97, 99	Campbell, Lt-Gen W. Pitcairn	112, 121–3
18th (Reserve) Bn (2nd London Welsh)		Cape Colony	46–7, 50, 54–5, 60, 63
	99, 104, 105	Cape Town	44, 46, 51, 105
19th (Service) Bn (Bantams)	95, 99	Cardiff	86, 88, 106
20th (Reserve) Bn	104	Carrog	14, *15*, 16, 18, 38, 79, 103
21st (Reserve) Bn	104, 119	Cecil, Lord Robert	144
22nd (Reserve) Bn	104	Cemaes	15, 16, 18, 19, 21–3, 40, 79, 84, 124
South Wales Borderers	88	Cemaes Life Saving Apparatus Station	
Welsh Army Corps	88–90, 92, 94, 170		19, *19*, 20
Welsh Guards	151	Cerrigydrudion	85
Welsh Horse	53	Cestyll, Cemlyn	79, 84
Welsh Regiment	88, 104	Chamberlain, Joseph	62, 66, 70–1
10th (Service) Bn (1st Rhondda)	86	Churchill, Winston	72, 124, 151
Australia	52, 56, 71, 145	Clynes, MP, J.R.	143, 146, 152
Banbury, MP, Sir Frederick	160	Cobham, Viscount	38, 74
Barkworth, A.E.	40	Colesburg	54
Barrett, Sgt Patrick	118–9	Colwyn Bay	85, 90, 91, 107
Bartlett family, Penarth	130	Compatriots Club	70
Basutoland	49, 63	Conscription Bill	144
Bechuanaland	63	Corn Production Act, 1917	133, 134, 140
Beit, Alfred	46, 60–2, 69, 79	Cornwallis-West, Mrs 'Patsy'	115, 118–9, 123
Belfield, H.C.	75	Cornwallis-West, Col W.C.	115, 118
Belper, Lord	74	Corvo, Baron (see Rolfe, Frederick William)	
Berry Lt Charles F.	55	Cowans, Lt-Gen Sir John	119, 121, 123
Bethel Chapel, Cemaes	15, 20	Cranworth, Lord	75, 79
Bethesda	85, 91	Cricieth	87–8
Bethune, France	105	Cuthbertson, Lt-Col E.B.	122
Bethune, Col E.C.	54	Dalgety, Col E.H.	49
Birch, Mr & Mrs	118–9, 121	Davies, Revd Glendower	52, 54
Blackbrooke estate	21, 50	Davies, Col David	92
Blaenau Ffestiniog	99	Davies, MP, Ellis W.	87, 115, 123, 124, 137
Bloemfontein	54	Davies, George M.Ll.	106, 107
Bodorgan	11	Davies, H.R.	91, 97
Bombay (Mumbai)	158	Davies, MP, Richard	12, 16, 31, 32, 52, 91, 147
Boston, Lord	85, 112	Davies, Capt Richard Lloyd	52
Boston, Lady	97	de Bucy, 11th Marquess	61
Brabant, Col E.Y.	46, 49	De Wet, Christiaan	49, 54, 55
Brace, MP, William	86, 143, 152	Deganwy	99
Brande Kraal	55	Delme-Radcliffe, Lt-Col	119
British South Africa Company	46, 60–7, 69, 71	Derby, Earl of	102, 104, 124
Brynddu	11, 12, 14, 18, 21, 22, 26, 36, 40, 49, 50, 79	Dickson, Gen H.E.	99
		Disestablishment of the Welsh Church	13, 92, 138, 140, 144–5
Brynsiencyn (see also Revd John Williams)	134, 141	Dolwyddelan	98
Bulkeley, William *diarist*	21	Dordrecht	47–8, 57
Caernarfon	91, 106	Douglas-Pennant, Violet	144
Cairns, 2Lt A.J.	128	Dunn, Col R.H.W.	90, 91
Cambrian Society, Cape Town	51	Durban	66

Dyffryn Aled PoW Camp, Llansannan 99
East African Estates Ltd 75–9, 88, 126, 146, 151, 152, 169
East African Protectorate 71–8
Ebenezer Chapel 15, 20, 21, 163–5
Edwards, George 142
Edwards, MP, J. Hugh 159
Edwards, O.M. 87
Egypt 148–50
Eisteddfod Môn 158
Elliott, Maj-Gen E.L. 55
Entebbe 72, 76
Evans, Beriah Gwynfe 106, 112, 114, 116
Evans, Ellis H. (*Hedd Wyn*) 126
Evans, Lt O.T. 53
Evans, L/Cpl Samuel 126
Evans, W.J. 106
Evans-Jones, Albert (Cynan) 106
French, FM Viscount John 55, 122, 123, 124
Gadlys Hotel 40
Gatacre, Lt-Gen Sir William 46–7
Gaza 126
Gazi Rubber & Fibre Estates Ltd 76
Gell, Philip Lyttelton 46, 60, 65, 79
Gifford, Lord 65
Goldman, Charles Sydney 69–71, 72, 74, 79
Graves, Robert 85
Grey, 4th Earl 46, 67, 79
Griffith, MP, Sir Ellis Jones 37, 44, 78, 85, 87, 135, 136, 137, 138, 140, 141, 171
Griffith, Capt Ll. Wyn 116
Grogan, Ewart Scott 69, 71, 72, 79
Government of Wales Bill 159
Gwalchmai 141
Haig, Gen Sir Douglas 116
Hanbury-Williams, Col J. 51
Harcourt, Lewis 75
Harlech 85
Henderson, MP, Arthur 135
Heneglwys 14
Henley-on-Thames 67, 148
Herbert, Maj-Gen Sir Ivor 90, 91
Holyhead 11, 20, 26, 85, 135, 141, 148, 150, 151, 160, 162, 164
Holyhead Trades & Labour Council 134, 135, 136, 139, 146, 148, 150, 152, 153
Howard, Revd J.H. 107
Howells, Lt J.W. 126
HMS *Tara* (see SS *Hibernia*)
Hughes, Capt F.B. 52–3, 55
Hughes, W. Bulkeley 11, 16, 18, 21
Hughes-Hunter, Col Charles 20, 22, 23, 25–6, 31–2, 49, 52, 84
Hughes-Hunter, Sarah 18, 21, 22, 39, 40, 84
Hughes-Hunter, Sir W.B. 160
India 16, 56, 158
Ireland 28, 39, 128, 149, 151, 165
Islington, London 18, 62
Jackson, Robert Newton 21
Jamestown 48
Jenkins, Revd J.G. (Gwili) 104
Jennings-Bramly, Maj A.W. 52, 55
Jersey 165
Jesus College, Cambridge 128
Job, Revd J.T. 92
Johannesberg 61–2, 69, 105
John, E.T. 153, 159, 164
Jones, MP, Haydn 87, 118
Jones, Sir Henry 87, 126
Jones, John Owen (see Ap Ffarmwr)
Jones, R.T. 142
Jones, Dr Thomas 85
Jones, MP, William 87, 136
Jones, W.J. (Brynfab) 134, 135, 138, 142, 147, 153–4, 160
Kenya 71–2, 75–6, 78–9, 126, 151–2, 169
Kitchener, FM Lord 50–2, 54–6, 55, 55, 56, 57, 84, 86, 88, 89, 90, 115, 116, 122
Kroonstad 54
Kikuyu tribe 73
Kilindini 72, 151
Kinmel Camp 102, 104, 106, 112, 114, 115, 119, 121, 122, 141, 144
Labour Party 134–5, 138–9, 142, 146–8, 150–4, 160, 164, 171
Leighton, MP, Stanley 38, 39
Levi, Prof T.A. 87
Lewis, Sir Henry 87
Lewis, MP, Thomas 31, 35–7, 147
Liberal Party 13, 16, 31–2, 36–8, 133, 135–7, 140, 153, 160–2, 170–1
Liberal Unionist Association 32
Limuru 73, 75
Liverpool 90, 92, 145, 160

Llanbadrig	14, 18, 32	Murray, Gen Sir Archibald	101, 115
Llanberis	87	Nairobi	71–3
Llandaff, Bishop of	106	Natal	46, 63
Llandudno	23, 90, 93, 95, *95*, *96*, 97–9, 102, 124, 136, 141, 145, 158	National Agricultural Labourers' & Rural Workers' Union	133, 142, 147
Llanfair-yng-Nghornwy	33	National Eisteddfod of Wales, Bangor	94
Llanfechell	11, 15, 19, 20–2, 26, 31, 33, 35, 36, 39, 40, 49, 52, 103, 130, 158, 163, *165*, *166*	National Eisteddfod of Wales, Birkenhead	126
Llangaffo	*159*	National Eisteddfod of Wales, Caernarfon	114
Llangefni	11, 14, 20, 32–4, 35, 36, 85, 133, 134, 137, 148, 158	National Farmers' Union	137
		National Fund for Welsh Troops	125
		National Union of Railwaymen	139
Llannerch-y-medd	34, 49, 135, 140, 141	Native Labour Commission	75
Lloyd, Lt-Gen Sir Francis	151	Neuadd	15–7, *17*, 26, 79, 163
Lloyd George, MP, Rt Hon David	44, 57, 87–9, 90–2, 94–5, 95,–6, 97–8, *98*, 99, 100, 102,114–7, 123, 138, 143, 150, 159, 161, 162, 170	Neuve Chappelle, battle of	105
		New Zealand	52
		Newborough	158
		Nicholson, FM W.G.	117
Lloyd George, Lt Gwilym	92	North Wales Heroes Memorial, Bangor	144
Lloyd George, Mrs Margaret	87, 125	North Wales Liberal Association	32
Lloyd George, Capt Richard	92	North Wales Quarrymen's Union	87, 142
London	18, 67, 74_5, 79, 84, 88, 90, 94, 101, 128, 161, 163	Oddfellows	21, 22, 79
		Orange Free State (Colony)	54–5, 60, 63
Lowry family, Llandyfaelog	130	Order of Mark Master Masons	23
Macdonald, MP, Ramsay	139, 143	Oswestry	38–9, 136
Mackinnon, Gen Sir Henry	95, *98*, 119, 121–2	Owen, Owen	38
MacLean, MP, Neil	143, 146, 147, 152	Parliamentary Labour Party	142, 143, 147, 148,150, 152, 153
Macpherson, J.I.	124		
Mametz Wood, Somme	116, 117, 130	Parys Mountain, Amlwch	11, 151
Markham, MP, Sir Arthur	114–6, 119, 122	Patagonia	17, 52, 66–7
Mashonaland	60, 64	Penhoek	47
Matabeleland	60, 64	Penrhyn Slate Quarry	87
Maxted, Capt H.R.	40	Pensarn	31
Maxwell, Gen Sir J. Grenfell	148, *149*	Pentraeth	152
Menai Bridge	11, 26, 145	Penmon	152
Middelburg	50, 56	Pershouse, Frederica Wilhelmina (see Thomas, Frederica Wilhelmina)	
Military Service Act, 1916	104		
Milner, Sir Alfred	38, 44, 46, 51, 60, 62, 63, 66, 69, 70, 79, 148, 149, 169	Pershouse, Frederick	21
		Pershouse, Wilhelmina Mary	21
Miners' Federation of Great Britain	143	Pershouse, Lt William Bradney	54
Min Menai Eisteddfod, 1920	158	Petrusburg	54
Mombasa	71–3, 78, 151	Philipstown	54
Morfa Conwy	25, 26, 94	Philipps, MP, Maj-Gen Sir Ivor	91, 95, 101, 116, 121, 123
Morgan, MP, D. Watts	86, 87, 143, 144		
Morris, Revd Richard	140, 147, *150*, 153	Pietersburg Hospital	62
Morris-Jones, Prof John	87, 104, 126	Plas Coch	11–12, 14, 16, 18–22, 32, 80, 160
Mostyn, Col Henry Lloyd	97, 112	Plas Newydd	11, 28

Plymouth, Earl of	74, 88–9, 95	Stanley, Sir Henry Morton	77–8, 169
Porthmadog	87	Stanton, Charles	86
Pretty, W.J.	136, 147, *150*	Stevenson, Frances	57
Prevention of Unemployment Bill	143	Stormberg	47
Price-Davies, VC, Brig-Gen Ll.A.E.	102, *102*	Sudan	148
Pritchard, Lt Hugh	91, 135–6, 140	Swansea	39, 86
Pritchard-Rayner, Capt John Henry	52	Tennant, H.J.	115, 122
Pwllheli	87, 98, 99, 117	Thomas, Frederica Wilhelmina	
Queenstown	47	(Lady Thomas)	21, 23, *29*, 50, 163–5
Rhodes, Cecil	41, 44, 46, 60, 61, 64, 79, 169	Thomas, Frederick Leyton Pershouse	21, 23, 50, *65*, 72
Rhodes Trust	61, 64, 67, 68	Thomas, Hugh	18, 79, 103, 136
Rhodesia	60, 64, 66–9, 71, 78–9	Thomas, MP, J.H.	139, 152
Rhoscomyl, Owen	53	Thomas, John Murray	17
Rhosgoch	49	Thomas, Tpr Joseph	55
Rhyl	90–1, 106, *107*, 112	Thomas, Lewis	147, *150*
Richard, MP, Henry	86	Thomas, Mina Margaret	22, 23, 65, 128, 163
Richards, Thomas	86	Thomas, MP, Sir Owen	6, *19*, 20, 23, 24–5,
Roberts, Evan	86, 92	27, 33, 47–8, 50, 53, 73–4, 97–8, 100, *107*,	
Roberts, MP, Sir Herbert	115, 118	117, *129*, 141, 149, 159, 164, 165, 166	
Roberts, Sgt Joseph Goodman	56	2nd Vol Bn, RWF 24–7, *24*, *25*, 27	
Roberts, R.J.	66–7	14th (Reserve) Infantry Brigade	102
Roberts, R. Silyn	93	43rd (Welsh) Division	90–9
Rodd, Sir James Rennell	*149*, 172	113th Infantry Brigade	99–102
Rolfe, Frederick William	67–9, 71	128th Infantry Brigade	90–9, *98*
Rowlands, Thomas	137, 147, *150*	Alderman, Anglesey County Council	37
Royal Charter	19	Ancestry	14–5
Royal Commission on Agricultural Depression	37–8	Anglesey Trading Company	40
Royal Commission on Labour	36	Bardic names	126, 158
Royal Commission on Land in Wales	39	Birth	14
Royce, W.S.	142, 143	Brabant's Horse	46-50, *47*, *48*
Ruthin	16, 85	Brigadier-general	90
Ruthin Castle	115, 119	Chief Officer Cemaes Life Saving	
St Asaph, Bishop of	106	Apparatus Station	19, *19*, 20
Sadler, Sir James Hayes	72, 74	Children	21–2, 53, 72, 93, 105, 125, 128
Salim, Sheik Ali Bin	78	Death	163
Sarn, Llŷn	99	Deputy Lieutenant of Anglesey	148
Shimoni	72, 75	Early politics	31–40
Shrewsbury	106, 125, 159	East African Estates Ltd	75–9
Skenfrith, Monmouthsire	21, 50, 72, 130	Education	16
Smuts, Jan Christiaan	48, 172	Farmer	17–18
Smuts, N.E.	48–9	High Sheriff of Anglesey	37
SS *Africa*	72	Hon brigadier-general	124
SS *Greek*	44	Independent denomination	20, 93
SS *Hibernia*	162–3	Justice of the Peace	37
SS *St Trillo*	145	Knighthood	124
SS *Sicilian*	46	Land agent	18, 39
SS *Tara*	148	Leaves Parliamentary Labour Party	153

Life in Pictures	161–2	Treves, Sir Frederick	78
Loss of command	112, 144	U-boats	99, 163
Marriage	21	Uganda	72, 78
Masonic	23	*Undeb Gweithwyr Môn*	133, *133*, 134, 135,
Member of Parliament	141–1	136, 137, 140, 141, 146, 147, 148, *150*,	
Military Court of Inquiry	116–24	150, 152, 153, 160	
Military Director of Agriculture	56	Uplands of East Africa Syndicate	72–5
Milner Mission to Egypt	148–9, 172	Valley, Anglesey	26, 27
O.T. Evans & Company	40	Victoria Falls	55, 64
Parliamentary candidate	37–9, 135–40, 160–2	Victoria, lake	71
		Vogelfontein	55
Personality	18	Walker, R.B.	142
Prince of Wales' Light Horse	50–6, *50*, *53*	Waterson, MP, A.E.	143
Publications	63, 67–9, 78	Welsh Church Temporalities Bill	145
Secretary Cemaes Regatta	23	Welsh Home Rule	138, 159–61, 171
Sword of Honour	97, *97*, 165	Welsh Independents, Union of	20, 105, 112
Uplands of East Africa Syndicate	72–5, *72*, *74*	Welsh Land Question	12, 13, 18, 39, 63–4, 149
		Welsh National Liberal Federation	39
Welfare of Soldiers	105–6, 125, 139, 145–6	Wepener, siege of	49, 57
Welsh Army Corps	88–90, 170	Westminster, Duke of	74
Thomas, Capt Owen Vincent	22, 23, 53, 65, 93, 125, 127, 128, 129	Wellington College	105
		Williams, Revd John (Brynsiencyn)	19, 85, 87,
Thomas, MP, Sir Robert J.	153, 159, 160–2, 164, 171	92, 98, 101, 102, 106, 107, 112, 124, 126, 139–40	
Thomas, Robert Newton	22, 23, 53, *53*, 54, 65, 72, *73*, *74*, 93, 125, *125*, 126, 129	Williams, G. Llywelyn	135
		Williams, Revd Thomas Charles	85, 92
Thomas, Thomas Owen	16–7, 66	Williams-Bulkeley, MP, Sir Richard	13
Thomas, 2Lt Trevor	22, *23*, 54, *65*, 93, 105, 129	Winchester	100–2, 172
		Wladfa, Y	17, 52, 66–7
Thomas, Capt W.	52	Workers' Union	133, 147, 150
Thomas, Tpr William	55	Wrexham	90, 106, 153
Thomas, William Robert	16	Wynne-Edwards, Col Thomas A.	*107*, *113*, 119, *120*, 121, *121*, 170, 172
Transvaal	44, 60–4, 66, 69, 79		
Transvaal Consolidated Land & Exploration Company	61	Yeldham, Maj Walter	32
		Zanzibar	72, 78, 151, 158
Trefriw	95	Zoutpansberg	66